Tourism in a VUCA World

Tourism in a VUCA World: Managing the Future of Tourism

EDITED BY

NASER UL ISLAM
Tata Institute of Social Sciences, India

MANJULA CHAUDHARY
Kurukshetra University Kurukshetra, India

AND

IZIDORA MARKOVIĆ VUKADIN
Institute for Tourism, Croatia

United Kingdom – North America – Japan – India – Malaysia – China

Emerald Publishing Limited
Emerald Publishing, Floor 5, Northspring, 21-23 Wellington Street, Leeds LS1 4DL.

First edition 2024

Reprints and permissions service
Contact: www.copyright.com

British Library Cataloguing in Publication Data
A catalogue record for this book is available from the British Library

ISBN: 978-1-83753-675-7 (Print)
ISBN: 978-1-83753-674-0 (Online)
ISBN: 978-1-83753-676-4 (Epub)

Printed and bound by CPI Group (UK) Ltd, Croydon, CR0 4YY

INVESTOR IN PEOPLE

Dedicated to the readers of tourism literature in pursuit of a seamless tourism experience in the VUCA world.

Contents

About the Editors

Naser Ul Islam, Ph.D., is an Assistant Professor of Tourism and Hospitality at Tata Institute of Social Sciences, Mumbai, India. His research interests primarily revolve around sustainable destination management, climatic change, destination attractiveness, and destination risk.

Manjula Chaudhary, Ph.D., is a Professor of Tourism and Director, Centre for Distance and Online Education (CDOE) at Kurukshetra University Kurukshetra, Haryana, India. She has also worked as Director at Indian Institute of Tourism and Travel Management under the Ministry of Tourism, Government of India. She has authored tourism management projects, policies, research papers, books, and articles in her interest areas of tourism management and marketing. With over 30 years of academic experience, she specialises in tourism marketing, tourist behaviour, and business communication.

Izidora Marković Vukadin, Ph.D., is a Senior Researcher at the Institute for Tourism in Zagreb, Croatia. As an expert in sustainable tourism, she participated in a number of European projects concerning the spatial development of tourism. Her research is focused on sustainable tourism development and management, impacts of tourism on protected areas and identity and environmental impacts of tourism.

About the Contributors

Ricardi S. Adnan is a Sociologist from the University of Indonesia and has worked professionally in private companies. He holds a Master's degree in Business Administration and a Doctoral degree in Industrial History. He developed a passion for tourism while mentoring postgraduate students researching the industry in 2018.

Frank Babinger is Associate Professor in Geography. He is specialised in tourism in coastal areas, sustainable tourism management and natural hazards in tourism destinations. He has published and presented papers at international conferences about those and other topics during the last 20 years.

Allegra Celine Baumann holds a Ph.D. in Sociology from TU Darmstadt, Germany. In her Ph.D. project, she analysed the impact of cruise tourism from a rhythmanalytic perspective using the case study of Dubrovnik. Allegra's research focuses on the interaction of tourism, urban infrastructure, and local life in cities.

Diana Baus works at the Institute for Tourism in Zagreb, Croatia, while finishing her Ph.D. at the University of Innsbruck in Austria. Her scientific research focuses on macroeconomic aspects of tourism, global value chains, sustainable supply chains, the development and application of circular economy in tourism, and the transfer of new technologies.

Jadwiga Berbeka, Ph.D., is a Professor at the Institute of Management at Krakow University of Economics (Poland). Prof Berbeka has authored or co-authored over 150 publications concerning innovation, business services, consumer behaviour, knowledge transfer, new technologies, and tourism. She reviews manuscripts for journals on the JCR list.

Krzysztof Borodako, Ph.D., is a Professor at the Institute of Management at the Krakow University of Economics (Poland). Prof Borodako is an author or co-author of over 160 publications concerning innovation, tourism, business services, new technologies, and event management. He has been the principal investigator in many research projects.

Irma Magaña Carrillo, holds a Ph.D. in Sciences, Trans-Pacific International Relations, a Master in Administration and a bachelor degree in Tourism Business Administration; is a tenured Professor at the Faculty of Tourism of the University of Colima. As a Member of the National System of Researchers of the National Council of Science and Technology of México, she specializes in Total Quality Management.

Dora Ivković is a Master's graduate in Tourism from the Faculty of Economics, Business, and Tourism at the University of Split, Croatia. With a keen interest in the tourism industry, Dora brings a fresh perspective grounded in academic excellence and is poised to make significant contributions to the field.

Hiromi Kamata is a Professor of Hospitality Management at the School of Business Administration, Hitotsubashi University. Her research interests include residents' attitudes towards tourism and repeat tourists. She has published in journals including *Tourism Review, Tourism Economics, Current Issues in Tourism,* and *Annals of Tourism Research Empirical Insights.*

Marko Koščak held the position of the Assistant Professor from 2014 to 2019 at the Faculty of Tourism University of Maribor, Slovenia, and from 2019 in the same Faculty as an Associate Professor. His academic interests are in the fields of Sustainable and Community Tourism, Geography of Tourism and Destination Management. He also provides professional consultancy services in regard to heritage, cultural, ethical, and responsible tourism as well as working with public, private, and EU organisations. In the past 30 years, he has worked as an Advisor to various institutions, including UNDP LoSD and various sustainable tourism initiatives in countries of W Balkans, EU, and Asia.

Jasenka Kranjčević is a senior research fellow at the Institute for Tourism, Zagreb, Croatia. She is also an Assistant Professor at the Josip Juraj Strossmayer University of Osijek Faculty of Civil Engineering and Architecture Osijek, where she gives lectures on the study course Rural Planning. Her research interests include rural development, spatial structure of villages, architectural touristic heritage, tourism history, and spatial distribution of tourism.

Damir Krešić has over 20 years of experience in the tourism sector, especially in destination management, strategic planning, and sustainable development. He graduated from Zagreb University with a degree in Finance and got his Ph.D. in Tourism. He is currently the Managing Director at the Institute for Tourism.

Dr Ante Mandić is an Assistant Professor at the University of Split, Croatia, and Affiliated Faculty at Colorado State University. He is an Associate Editor for the *Journal of Ecotourism* and Coordinator of knowledge development at the International Union for Conservation of Nature WCPA TAPAS. His expertise lies in sustainable tourism in nature-based destinations.

Carlos Mario Amaya Molinar is a tenured Professor at the Faculty of Tourism of the University of Colima. He holds a Ph.D. in Tourism, Law and Business by the University of Girona, a Master in Finance from the University of Colima and a bachelor degree in Sociology from the National Autonomous University of Mexico. He has research in subjects like tourism competitiveness, information technologies in tourism and community-based tourism.

Tony O'Rourke works with the Green Lines Institute for Sustainable Development in Portugal. Since retiring in 2011, he has taught part-time at the MSc and MBA levels as a visiting/part-time Professor and also carried out advisory work for Co-operatives UK. His current academic interests are in the fields of Sustainable and Responsible Local Tourism, Financing of Local Tourism/Destination Management organisations and the creation of tourism credit co-operatives.

Ana Portolan is Associate Professor and works at the Department of Economics and Business Economics, University of Dubrovnik. Her research interests include tourism impacts, competitiveness in tourism, sustainable tourism, and peer-to-peer tourist accommodation. She also publishes on local residents' attitudes towards tourism impacts with emphasis on World Heritage Sites.

Michał Rudnicki, Ph.D., is an Assistant Professor at the Institute of Management at Krakow University of Economics (Poland). He has authored or co-authored over 70 publications concerning innovation, business services, knowledge transfer, tourism, and new technologies. He has been the principal investigator in a few research projects.

Sandra Sánchez-Arcediano is a Ph.D. student in Tourism. She is specialised in tourism destination planning and management. She is currently specialising in risk management in coastal tourism destinations and tourism vulnerability analysis. She is very interested in the study of tsunamis, analysed from a tourist perspective.

Marino Stanković works as a Professor Assistant at the University of Dubrovnik, Department of Economics and Business. His interests are in the fields of the tourism industry and statistical analysis. He also publishes on sustainable tourism and marketing in tourism.

Dina Stober is an Associate Professor at the Josip Juraj Strossmayer University of Osijek Faculty of Civil Engineering and Architecture Osijek. Her academic and professional field is urban planning and design, focusing on urban planning, rural planning, revitalising cultural heritage, industrial buildings, and heritage.

Wataru Uehara is a Professor of Marketing at the School of Business Administration, Hitotsubashi University. His research interests include consumer behaviour, marketing management, and tourism. He has published in several academic journals, including *International Journal of Marketing & Distribution*, *Tourism*, and *Annals of Tourism Research Empirical Insights*.

Damjan Zovko, Faculty of Economics & Business, and University of Zagreb. Damjan Zovko is a student at the Faculty of Economics and Business of the University of Zagreb. He actively deals with issues of integrated environmental topics, such as resource efficiency and sustainable production and consumption. His particular areas of interest are decoupling economic growth from environmental pressures, statistics, commercial law, and corporate reporting on environmental, social, and governance issues.

Mira Zovko, Ph.D. is an Expert Advisor-Specialist for environmental and climate issues, and tourism sustainability in the Ministry of tourism and sports of the Republic of Croatia. She has over 20 years of experience in environmentally related public health issues, sustainable development, and reporting on the environment and nature as an editor of the State of the Environment Report in the Republic of Croatia, a collaborator in the creation of the European State of Environment Report (EEA), and as a member of the Steering Committee on the Future of Global Environment Outlook (UNEP).

Snježana Boranić Živoder is a Research Associate at the Institute for Tourism, Zagreb, Croatia. Her research interests include destination management and marketing, destination branding, sustainable tourism, and behavioural science. She has published in several academic journals, including *Journal of Destination Marketing & Management*, *Acta Turistica*, and *Tourism*.

Preface

Global tourism witnessed the worst-ever crisis during the COVID-19 pandemic when tourist arrivals nosedived. This sudden threat compounded the existing problems of the tourism industry, which was trying to balance the ecological, economic, political, technological, and social concerns at destinations. This ambiguity of the tourism landscape challenged the strategic decision-makers to adopt 'Innovation and Creativity' as a way of life. It was the innovative approaches that gave solutions to unprecedented pandemic times in the form of 'tourism with restrictions'. This also led to the learning that possible future environments may be more threatening, requiring a completely new approach to strategic management.

The book emerges as a timely contribution to strategic management in tourism that looks at the future of tourism in a volatile, uncertain, complex, and ambiguous (VUCA) environment. Through this book, an attempt has been made to understand the strategies and plans of tourism stakeholders during VUCA times. The diversity of strategies and plans of tourism stakeholders in equally diverse settings makes this book an invaluable guide for tourism and hospitality administrators, academicians, and students. The rich collection of articles on different dimensions of destination planning and management under VUCA adds to the appeal of this book for destination management organisations and all other tourism stakeholders.

Coverage and Structure

The book offers a strategic outlook on tourism. It is divided into 3 thematic parts as sections and has 16 chapters. The different chapters raise the relevant issues of management in turbulent environments. Each chapter takes up a unique challenge encountered at a different site, offers analysis, and provides a way forward.

'Rethinking Tourism' is the first section and includes chapters relating to newer perspectives of tourism in current times, particularly concerning the high impact and high importance areas of sustainable tourism, climatic changes, and technology.

'Community Perspectives and Tourist Behaviour in VUCA' is the second section, including contributions on unexpected and unforeseen behavioural aspects of the community and tourists during VUCA times. This very interesting part discusses the unusual acceptance of tourism by stakeholders during the pandemic and among biothreats. Pro-environmental tourist behaviours and nudging are discussed as opening new dimensions.

The third section on 'Organisational and Strategy Transformation Under VUCA' carries the discussion forward to include chapters on pro-active and reactive models and action plans in the face of VUCA challenges. Managing destination branding and reputation; organisational change and management, and case studies on business approaches under risk are highlights of this part.

The different contributions to the diversity of management approaches under turbulent times showcase human ingenuity and hope for a brighter future, even during the VUCA environment. This book offers an understanding of volatile, uncertain, complex, and ambiguous events bordering crisis and contingent solutions as a way forward. The discussions on situation analysis, new idea generation, and management of tourism are exciting and provide an in-depth understanding of relevant issues, making it a 'Guidebook' for all stakeholders in tourism ranging from graduate students to top managers, government to private players, businesses to community and many others.

Keywords: VUCA; sustainable tourism; tourism risk; tourism adaptation; strategic management

Highlights

The book appreciates Innovation, Creativity, and Resilience in the Strategic Management of tourism in the VUCA world.

The book presents novel situations and solutions to overcome the high-risk VUCA circumstances.

The book addresses the need for a strategic reevaluation of the tourism industry in the face of VUCA.

The book showcases diverse management approaches during turbulent times, demonstrating human ingenuity and optimism for a brighter future.

The book will interest a complete generation of tourism and hospitality professionals, academics, policymakers, and tourists who have seen the extremely tough COVID-19 pandemic times. The cases and discussion in the book will stay relevant and offer solutions in times to come as risk events continue to rise, such as extreme weather, geological disturbances, and pockets of the world breaking into war.

Chapter 1

Introduction: Tourism in a VUCA World

Manjula Chaudhary[a] and Naser Ul Islam[b]

[a]*Kurukshetra University Kurukshetra, Haryana, India*
[b]*Tata Institute of Social Sciences, Mumbai, India*

Abstract

Business environment has had a considerable influence on the strategic and operational choices of organisations since the beginning of industrialisation. The faster pace of change in the environment and unpredictability was observed in the advancement of the industrial ages. Strategic management thinkers studied the organisational context of turbulent environments including volatile, uncertain, complex, and ambiguous (VUCA). Ambiguity in a volatile, uncertain, and complex environment changed the rules of business altogether from structured organisations to flexible ones with living entity-like responsiveness. Strategic leadership has emerged as the radar to see solutions in unpredictable environments. The inherent vulnerability of tourism to the vagaries of outside forces makes it imperative to accept and prepare for VUCA. The future of tourism will rest in flexible, agile, innovative, and resilient business models.

Keywords: VUCA; strategic management; IA 4.0; agile and living organisations; tourism

Introduction

The business environment has always been the pervasive factor behind the success of organisations. Top management thinkers laid out its significance and developed the different tools of environmental scanning to gain the right traction for strategic and operational decision-making. The research and practice of management in almost every functional area dealt with the changing environment. New strategic approaches were developed to enhance the competitiveness and survival of business entities. Porter's different models on strategy suggest ways

Tourism in a VUCA World: Managing the Future of Tourism, 1–7
Copyright © 2024 by Manjula Chaudhary and Naser Ul Islam
Published under exclusive licence by Emerald Publishing Limited
doi:10.1108/978-1-83753-674-020241001

to add value in a competitive environment (Mathews, 2013). In a discussion on the success and failure of corporations, Drucker (2017) emphasised the realignment of an organisation's behaviour in line with the new realities of its environment. Environmental change was taken as the only permanent thing though its dynamics varied across time and space. Todnem By (2005) noted that studies on change management identify change as an ever-present element that affects all organisations, and the pace of change has never been greater than in the current continuously evolving business environment. The frequency of unexpected events of global order has increased in recent times. World Economic Forum (2023) reported that the pace of change is much faster and more disruptive in the current time and identified pandemic and technological revolution as fundamentally changing the business world.

The VUCA World in the Industrial Ages

In the field of management, the construct of a turbulent environment was identified as a 'turbulent field-ground in motion' as one of the causal textures of an organisation environment requiring a high level of adaptation (Emery & Trist, 1965). This work was carried forward by other strategic management researchers to identify the causal relationship between organisational strategies and environmental disturbances. Ansoff (1987) laid stress upon 'Strategic Issue Management' for acceptance of new and unfamiliar issues concerning a business enterprise and an early warning system for crisis who also found that the quintessential relationship of environment-capability-strategy has withstood the test of time. A number of new organisation theories were developed that were divergent from traditional theories. Open systems theory recognises the interdependence of organisations and their environment with permeable and variable boundaries (Scott, 1981). Chaos theory was developed and used for complex, non-linear, dynamic systems where long-term planning cannot be made due to the absence of equilibrium (Levy, 1994). Complexity theory recognises that organisations co-evolve with their environments, and strategic management is about a process in permanent flux, with action and learning feeding back to each other in a succession of iterations (Pina e Cunha & Vieira da Cunha, 2006). A good amount of literature on strategic management is devoted to the balance between the environment and organisations (Guerras-Martin et al., 2014). VUCA is a later formulation of a turbulent environment where ambiguity changes the game altogether as cause and effect are unknown altogether (Bennett & Lemoine, 2014a, 2014b).

To address the impact of continuing environmental changes on business, many studies were conducted in the concerned areas of management of change, organisational strategy, and operational management. Reed (2022) proposed a mindset of continuous operational improvement and strategic renewal to address environmental transitions with the objective of revealing new relationships involving operations, strategy, and performance. Agility in organisations and an agile mindset are offered as the solution around VUCA drivers (Eilers et al., 2022). The explicit focus on the human dynamics of such an endeavour of managing VUCA was suggested through three sets of interrelated actions: identifying your

VUCA, defining obstacles to agility, and implementing agility-enhancing practices (Baran & Woznyj, 2020).

The challenge was accepting sudden changes and associated risks, foreseeing patterns, devising contingency plans, and being ready for quick actions. Jarrett (2000) found that acceptance of risks for the potential of reward was an essential part of entrepreneurial business.

The history of industrialisation is witness to environmental changes. The journey of industrialisation from Industrial Age (IA) 1.0 to IA 4.0 suggests a distinct pattern wherein every new age had a shorter period and a greater disruptive effect on work and society. IA 1.0 is considered to have begun in the 18th century in 1740 and is marked by the mechanisation, use of steam, and its profound effect on urbanisation. The IA 2.0 began in the 19th century in 1870 and remained in force till 1914. This created mass manufacturing by the use of electricity and assembly line production. More changes came in the 20th century, around the 1950s, with IA 3.0, which produced electronics, computers, and information technology. This led to the spread of the digital economy, which was thought to be a big business challenge. Gates and Hemingway (2000) introduced and advocated the concept of the digital nervous system to unite all systems and processes for success in the digital economy. The current IA 4.0 that began in the 21st century in 2000 through the coming of Cyber and Physical Systems (CPS) had exponential velocity, scope, and impact, transforming production, management, and governance (Klaus, 2016). Grabowska and Saniuk (2022) study on business models in IA 4.0 found the creation of new open business models that allow the introduction of open innovations, rapid reorganisation of processes, and very flexible adjustment of the functioning of companies to new conditions and dynamically changing competitive and common environments.

Twenty-first century, marked by unexpected and fast-paced planned and unplanned interventions, has been dubbed as VUCA times and VUCA world by the researchers wherein the evolution of the cyber world, artificial intelligence, and disruptions like COVID have fast-paced countries, societies, and economies to completely new operative models (Taskan et al., 2022).

Leadership in VUCA Times

In VUCA situations, leadership becomes important. Leaders must deal with growing uncertainty, complexity, and ambiguity in their decision-making environments and with external volatility, and business leaders who stay focused on their mission and values and have the courage to deploy bold strategies building on their strengths will be the winners (George, 2017). How decision-makers observe and respond to a shock event depends on how they perceive it, and actor responses are also likely to vary depending on whether they view the occasion for decision-making as having a negative (threat) or positive (opportunity) impact (Eden et al., 2021). Begeç and Akyuz (2023) found that leaders for technology-intensive collaborative ecosystems should possess a holistic view that can oversee multiple players, dimensions, components, processes, dependencies, and interactions while understanding the VUCA challenges in managing the transformation. The governance and management strategies adopted at different levels during the COVID pandemic prove the importance of leadership and unique strategies. A study in Australia identified responsible leadership associated with innovations that serve the broader public good overcoming the different challenges posed by the crisis, as a pathway for transforming the tourism and hospitality industry towards a more sustainable and community-centred 'new normal' (Yildiz et al., 2023). Leadership role has been found to be critical in crisis management (Smits & Ezzat Ally, 2003).

Tourism in a VUCA World

The new dynamics of the IA 4.0 business world regarding management, change, organisational adaptations, and leadership were observed in the tourism industry too. The tourism industry has faced more heat from the VUCA world for having networked business models and a good presence of small- and medium-sized enterprises (SMEs). In the last decade, SMEs have been experiencing organisational challenges in adjusting to an increasingly VUCA environment ruffled by Schumpeter's gale of creative destruction (Santoso et al., 2020). Many technological advancements will happen in this IA 4.0 age, especially in implanted and wearable technologies, unmanned vehicles, as well as more humanoid robots, artificial intelligence, AI-based systems, robots, and intelligent decision-makers (Oztemel & Gursev, 2020). These developments will have tourism participating in their use and also being impacted in turn. Gössling (2021) identified usurpation (2016–2020, ongoing) as a stage of ICT adoption in the tourism industry coinciding with the growing dependence of individuals on ICT for participation in social and professional life, placing caution against the expansion of power and control mechanisms by a limited number of dominating platforms on a global scale posing the risk of barring critical opinion from the individual entangled with the ICT economy and social media dependent digital identities.

The IA 4.0 has primarily touched manufacturing and, consequently, services that are delivered through the inclusion of tangibles in the delivery chain. Tourism service delivery has different business models combining tangibles and intangibles and has undergone immense changes in current years regarding the use of technology such as robots in restaurant service, robot cleaning devices, etc. The adoption of technology gained momentum during COVID-19 when the concept of touchless service was introduced (Iskender et al., 2022). The components such as augmented reality, the Internet of Things, artificial intelligence applications, and big data make it possible to create a service difference in tourism as in other sectors (Dalkiran, 2022). The advent of the fourth industrial revolution, the evolution of technological devices, and the development of the internet are having a profound impact on tourism, qualifying the current period as the 'era of Tourism 4.0', where the digital revolution is modifying the behaviour of tourists, businesses and tourist destinations, projecting them towards a smart perspective to co-create value for tourists, workers, and local communities (Pencarelli, 2020). Chaudhary and Islam (2023) noted that the architecture of tourism will evolve consistently with the advancements in future technologies, and the increased investments in 5G technology will bridge the digital divide creating equitable access for extended tourist experiences and will also bring transparency and openness to all businesses.

Rate et al. (2018) emphasised the need for a greater depth of understanding in tourism, far beyond what suffices for many other industries, concerning the influence of the environment considering the special relationship between tourism and its marketing environment. Speakman and Sharpley (2012) found the relevance of basic tenets of chaos theory in the crisis management of tourism destinations. Tourism is a dynamic system with many interrelated parts, and change in any one of these will cascade to the whole system. The history of the VUCA environment is witness to the fact that it significantly impacts tourism, and only the flexible, adaptive, and innovative response strategies prevent the tourism business from going downhill.

The world-over response of the tourism industry during COVID-19 and its subsequent bounce back is a lesson in handling VUCA disruptions. The new reality of the VUCA world must be accepted to give newer solutions in tourism. The interactive digital technology using real-time collaboration of all tourism stakeholders will be able to generate effective live responses to threats emerging from VUCA reality. Grewatsch et al. (2023) suggested systems thinking to help strategy scholars investigate co-evolutionary dynamics, advance processual insights, and recognise tipping points and transformative change of wicked problems in place of reductionist thinking that examines parts to understand the whole systems thinking considers the context in which parts are embedded. Major and Clarke (2022) noted the idea of considering tourism as an organic living system as a new regenerative paradigm concerning the influence of environment grounded in living systems theory wherein Michelle Holliday's universal design principles for life; divergent parts, relationships, and structures, the emergent whole and life; resonate for tourism. Antonacopoulou (2018) also discussed a similar living and human approach in view of VUCA conditions calling for VUCA responses (primer), VUCA learning leadership, and proposed sensuous learning for a new learning organisation having a new form of intelligence. And the future of strategic management in tourism in the VUCA world may lie in living, agile organisations. Systems thinking is considered important to help understand and manage the interconnected tourism business (Postma & Yeoman, 2021).

Conclusion

The literature on strategic management developed for manufacturing organisations provides directions to the tourism industry for growth and sustenance under VUCA conditions. The earlier models of management considered the environment as predictable, later changed to the predictability of alternate probabilities and nonpredictable VUCA. The structured management outlook evolved towards a fluid and dynamic one as a response strategy to the VUCA world. This changed every aspect of organisational management, specifically structures, procedures, mindset, and all the related flows. The future of tourism will lie with 'learning, living, organic' organisations that can effectively leverage new technology and continually develop strategic capabilities. Apt is the comment of Wilkinson and Kupers (2013) that success in the future depends on the future success of decisions, which cannot be known in advance, but a sustained scenario practice can make leaders comfortable with the ambiguity of an open future to counter hubris and foster quick adaptation in times of crisis.

References

Ansoff, H. I. (1987). The emerging paradigm of strategic behavior. *Strategic Management Journal*, *8*(6), 501–515.

Antonacopoulou, E. (2018). Organisational learning for and with VUCA: Learning leadership revisited. *Teoria e Práctice em Administração*, *8*(2), 10–32.

Baran, B. E., & Woznyj, H. M. (2020). Managing VUCA: The human dynamics of agility. *Organizational Dynamics*, *50*(2), 1–11.

Begeç, S., & Akyuz, G. A. (2023). Requirements of collaborative and transformational leadership in digital ecosystems: Techno-orchestrating leaders in a VUCA world. *Revista de Administração de Empresas*, *63*(5), 1–30.

Bennett, N., & Lemoine, J. (2014a). What VUCA really means for you. *Harvard Business Review*, *92*(1/2), 1.

Bennett, N., & Lemoine, G. J. (2014b). What a difference a word makes: Understanding threats to performance in a VUCA world. *Business Horizons*, *57*(3), 311–317.

Chaudhary, M., & Islam, N. U. (2023). Tourism 4.0 and evolving architecture of tourism – A perspective. *Journal of Hospitality Application & Research*, *18*(2), 95–103.

Dalkiran, G. B. (2022). The effects of Industry 4.0 components on the tourism sector. In İ. İyigün & Ö. F. Görçün (Eds.), *Logistics 4.0 and future of supply chains. Accounting, finance, sustainability, governance & fraud: Theory and application*. Springer. https://doi.org/10.1007/978-981-16-5644-6_14

Drucker, P. F. (2017). *The theory of the business (Harvard Business Review Classics)*. Harvard Business Press.

Eden, L., Hermann, C. F., & Miller, S. R. (2021). Evidence-based policymaking in a VUCA world. *Transnational Corporations Journal*, *28*(3), 159–182.

Eilers, K., Peters, C., & Leimeister, J. M. (2022). Why the agile mindset matters. *Technological Forecasting and Social Change*, *179*, 121650.

Emery, F. E., & Trist, E. L. (1965). The causal texture of organizational environments. *Human Relations*, *18*(1), 21–32. https://doi.org/10.1177/001872676501800103

Gates, B., & Hemingway, C. (2000). *Business at the speed of thought: Succeeding in the digital economy*. Penguin UK.

George, B. (2017). VUCA 2.0: A strategy for steady leadership in an unsteady world. *Forbes Magazine*, 1–5.

Gössling, S. (2021). Tourism, technology and ICT: A critical review of affordances and concessions. *Journal of Sustainable Tourism*, *29*(5), 733–750.

Grabowska, S., & Saniuk, S. (2022). Business models in the industry 4.0 environment – Results of web of science bibliometric analysis. *Journal of Open Innovation: Technology, Market, and Complexity*, *8*(1), 19.

Grewatsch, S., Kennedy, S., & (Tima) Bansal, P. (2023). Tackling wicked problems in strategic management with systems thinking. *Strategic Organization*, *21*(3), 721–732. https://doi.org/10.1177/14761270211038635

Guerras-Martin, L. Á., Madhok, A., & Montoro-Sánchez, Á. (2014). The evolution of strategic management research: Recent trends and current directions. *BRQ Business Research Quarterly*, *17*(2), 69–76.

Iskender, A., Sirakaya-Turk, E., Cardenas, D., & Harrill, R. (2022). COVID or VOID: A systematic literature review of technology adoption and acceptance in hospitality and tourism since the breakout of COVID-19. *Tourism and Hospitality Research*, 14673584221133667.

Jarrett, E. L. (2000). The role of risk in business decision-making, or how to stop worrying and love the bombs. *Research-Technology Management*, *43*(6), 44–46.

Klaus, S. (2016). The fourth industrial revolution. *World Economic Forum*.

Levy, D. (1994). Chaos theory and strategy: Theory, application, and managerial implications. *Strategic Management Journal*, *15*(S2), 167–178.

Major, J., & Clarke, D. (2022). Regenerative tourism in Aotearoa New Zealand – A new paradigm for the VUCA world. *Journal of Tourism Futures*, *8*(2), 194–199.

Mathews, J. (2013). The competitive advantage of Michael Porter. In M. Witzel & M. Warner (Eds.), *The Oxford handbook of management theorists*. OUP Oxford. https://doi.org/10.1093/oxfordhb/9780199585762.013.0022

Oztemel, E., & Gursev, S. (2020). Literature review of Industry 4.0 and related technologies. *Journal of Intelligent Manufacturing*, *31*, 127–182.

Pencarelli, T. (2020). The digital revolution in the travel and tourism industry. *Information Technology & Tourism*, *22*(3), 455–476.

Pina e Cunha, M., & Vieira da Cunha, J. (2006). Towards a complexity theory of strategy. *Management Decision*, *44*(7), 839–850.

Postma, A., & Yeoman, I. S. (2021). A systems perspective as a tool to understand disruption in travel and tourism. *Journal of Tourism Futures*, *7*(1), 67–77.

Rate, S., Moutinho, L., & Ballantyne, R. (2018). The new business environment and trends in tourism. In L. Moutinho & A. Vargas Sánchez (Eds.), *Strategic management in tourism* (pp. 1–15). CABI.

Reed, J. H. (2022). Operational and strategic change during temporary turbulence: Evidence from the COVID-19 pandemic. *Operations Management Research*, *15*, 589–608. https://doi.org/10.1007/s12063-021-00239-3

Santoso, A. S., Soh, P. H., Larso, D., & Chen, J. (2020). Strategic entrepreneurship in a VUCA environment: Perspectives from Asian emerging economies. *International Journal of Entrepreneurial Venturing*, *12*(4), 343–353.

Scott, W. R. (1981). Developments in organization theory, 1960–1980. *American Behavioral Scientist*, *24*(3), 407–422.

Smits, S. J., & Ezzat Ally, N. (2003). "Thinking the unthinkable" – Leadership's role in creating behavioral readiness for crisis management. *Competitiveness Review: An International Business Journal*, *13*(1), 1–23.

Speakman, M., & Sharpley, R. (2012). A chaos theory perspective on destination crisis management: Evidence from Mexico. *Journal of Destination Marketing & Management*, *1*(1–2), 67–77.

Taskan, B., Junça-Silva, A., & Caetano, A. (2022). Clarifying the conceptual map of VUCA: A systematic review. *International Journal of Organizational Analysis*, *30*(7), 196–217.

Todnem By, R. (2005). Organisational change management: A critical review. *Journal of Change Management*, *5*(4), 369–380.

Wilkinson, A., & Kupers, R. (2013). Living in the futures. *Harvard Business Review*, *91*(5), 118–127.

World Economic Forum. (2023). The key market trends changing the ways businesses work. *World Economic Forum*.

Yildiz, M., Pless, N., Ceyhan, S., & Hallak, R. (2023). Responsible leadership and innovation during COVID-19: Evidence from the Australian tourism and hospitality sector. *Sustainability*, *15*(6), 4922.

Part I

Rethinking Tourism

Chapter 2

Management of Trends in Sustainable and Responsible Tourism Post-2023

Marko Koščak[a] and Tony O'Rourke[b]

[a]*Faculty of Tourism University of Maribor, Slovenia*
[b]*Green Lines Institute for Sustainable Development, Barcelos, Portugal*

Abstract

A key lesson from the COVID-19 pandemic was the extent to which the collapse of tourism activity underlined the sensitivity of the industry with regard to mass and over-tourism. In previous decades, we were aware of the effects of such events as terrorist attacks and environmental disasters; the pandemic provided a display of the fragility of tourism. It represented a wake-up call for us to pause and reflect on whether the type of industry tourism had become, was entirely fit for purpose and to imagine what the 'new normal' tourism would be. The problem apparent since the middle of 2022, as pandemic restrictions lessened and tourism destinations re-opened, was that there would be no 'new normal' as in many cases there would be a return to the 'old normal', as mass tourism destinations refilled with visitors and environmental degradation resumed. The sense of fragility continued, no longer impelled by the pandemic, but by new critical events in the post-pandemic world – war in Ukraine, the energy crisis, the consumer inflation crisis and rising interest rates in advanced economies, and the slowing of real economic growth. In addition, in 2023, we became even more aware of dangers from an over-heating planet – such as floods and extreme weather conditions. The longer-term prospect of many popular tourism resorts being effectively wiped out is no longer an obscure threat but a potentially concrete reality. This chapter will look at how we manage trends towards a more sustainable and responsible form of tourism.

Tourism in a VUCA World: Managing the Future of Tourism, 11–25
Copyright © 2024 by Marko Koščak and Tony O'Rourke
Published under exclusive licence by Emerald Publishing Limited
doi:10.1108/978-1-83753-674-020241002

Keywords: COVID-19 pandemic; critical factors; Dolenjska &
SE Slovenia; fragility; green & niche tourism; inflationary effects;
planning; post-pandemic tourism recovery & management;
sustainable & responsible tourism; vineyard tourism

1. Introduction

In this chapter, we will examine some of the developments from the perspective of the immediate post-COVID-19 period (2022–2023) as well as potential developments over the medium term (2024–2027). Central to this is a case study indicating aspects of local sustainable tourism through the pre-pandemic, pandemic and post-pandemic periods. This will stimulate consideration of the following issues:

- A restoration of confidence by consumers in the travel infrastructure at a local level.
- Alternatives to mass tourism have begun to occur at a local level.
- Engagement in the wider travel and tourism sector to seek and measure medium to longer-term capacity planning.
- A solid and structured pursuit of sustainability and responsibility among local tourism destinations.

It is important to understand that tourism is a complex eco-system of many players in which large multinational corporations operate alongside small companies (Koščak & O'Rourke, 2023). We are aware that probably 80% of tourism enterprises are in the SME sector, the majority of which may be defined as in the Micro and Small Enterprise (MSE) sector. All are seeking to generate income and economic effect, which is often a main priority for enterprise owners. At the same time other equally important components, such as social and environmental changes (e.g. global warming and climate change) are neglected or forgotten in everyday destination management. Tourism is regarded as one of the most important sectors in which destinations are able to generate positive economic effects, employment opportunities and well-being for the local labour force. This happens in many different types of areas and regions – urban centres, islands, coastal, rural and remote areas for many of which tourism is an economic backbone of the economy (Koščak & O'Rourke, 2021).

Our initial comments are focused on the fragility of the recovery process, the immediate perspective for sustainable and responsible tourism as well as the longer term. This inevitably focuses on the global environment but requires us to understand that global trends have a clear and dramatic impact at a local sustainable level.

Sustainable tourism is one of the approaches to the development of the tourism sector, which should assist the decision-maker in tourism to best balance its positive and negative effects on current and future populations. Sustainable tourism is defined by the United Nations World Tourism Organization (UNWTO, 1998) as 'tourism that takes full account of its current and future economic, social and environmental impacts, addressing the needs of visitors, the industry, the environment and host communities'. Sustainable tourism is not a 'niche tourism sector'; sustainable tourism principles can apply to all types of tourism including eco-tourism, agri-tourism and even mass tourism. Sustainable tourism principles recognise that tourism must balance economic, social and environmental issues in order to maximise benefits for destination communities.

Therefore, sustainable tourism should (Koščak & O'Rourke, 2023; UNEP & UNWTO, 2013):

- Make optimal use of environmental resources, maintaining essential ecosystems and helping to conserve biodiversity;
- Respect socio-cultural authenticity, conserve built and living cultural heritage and contribute to cross-cultural understanding and tolerance; and
- Ensure long-term socio-economic benefits, fairly distributed to all community stakeholders, including stable employment and income-earning opportunities, social services and poverty alleviation.

1.1. The Fragility of the Recovery Process (2022–2023)

The recovery of tourism from the spring of 2022 has been fragile and synchronistically connected with global economic trends. Global growth of 3.2% in 2022 (OECD, 2023) was significantly below what had been anticipated at the beginning of 2022, as prospects of COVID-19 recovery appeared. Tourism is to an extent regulated by the ability of consumers to engage in tourism activity; there was undoubtedly a surge of demand as post-COVID-19 restrictions were lifted from Spring 2022 across the advanced economies. However, substantive growth was impacted by the effects of the war in Ukraine and the consequential energy crisis; whilst the latter had a negative effect on the cost of living across those advanced economies.

The use of the interest rate tool by G7 central banks resulted in borrowing costs increasing and impacting tourism in terms of the costs of servicing loans and the availability of credit for financing post-COVID-19 recovery. There is also evidence of higher pricing by travel industry sectors, particularly in the mass tourism market, as they seek to recover income flows from the significant losses incurred from 2020 to 2022. This dramatic rise in pricing, prompted by cost inflation pressures, became evident in the latter part of 2022 as consumers began to book vacations into 2023 and found vacation travel and accommodation costs had doubled above pre-pandemic levels (authors' estimates).

If we look at specific markets for inbound European tourism, we can see that the US economy is likely to continue to have a decline in economic growth; potentially falling from 5.1% in 2021 (IMF WEO, 2022) to a predicted 1.5% in 2022 and 1.0% in 2023 (authors estimates). The Euro Area will decline from 5.2% in 2021 to 3.2% in 2022 and 0.5% in 2023; a recovery to 1.0% growth is unlikely to take place until 2025 (authors' estimates).

Falling economic growth indicates less capacity for consumers to spend on tourism, particularly as they wrestle with higher energy prices and escalating food costs. This may affect both domestic and overseas tourism destinations, as consumers seek tourism destinations that through currency devaluations offer better cost potentials. This is already evident in such tourism destinations as Turkey, as the huge devaluation of the currency has made tourism opportunities significantly cheaper.

1.2. The Immediate Perspective (2023)

In 2023, it is likely that tourism in the advanced economies will continue to be affected by economic and financial trends:

(a) Monetary policy determined by the major central banks will ensure that interest rates remain at above historic levels. This implies continuing pressure through 2023 on lending and the cost of lending for tourism enterprises. This will impact strongly on micro & small enterprises, whose borrowing capacity is already diminished.

(b) A new level of sensitivity is the challenge to banking stability. The March 2023 crisis affecting Credit Suisse had a significant effect on the lending appetite of mainline banking institutions as they sought to protect their solvency base. Although not matching the turmoil of the 2007–2009 period, it is likely that banks will tend to view lending activity more carefully. As always enterprises in local sustainable tourism will find themselves at the most negative edge of such trends. We should therefore compute this possibility into our analysis of underlying trends impacting the local sustainable tourism sector beyond 2023.

(c) In positive terms, cost sensitivity may well be a factor that helps and supports local sustainable tourism. Focusing on the sustainable and ethical tourism market, cost sensitivity may be less important than it is for the mass tourism/inclusive package tourism sector. In the sustainable and responsible tourism market, the objective may be seen as a vacation experience which satisfies needs and concerns about sustainability and the ethical credentials of the destination. Clearly, this may well be more achievable for what we would describe as the 'silver market', financially stable tourists with ethical and sustainable instincts who are in the 65+ age category (i.e. the 'baby boomers') and who have sufficient financial resources to be able to indulge in locally centred sustainable tourism.

1.3. The Medium Term (2024–2027)

We should take account of the following issues over the medium term:

(a) Inflation is unlikely to diminish significantly affecting not only the ability of tourism sector owners to manage costs in a timely and efficient manner but also relating to the propensity for tourism expenditure as inflation bites into disposable income. OECD suggests that headline inflation in the G20 economies will only moderate into the second half of 2024, declining to 4.5% in 2024 from 8.1% in 2022 (OECD, 2023).

(b) Food price inflation will continue to have an impact on the tourism sector over the medium period. Prices in the advanced economies (UN Food & Agriculture Organisation, 2023) are likely to remain at some 40% above the 2019 level.

(c) Job vacancies in a number of key economies remain a matter of concern; whilst nominal wage growth in the Euro area dipped during 2022, there are increasing pressures from trade unions for the restoration of parity in terms of inflation matching. Whilst this does not immediately affect the micro/small sector of tourism, it has an effect on the medium/large sector which then has the capacity to filter down into the MSE sector.

(d) The immediate expansion of global economic growth in 2021 to 6.0% was followed by a decline to 3.2% in 2022 and 2.7% in 2023 (IMF, 2022). Yet we would suggest (authors' projections) that G20 growth – a key element in tourism expenditure – will only reach 2.5% in 2025. Thus, over the medium term, the global economic situation will limit tourism growth and development.

(e) Nonetheless, we should also be aware of the green investment uptick. We have estimated that green sustainable investment across the advanced economies will grow by 220% from 2022 to 2030 (estimated on 2021 real prices). Undoubtedly much of this investment will be directed into SME projects, but should also have a useful trickle-down effect in the MSE tourism sector (authors' projections).

2. Case Study

The case study provides a number of good practices from selected tourism destination that we believe could help us to illustrate how a rethinking of the sustainability paradigm may be applied to tourism destinations worldwide. Namely, the post-pandemic discourse of sustainability has shifted towards bringing understanding of how experiential approaches in product design, security, general and personal hygiene, social distance, 'green' – away from the mass visit and towards the preserved environment, conditions for the well-being of guests and addressing nearby markets should be considered for sustaining tourism on the long run (Koščak & O'Rourke, 2023; One Planet Sustainable Tourism Programme, 2020).

2.1. Vineyard Retreats in Dolenjska, SE Slovenia

Slovenia is a country where heritage and tradition are cherished, which is also manifested through the '*Vineyards Retreats*' touristic project, developed 13 years ago in the South-East of Slovenia, in the region of Dolenjska. Vineyard retreats are smaller tourist facilities located in the midst of vineyards offering magnificent panoramic views. A wine cellar with stored wines lies under a modern furnished apartment. In various regions of the world, such a local tourism concept as that of vineyard retreats is known as 'green tourism'. Green tourism – in contrast to 'eco-tourism', which relies on travel to distant locations – seeks to provide recreational attractions and hospitality facilities to local people within their local regions, thereby reducing tourism-related travel.

Vineyard retreats were launched on the domestic and foreign touristic markets in 2010. Guests explore Slovenia's natural and cultural heritage, its traditions as well as everyday life during their stay. These retreats complement the amazing nature, beautiful cultivated landscapes, warm hospitality and cleanliness of the surroundings. In particular, visitors are able to enjoy the local cuisine as well as wines, some of which are then purchased for consumption at home.

2.2. Going for Sustainability, Green & Niche Tourism

The general global trend in the consumption segment (agriculture, cuisine and the energy sector and tourism) is to seek products that comply with the principles of respect for sustainability and environmental protection. This also applies to the niche sector of wine-growing/wine-making. The experience of pioneering countries in this field indicates that sustainability and integrated production are becoming increasingly important factors for the industry. Their experience also shows that the proportion of sustainable products in the portfolio of tourist products is required to expand in the future. However, a few conscientious individuals are not sufficient; instead, a well-planned and organised approach is required that will allow the concept of sustainability or sustainable production to become an integral part of the comprehensive story of a given wine and tourist destination. Sustainability is an opportunity for wine tourism; however, its economic feasibility must also be considered. If these trends are to be economically viable, winegrowers will ignore them at their peril. Vineyards and wine are components of a cultural heritage, which is connected to history and has been an essential element for the economic, social and cultural development of different wine regions. Wine culture has grown as part of the life, culture and diet of these regions since time immemorial. As a cultural symbol, the importance of wine has changed over time, moving from an imperative source of nutrition to a cultural complement to food and conviviality and compatible with a healthy lifestyle. Promoting wine culture adds authenticity to its origins and creates a product strongly linked to gastronomy, the pleasures of taste as well as the underlying heritage (Koščak & O'Rourke, 2023).

In terms of volume, we understand that at least in Slovenia, wine tourism is a niche product. Niche tourism refers to how a specific tourism product may be tailored to meet the needs of a particular audience/market segment. Locations with specific niche products are able to establish and position themselves, as niche tourism destinations. Niche tourism, through image creation, helps destinations to differentiate their tourism products and compete in an increasingly competitive and cluttered tourism environment. Through the use of the niche tourism life cycle, it is clear that niche products will have different impacts, marketing challenges and contributions to destination development as they progress through it. This is also extremely important and an opportunity in the post-COVID-19 environment, where safety will concern many visitors, who will wish to select destinations and products displaying a minimum level of risk to increasing volumes of visitors (Koščak & O'Rourke, 2021).

2.3. Positive Effects of Such Products

Tourism in vineyard retreats has exceptionally positive effects:

- preservation and restoration of the traditional housing heritage, without interventions in the existing space;
- new, unique accommodation facilities;
- the wine is marketed together with the facility;
- vineyards are preserved despite the recent trends of cutting down vines in the Dolenjska region (as well as across Slovenia).

It is unrealistic to expect Dolenjska to compete in wine tourism with other regions and countries as a wine-growing area given its quality, production volume, natural and cultural potential, reputation in the tourist market and the current marketing input in the field of tourism. However, it is necessary to point out that the 'Tourism in Vineyard Cottages' tourist package was a major step forward. It proved that systematic work and cooperation could help the Dolenjska tourist destination become more recognisable in this segment of its tourist industry (Koščak & O'Rourke, 2020).

Nevertheless, additional research into tourist markets, more coordinated activities and approaches are required for the successful future development of wine tourism in Dolenjska. It is important to integrate and unite all stakeholders in the tourist industry – both private and public – as well as the enthusiasts, in order for them to work together in a co-ordinated manner. This includes the co-operation of stakeholders – wineries, hotels, tour operators, restaurants, wine cellars, farmers, food producers and wine merchants. All require to be guided in a determined way by an analysis and assessment of whether wine tourism may be integrated across the various sectors and place the idea of a sustainable product, including wine and food. The main objective should be how to turn this into a convincing and marketable tourist product (Koščak & O'Rourke, 2020).

2.4. Pre- and Post-COVID-19 Trends and Statistics

The level of disruption caused by the COVID-19 pandemic has been far more severe than previous global challenges (e.g. SARS or the 2008–2009 financial crisis) and has brought fundamental changes to the travel industry worldwide. The global health crisis left governments across the advanced economies facing public health emergencies, struggling to support their economies and creating a severe effect on the tourism sector. The fundamental nature of tourism changed and recovery of the sector continues to be as gradual as the engagement of affected economies varies (European Travel Commission [ETC], 2020; Koščak & O'Rourke, 2021).

In addition, there are new challenges for sustainable tourism, which relate not only to post-COVID-19, but the current energy crisis, the cost of living crisis driven by inflation as well as problems with lack of resources in many tourism destinations (e.g. financial, managerial and structural). Tourism planning and management should therefore provide a strategy for the sustainable development of tourism destinations. It is critical that conflicting interests are examined and resolved with mutually acceptable and participative planning solutions ensuring the compatibility of different strategies and the long-term satisfaction of all stakeholders in the tourism destination. Local people at tourism destinations are the most important stakeholders, as they provide local resources to visitors in exchange for economic benefits and an improved quality of life. Adequate returns on the resources utilised by tourists must be achieved. Measures should be taken to rationalise, regulate and legislate on the use of economic, socio-cultural and environmental impacts. Appropriate types and levels of tourism activity should therefore be determined according to the goals and objectives established through a coherent and well-orchestrated planning process that examines all vulnerabilities and involves all stakeholders (Buhalis, 2000; Koščak & O'Rourke, 2023; Peters et al., 2018).

Vineyard cottage tourism, covering Slovenia's south-eastern regions of Dolenjska, Bela krajina and Kozjansko-Obsotelje, brings together some 50 owners of vineyard cottages, who have outsourced their accommodation capacities for tourist purposes. In 2017, the Slovenian Tourist Board committed itself to make Slovenia: 'A green boutique global destination for high-end visitors seeking diverse and active experiences, peace, and personal benefits. A destination of five-star experiences' (Slovenian Tourism Strategy 2017–2021). The green, boutique and sustainable tourism certainly belongs to the product Vineyard cottage tourism. The brand of vineyard cottages looks forward into the cultural and natural heritage of our country. Owners of vineyard cottages sought to transform their abandoned cottages into environmentally friendly tourism accommodations connected into an innovative tourist product. Vineyard Retreat Tourism was in 2011 given the award of the second most innovative tourist product in Slovenia by the Slovenian Tourist Board.

In 2012, the Dolenjska Destination Management Organisation (VisitDolenjska, 2012) selected five key tourism products intended for future development in domestic and foreign markets as new but the most promising tourist products – Natural and Cultural Heritage, Active Holidays, Health and Relaxation, Food & Wine, Tourism in the Vineyard Cottages. Statistics from 2010 onwards indicate that Vineyard Cottage Tourism has seen overall annual growth in volume and an increase in visits from different tourism markets. The number of overnight stays is more or less consistently growing, indicating that vineyard cottage tourism is on the rise whilst tourists seek peace, nature and sustainable tourism products at the destination (Fig. 1).

2.5. Vineyard Tourism – Achievements

From this evidence, it is clear that this product did not suffer significantly from the effects of COVID-19 pandemic. In the late spring of 2020, there were around 40% less visitors compared with previous seasons. However, after the all-year

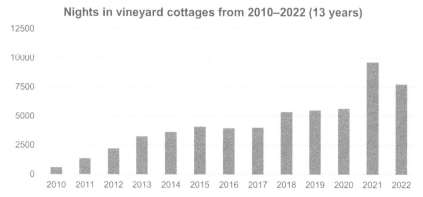

Fig. 1.   Vineyard Tourism Statistics (2010–2020). *Source*: VisitDolenjska Novo mesto (2023).

data for 2020 was released, it is clear that guests from the foreign markets were in the minority and the domestic market was the most important in the 2020 tourist season. This was due to the tourism voucher scheme, introduced by the Slovenian government, which demonstrably rescued the tourism season. As we see from the figures in 2021, the individual and boutique products were very appealing for the visitors, with the majority being from the domestic market. Data in 2021 indicate a 68% growth, an impressive result for the full year of the COVID-19 pandemic period. However, it could be concluded that those visitors who sought peace, tranquility, green and social distance including destinations away from mass tourism, are most likely to continue to select such niche products and local destinations.

The following issues relate to the post-2022 period and future tourism development. Experience indicates that the destinations successfully surviving the pandemic were those guaranteeing individual safety and distance and a high-quality natural environment. Before 2020, the key factors for the development of sustainable tourism, globally and in Slovenia, were related to (Koščak & O'Rourke, 2020; UNEP/UNWTO, 2013):

- responsible management;
- searching for added value to local products and services;
- safety and social responsibility;
- accessibility for all;
- assessment of the load-bearing acceptability of the environment;
- excessive tourism or 'overtourism';
- participatory planning;
- partnership approach.

We propose that these key factors remain critical for the future development of sustainable tourism. Nonetheless, the following new trends and actions are important in ensuring the following development in tourist destinations (Koščak & O'Rourke, 2023):

- new experiences;
- safety;
- general and personal hygiene;
- social distance;
- 'green' – remote from mass visits and preserved environment;
- conditions for good psycho-physical well-being of guests;
- addressing nearby markets.

Undoubtedly, this concerns long-term development and both providers and visitors must understand that the satisfaction of both is the key to ensuring the sustainability of the product. Despite everything, the rich natural and cultural heritage, where we can place the products of wine tourism in Dolenjska, represents a great opportunity and, above all, a challenge for better cooperation of all stakeholders.

It is likely that the tourism of past decades – e.g. the mass movement of tourist invasions – will be ahistorical image. Regrettably, mass tourism during and immediately after the pandemic appears to have created an open wound in many European economies with constant reinfection by the hordes of consumer tourists. The mass tourism phenomena require drastic changes and fundamental rethinking. The future will show if new forms and proposed long overdue changes to a scientific, human, rational and conservative niche tourism will be the single, practical cure for our collapsing tourism industry. The product 'Vineyards retreats' exactly matches all elements of that niche tourism, which to Winegrowers Associations, stipulates the future of sustainable tourism in advanced economies (Koščak & O'Rourke, 2023).

This requires a long-term commitment, whereby providers of services and visitors must understand that the satisfaction of both is key to ensuring the sustainability of the product. Nevertheless, the rich natural and cultural heritage that includes wine tourism products in Dolenjska represents an opportunity and a challenge for better cooperation among all stakeholders. The challenge for the future lies in following the principle 'Act cooperatively, promote the collective and deliver the individual'.

3. Discussion and Conclusions

3.1. Evaluating the Situation

In the immediate post-pandemic period, it was assumed that after the period of pausing and reflecting, tourism would recover through a major change in the habits and format of tourism activity. The pandemic created a sense of concern regarding health and safety issues surrounding the flow of large numbers of tourists to mass tourism resorts. In that immediate aftermath, a progressive memory lapse appeared to have indulged the mass tourism industry and its customers, as the big resorts and city centres once more filled with consumers. However, by the later months of 2022, it became evident that dynamically increasing energy prices and rampant cost of living inflationary trends, were placing a brake on economic growth in the advanced economies. By the late spring of 2023, this was also a driver of significant cost increases in inclusive tourism holiday packages and in the cost of holiday flights. Increasing interest rates also began to impact citizens disposable income. At the same time as the war in Ukraine passed into its second year, other global trends became dominant. Examples were the developing climate crisis – floods, storms and excess temperatures – and the economic migratory trends from Africa and Asia into Europe and from Central and South America into the USA. Added to this, many European countries and the UK have endured strikes by discontented travel workers, which have disrupted tourism.

At this time, we have no easy way of speculating as to the outcome of these trends. In advanced economies as disposable income shrinks in real terms and as inflation makes savings progressive of less value, may we discern that tourists from the advanced economies are changing habits? Are they, for example:

(a) Considering rural holidays in their home country on the basis of lower travel costs and the environmental benefits?
(b) Abandoning long-haul holidays (i.e. inter-continental) for short-haul (i.e. in the same continent?
(c) Using rail or car travel, especially for domestic or short-haul holidays, in place of air travel?

COVID-19 has emphasised the need to strengthen resilience in the tourism sector and awaken a sense of unity and interconnectedness among tourism stakeholders. The crisis highlights the fragility of the natural environment and the need to protect it, as well as the intersections of tourism economics, society and the environment. It represents an opportunity to accelerate sustainable consumption and production patterns and build back better tourism (One Planet Sustainable Tourism Programme, 2020). The case study therefore poses an interesting alternative – to look at the opportunities for tourism development in niche activities in local tourism destinations. Such destinations aim to provide tourist experiences which are environmentally sound and sustainable, whilst also being ethically responsible and respectful of the local culture and heritage.

3.2. Assessing the Case Study

3.2.1. What Lessons May We Be Able to Learn from the Case Study?

The case study example shows that the post-pandemic discourse of sustainability has shifted towards bringing understanding of how experiential approaches in product design, security, general and personal hygiene, social distance, 'green' – away from the mass visit and towards the preserved environment, conditions for the well-being of guests, and addressing nearby markets should be considered for sustaining tourism on the long run. Of course, this also entails the transformation of the development strategies and the search for new development paradigms, which can no longer bypass the principles of sustainable and responsible tourism or be allowed to move away from them.

The pandemic has served to demonstrate the importance of tourism as an economic force and a provider of livelihoods, raising awareness of this at the highest levels of government and amongst the public at large. However, it has also thrown light on the fragility of the sector, which is highly fragmented and interdependent, with a heavy reliance on micro and small enterprises. Furthermore, it has shown that tourism development can be imbalanced, leading to an over-dependence on the sector in some economies. Despite tourism's clear potential as a driver for positive change, it is widely accepted that rapid or unplanned tourism growth can result in a range of negative impacts, including in the use of land, water and other non-renewable resources, the generation of waste and a significant contribution to global greenhouse gas emissions. Pressure on local communities has occurred in some areas, arising from high visitor volumes and weak management, and the quality of jobs in the sector can be inconsistent. Many businesses and destinations have been unable to develop and manage tourism to their full advantage owing to a lack of planning, co-ordination, skills and resources and a failure to make the most of new opportunities offered by digitalisation.

3.2.2. Are We Able to Discern Any Critical Success Factors in the Case Study Which May Be Applied to Other Niche Sectors in Local Tourist Destinations or Indeed to Local Tourism Destination Management as a Whole?

As we stated in the case study the following new trends and the implementation of measures, such as new experiences in green destinations, safety, general and personal hygiene, social distance, 'green', remote from mass visits and preserved environment, conditions for good psycho-physical well-being of guests, addressing nearby markets and others will be important for the sustainability of local destinations. The rich natural and cultural heritage, where we can place the products of wine tourism, such as in Dolenjska, represents a great opportunity and, above all, a challenge for better cooperation of all stakeholders in the destination. The product 'Vineyards retreats' is exactly matching all elements of the niche tourism, which is, to Winegrowers Associations the future of sustainable tourism in Europe and globally (Koščak & O'Rourke, 2023).

3.2.3. Are We Able to Determine If There Are Critical Failure Factors Which May Block the Application of the Case Study to Other Sectors in Local Tourism Destinations

Local tourism destination management is the process of managing a tourist destination, or area, to ensure that it is well maintained and attractive to visitors. It involves creating an attractive environment, providing facilities and services and promoting the destination to potential visitors. It is important to ensure that the destination is a safe and enjoyable experience for visitors.

Local sustainable tourism should focus on community-based tourism and the development of locally owned businesses. This should include initiatives such as the promotion of local cultural heritage, the development of local products and services and the promotion of sustainable transportation options such as walking, biking and public transport. Local governments should also provide incentives to local businesses to encourage them to adopt sustainable practices. Additionally, local communities should be encouraged to participate in tourism activities as a way to generate income and create employment opportunities. Finally, governments should invest in educational programs to help local people understand the importance of sustainable tourism and how to implement it. The following key steps should be considered in order to avoid critical failure factors in the destination (Hoffman, 2014; Koščak & O'Rourke, 2023):

(a) *Establish clear objectives:* Establish objectives for the destination that are realistic and achievable. These objectives should include improving the visitor experience, enhancing the destination's appeal and increasing visitor numbers in manageable volume.
(b) *Develop a strategy:* Develop a strategy to achieve the objectives of the destination. This should include an assessment of the current situation, the desired outcomes and the resources and actions necessary to achieve them.
(c) *Develop a plan*: Develop a plan that outlines the steps necessary to achieve the desired objectives. This should include a budget, timelines, resources and an evaluation plan.
(d) *Manage facilities and services*: Ensure that the destination is well maintained and that all facilities and services are provided. This includes managing public areas, ensuring that necessary services are available and promoting the destination.
(e) *Promote the destination*: Promote the destination through advertising, public relations and social media.

3.2.4. How Do We Match the Flows of Rising Demand Indicated in the Case Study with the Need to Manage Footfall and Create Protection of the Natural and Cultural Heritage (Tangible and Intangible) from Excess Tourism?

Some of the following steps and measures will be important (eTurbonews, 2022):

(a) *Establish Visitor Limits:* Establish visitor limits and create a monitoring system that tracks how many visitors are in the area at any given time and how long they stay. This will help manage the number of visitors and prevent overcrowding.
(b) *Charge Fees*: Charge fees to visitors in order to discourage over-tourism and to generate revenue that can be used to protect the natural and cultural heritage.
(c) *Promote Sustainable Practices*: Promote sustainable practices such as carpooling, using public transportation, or walking/biking to help minimise environmental impacts from tourism.

(d) *Implement 'Leave No Trace' Policies*: Implement 'leave no trace' policies to ensure that visitors are respectful and mindful of nature and cultural sites.
(e) *Educate Visitors*: Educate visitors on the importance of protecting the natural and cultural heritage of the area. This can be done through brochures, signs and other materials.
(f) *Monitor the Impact of Tourism*: Monitor the impact of tourism on the natural and cultural heritage by conducting regular assessments and evaluating the effectiveness of the methods being used to protect them.
(g) *Engage Local Communities*: Engage local communities and involve them in the protection.

3.2.5. It is Important That Destination Management (DMO) Directs the Destination Products in a Sustainable and Responsible Manner, by Distributing Tourist Flows and Volumes to Different Destination Products Such As (Koščak & O'Rourke, 2023):

(a) *Agritourism:* Agritourism is a good way to capitalise on the rural landscape and local produce of a destination. Visitors can learn about the local agricultural practices, pick-your-own fruits and vegetables and sample traditional dishes made with local ingredients.
(b) *Eco-tourism*: Eco-tourism is becoming increasingly popular among tourists, who are looking for environmentally conscious ways to explore local destinations. Eco-tourism activities could include bird watching, nature walks and kayaking through local rivers or lakes.
(c) *Cultural Tourism*: Cultural tourism is a great way to learn about the history and traditions of a destination. This could include guided tours of cultural sites, such as monuments, museums and archaeological sites. It could also include cultural activities, such as traditional events, folklore and cultural workshops.
(d) *Adventure Tourism*: Adventure tourism is a great way to attract thrill-seekers to a destination. This could include activities such as trekking, mountain biking, rafting, canoeing and others.
(e) *Food Tourism*: Food tourism is becoming increasingly popular among tourists. Visitors can learn about the local cuisine, take cooking classes, and take part in food and wine tastings.

All these are part of the Dolenjska destination product mix and can be well inserted in sustainable itineraries, which offer a stay for 3–4 days in the destination.

References

Buhalis, D. (2000). Marketing the competitive destination of the future. *Tourism Management, 21*(1), 97–116.
European Travel Commission. (2020). *Handbook on Covid-19 recovery strategies for national tourism organisations*. ETC & Toposophy Ltd.

eTurbonews.(2022). *Report*.[Online].https://eturbonews.com/tourists-no-longer-concerned-about-covid-19/

Hoffman, M. L. (2014). From sustainability to resilience: Why locality matters. *Research in Urban Sociology*, *14*, 341–357. https://doi.org/10.1108/S1047-004220140000014015

International Monetary Fund. (2022). *World Economic Outlook: Countering the Cost-of-Living Crisis*. Washington, DC.

Koščak, M., & O'Rourke, T. (Eds.) (2020). *Ethical & responsible tourism – Managing sustainability in local tourism destinations* (1st ed.). Routledge.

Koščak, M., & O'Rourke, T. (2021). *Post-pandemic sustainable tourism management – The new reality of managing ethical and responsible tourism*. Routledge.

Koščak, M., & O'Rourke, T. (Eds.) (2023). *Ethical & responsible tourism – Managing sustainability in local tourism destinations* (2nd ed.). Routledge.

One Planet Sustainable Tourism Programme. (2020). *One planet vision for a responsible recovery of the tourism sector*. en-brochure-one-planet-vision-responsible-recovery.pdf (amazonaws.com).

OECD. (2023). OECD Economic Outlook, Interim Report September 2023: Confronting Inflation and Low Growth, OECD Publishing, Paris, https://doi.org/10.1787/1f628002-en.

Peters, P., Gössling, S., Klijs, J., Milano, C., Novelli, M., Dijkmans, C., Eijgelaar, E., Hartman, S., Heslinga, J., Isaac, R., Mitas, O., Moretti, S., Nawijn, J., Papp, B., & Postma, A. (2018). *Research for TRAN Committee – Overtourism: Impact and possible policy responses*. European Parliament, Policy Department for Structural and Cohesion Policies, Brussels.

UN Environment Programme & UN World Tourism Organization (UNEP & UNWTO). (2013). *Making tourism more sustainable – A guide for policy makers*. UNWTO.

UN FAO Food Price Information (2023). https://www.fao.org/worldfoodsituation/en

World Tourism Organization (WTO). (1998). *Guide for local planner authorities in developing sustainable tourism*. UNWTO.

Web Data

Slovenian Tourism Strategy 2017–2021, Government of the Republic of Slovenia (2017). https://www.slovenia.info/uploads/publikacije/the_2017-2021_strategy_for_the_sustainable_growth_of_slovenian_tourism_eng_web.pdf

VisitDolenjska (2012). https://www.visitdolenjska.eu/en/

VisitDolenjska (2023). https://www.visitdolenjska.eu/en/

Chapter 3

The New Realities of the Tourism Industry in the Era of Global Climate Changes

Mira Zovko[a] and Damjan Zovko[b]

[a]*Ministry of Tourism and Sports, Zagreb, Republic of Croatia*
[b]*Faculty of Economics & Business, University of Zagreb, Croatia*

Abstract

The global energy transition is a process without historical experience that affects all participants in the technological chain of energy management, citizens and business entities. This increasingly dynamic process is aimed at decarbonisation of the entire economy, social stability and human well-being. We are witnessing the rapid development of more energy-efficient technologies, clean energy sources and stricter rules regarding the greenhouse gas (GHG) emissions. The data clearly show changes in the Earth's climate system. Their consequences represent the most urgent threat to the longevity of tourism, which is one of the five most threatened economic sectors. At the same time, tourism continues to have a significant contribution to climate change due to growing GHG emissions, primarily from transport and accommodation facilities.

This chapter seeks to provide an overview of the drivers of GHG emissions and societal responses aimed at addressing tourism-related carbon emissions. It also offers an overview of climate and energy public policies and possible solutions towards a net-zero carbon future for the tourism industry. The purpose of this review is to empower tourism practitioners with current knowledge funded in global and European decarbonisation strategies and encourage them to reflect and create a new and more effective solution.

Keywords: Low-carbon tourism; climate policy; energy policy; climate change mitigation; decoupling

Tourism in a VUCA World: Managing the Future of Tourism, 27–42
Copyright © 2024 by Emerald Publishing Limited
All rights of reproduction in any form reserved
doi:10.1108/978-1-83753-674-020241003

1. Introduction

It is widely accepted that the main cause of ecosystem degradation is the deple-
tion of natural resources, which is the consequence of human activities such as
intensive agriculture, deforestation and soil sealing for the construction of human
settlements and related infrastructure. Accelerated climate changes and global
warming additionally affect the vulnerability of ecosystems, and consequently
human well-being (World Economic Forum [WEF], 2023). Impacts of climate
changes are intrinsically linked to the loss of natural resources that manifests in
significant decline of biodiversity and the change of chemical composition of
marine and water resources, including degradation of soil and melting of ice in
cold regions. In the Sixth Assessment Report of the Intergovernmental Panel on
Climate Change (IPCC) (2022a), scientists estimated that most of the impacts of
climate change affect drinking water sources. Drought, floods and degradation
of water and terrestrial ecosystems will cause increased risk to the freshwater
quality. Rising temperatures allow the spread of vector-borne diseases and the
increased number of days per year with a maximum temperature above 35 °C
cause an increase in frequency of extreme heat and fires. Climate changes also
decrease crop productivity threatening food supplies. Frequent occurrences of
extreme weather conditions adversely affect human health and property. According to estimates of climate-related risks, the IPCC indicates that the window to
address the climate crisis is closing rapidly (IPCC, 2022a).

For more than three decades, it appears that environmental governance has
attempted to alter business-as-usual and behavioural patterns of the global population towards sustainable choices. All economic sectors, including tourism, are
steered by public policies and initiatives to decouple economic growth from GHG
emissions and unsustainable usage of natural resources. Decisions should be
made in favour of projects and activities that are in line with the Paris Agreement
and associated climate and energy policies (EC, 2021a).

In the context of global and EU climate efforts, this chapter systematises
opportunities and challenges of tourism's energy transition. It highlights some of
the most creative and successful solutions. The purpose of this review is to raise
the awareness of tourism experts regarding net-zero carbon future and ways of
improving their business in accordance with upcoming requirements.

2. Drivers of Carbon Emissions in the Tourism Industry

2.1. Tourism in the Context of the Global Energy Transition

Global economic growth requires increased energy consumption. Carbon emissions mainly arise from industrial processes, combustion of fossil fuels in motor
vehicles and stationary sources (e.g. power plants, home heating and cooling), but
they are also incorporated into numerous goods and services (Perera, 2017). After
two years of extreme variability in industrial production, disruptions in energy
use and fuel trade flows, global energy-related GHG emissions rose by 0.9% (or
321 Mt CO_2 eq.) and GDP grew by 3.2% in 2022. According to the same source,
around 60 Mt CO_2 eq. could be attributed to cooling and heating requirements in

extreme weather conditions. Reduction in industrial production, increased use of renewable energy sources and the increasingly widespread use of electric vehicles and heat pumps helped prevent an additional 550 Mt of CO_2 eq. (IEA, 2023).

The tourism industry is a widely recognised economic sector with an estimated 4.4% growth rate between 2023 and 2027 (Statista, 2023). Depending on the estimates, the carbon footprint of tourism ranges between 5% and 10% of global emissions (Lenzen et al., 2018; UNWTO, UNEP & WMO 2008; WTTC, UNEP & UNFCCC, 2021). Recent projections revealed that compared to 2016 GHG emissions from the tourism industry could increase by 25% until 2030 (UNWTO & ITF, 2019). The European Travel Commission (ETC) warns that by 2050, GHG emissions from the tourism could increase by 170% if the decarbonisation process is not accelerated (ETC, 2018).

As a key part of the tourism industry, passenger transport is the largest contributor to carbon emissions. Three-quarters of tourism's GHG emissions are generated from aviation and road transport, which amounts to 5% of all global energy-related GHG emissions (UNWTO & ITF, 2019). The aviation industry is expected to triple the use of fuels and double GHG emissions by 2050 (ATAG, 2021; ICAO, 2020). Nevertheless, the potential of more sustainable fuels in aviation is significant, although they represent only 0.05% of the total fuel consumption in this type of transport (Eurocontrol, 2022). The IPCC urges immediate action to cut GHG emissions from transportation in order to stabilise the climate, particularly with regard to the production of 'clean carbon' alternative fuels (IPCC, 2014). According to the Cruise Lines International Association (CLIA, 2020), the number of cruise passengers increased by 10% in the period 2008–2018. The weighted average value of energy consumption per night per cruise passenger is 12 times higher than the value for a land-based hotel (1,600 MJ) (Howitt et al., 2010). Decarbonisation of the cruise industry is ongoing through the introduction of alternative carbon-clean fuels, such as liquefied natural gas (LNG) and other bio and synthetic hydrogen-derived fuels (Wang et al., 2023a). Additionally, decarbonisation strategies frequently take into account additional measures including fleet optimisation, energy efficiency and itinerary efficiency. Since international shipping and flight travel account for 5% of global emissions (UNEP, 2022) the production and use of more sustainable fuels (particularly synthetic ones), as well as the development of green ports are critical in accelerating the decarbonisation of air and maritime transportation.

Accommodation as an integral part of the tourism value chain accounts for around 20% of the sector's GHG emissions (UNWTO, UNEP & WMO, 2008). It mainly comes from purchased services with a share of 55%, while energy consumption in tourism-related facilities is the second important source of carbon emissions with a share of 37% (WTTC, 2021). Depending on the types and approaches to energy consumption, different tourist facilities have variable energy intensities (Gössling & Lund-Durlacher, 2021). Among all categories of tourist accommodation, hotels are the biggest energy consumers, mostly due to heating, cooling and food preparation. They usually rely on 24-hour functions that are often characterised by reckless energy waste for business operations and unsustainable behavioural patterns of visitors (Deng, 2023). Besides, disruptive innovations that offer accommodation on digital platforms (such as AirBnB), as well as the constant interest in second homes represent additional sources of carbon emissions (Zervas et al., 2017).

2.2. Heterogeneity in the Emission Profiles of the Tourism Industry

The carbon footprint of the tourism industry encompasses the direct and indirect emission of tourist activities and its embodiment in the goods and services. Tourists and travellers generate direct emissions from tourism consumption, whereas indirect emissions are the result of suppliers entering the tourism industry. Because indirect carbon demands frequently are omitted from the calculation, previous estimates of the carbon footprint of tourism were frequently inaccurate (Volpi & Paulino, 2018). It is challenging to estimate indirect emissions since they arise from any industry involved in the supply chain that produces a tourism-related good and service. Today, there is an urgent requirement to determine the total carbon footprint of a travel and tourism package and publicly reveal the overall carbon emission estimation. Travel and tourism activities may include specific NACE (rev.2) economic activities, such as Land transport and pipeline transport (H49), Water transport (H50), Air transport (H51), Accommodation and food service activities (I), Travel agencies, tour operators and other reservation services and related activities (N79), Office activities, administrative, office and other auxiliary business activities (N82); Creative, artistic and entertainment activities (R90); Libraries, archives, museums and other cultural activities (R91); Gambling and betting (R92) and Sports, entertainment and recreational activities (R93) (EC, 2021b). It is obvious that kind of heterogeneity in the emission profiles of tourism supply represents a challenging effort to decrease carbon emissions through the entire value chain. It requires a holistic and interdisciplinary approach with consensus over differing operational structures and commitments to agreed metrics.

2.3. Gradual Decoupling of Economic Growth and GHG Emission

Traditionally, economists and environmental scientists support decoupling as a measure of efficient natural resource use in the context of constant economic growth (Adriaanse et al., 1997; Matthews et al., 2000). According to IPCC (2022a), decoupling refers to economic growth that is no longer closely correlated with the use of fossil fuels. Many scholars agreed that the decoupling of economic growth (expressed as GDP) from air pollutants (GHG emissions, ozone precursors and/or acidifying substances) represents a measure of effects generated by variety of industries on the environment (Ward et al., 2016; Zovko & Zovko, 2020).

According to the Report of the Working Group on Decoupling to the International Resource Panel, both relative and absolute decoupling are possible (UNEP, 2011). Relative decoupling is apparent when emissions are lowered at a slower rate than the rate at which economic activity is growing. Absolute decoupling refers to the overall reduction in emissions even when the economy expands. Relative decoupling is typically more prevalent in economies around the world (Haberl et al., 2020). Unlike relative decoupling, absolute decoupling of GHG emissions from economic growth is quite difficult to achieve because fossil fuels remain the main source of energy. This would only be feasible if there is a simultaneous absolute quantitative decrease in carbon emissions across all economic sectors within a parallel increase in economic efficiency (Umpfenbach, 2015).

In the last 10 years, a growing number of countries have reduced their GHG emissions according to their mitigation strategies (IPCC, 2022b). However, their annual decline in GHG emissions is relatively small compared to the global growth of the emissions observed over the recent decade. Complementary evidence suggests that countries have decoupled territorial GHG emissions from GDP, but fewer have decoupled consumption-based emissions from GDP. The decoupling has mainly occurred in countries with high GDP per capita and high GHG emissions per capita, which is not sufficient to tackle the climate crisis. According to the same source, there is an urgent need to enhance urban mitigation activities given the dual issues of increased urban carbon emissions and future estimates of more frequent extreme climate events. However, the above-mentioned challenges prevented the decoupling of economic growth from GHG emissions. According to IEA (2023), the GHG emissions intensity expressed in the metric tonnes of CO_2 eq. per unit of economic value (or product produced) has slowed compared to the previous decade.

The empirical data suggest that tourism boosts economic growth and GHG emissions (Jiaqi et al., 2022; Lawal et al., 2018). The fact that tourism mainly relies on fossil fuels leading to the conclusion that GHG emissions of the tourism industry are related in a causal way. Accordingly, it is obvious that consumption-based emissions are associated with the travel and tourism demands, which are being transformed due to the interests of visitors, but also regarding current climatic conditions. For example, in the last few decades, urban tourism has grown significantly (Page & Duignan, 2023; UNWTO & WTCF, 2018). Due to the growth of urban tourism in cities, carbon emissions from transportation, accommodation, catering and shopping related to tourist activities are increasing (Tian, 2023). It seems that this type of tourism enhances the unused potential of low-carbon development of urban areas. On the other hand, a recent European study (EC & JRC, 2023) reveals that the north-south pattern in tourism demand changes regarding seasonal and regional distributions. While Southern regions face a significant decrease in tourist demand during the summer season, Northern areas register an increase during the summer and early autumn season.

As a result, these changes and increases in travel and tourism activities will unavoidably slow the eventual decoupling of economic growth from GHG emissions in most of the urban tourism destinations. Therefore, it is crucial to implement low-carbon strategies as soon as possible (Zhang & Zhang, 2020), particularly in light of the noticeable rise in the frequency of extreme weather conditions. Local economic competitiveness funded on green and digital solutions with sustainable visitor behaviour may contribute to lowering urban carbon emissions and resilience of overall tourism.

3. Societal Responses to Lowering Tourism-Related GHG Emissions

3.1. International and EU Climate Policy to Tackle Global Climate Crisis

Progress in mitigating climate change has been ongoing since 1992 when signatory countries to the United Nations Framework Convention on Climate Change (UNFCCC) committed to adopting national climate policies (UNFCCC, 1992). Since then, scientists and policy makers have intensified their efforts to structure public policies and initiatives aimed at mitigating and adapting to climate change. The Paris Agreement was ratified in 2016 by 196 signatory nations on the Conference of the Parties (COP) 21 with the consensus to limit global warming no more than 1.5 °C, to reduce carbon emissions by 45% until 2030 and reach net zero by 2050 (UN, 2016). Getting to net zero requires all governments to strengthen their Nationally Determined Contributions (NDCs) and take urgent action to reduce carbon emissions.

In 2021, The Glasgow Climate Pact was adopted at the UNFCCC COP 26 held in Glasgow. It was the call for all governments to improve their Nationally Determined Contributions (NDCs) by reviewing and strengthening their 2030 emission reduction targets, by the end of 2022 (UNFCCC, 2021). The latest IPCC's Sixth Assessment Report unambiguously confirmed that the atmosphere, ocean, and land have warmed due to human influence. Those changes have occurred rapidly across the globe in the cryosphere, atmosphere, ocean, and biosphere (IPCC, 2022b). All around the world climate change is causing climate extremes with adverse impacts on all industries, including the travel and tourism sector. The tourism industry is particularly vulnerable due to extreme weather events like heat waves, heavy rainfalls, droughts, and tropical cyclones. According to IPCC (2022a) tourism is one of the five most threatened economic sectors along with agriculture, forestry, fishery and energy. Over the next several decades or longer, many natural and human systems will confront additional serious risks (WEF, 2023).

European goal is to become the first climate-neutral continent. In 2019, EU member states reported that they have already adopted or planned to adopt 1,925 national policies and measures to reduce GHG emissions through progress in energy efficiency and renewable energy (EEA, 2019). Recently, EU delivered a comprehensive development strategy – EU Green Deal and announced the establishment of the EU Taxonomy as a classification tool for sustainable investments. In its impact assessment Stepping up Europe's 2030 climate ambition – investing in a climate-neutral future for the benefit of our people the EC has recognised that its current policies and national measures will result in only 45% reduction of carbon emissions by 2030, if fully implemented (EC, 2020). According to the same source, the projections showed that by simply continuing to implement the existing EU legislation GHG emissions would be reduced by 60% until 2050, which is not sufficient.

Therefore, the European Commission introduced the EU Climate Law as a legally binding regulation with a long-term requirement for EU member states to reach zero net GHG emissions by 2050, and a short-term objective of cutting emissions by 55% until 2030 (EC, 2021c). Accordingly, provisions of the EU Green Deal and EU Climate Law required the strongest harmonisation of EU policy. In order to decarbonise the entire European economy, the EC started the alignment process by developing a set of new legislative documents and reforms. Climate, land use, energy, transportation and taxation are the five policy areas of Fit for 55 policy package (EC, 2021d). This combination of regulatory provisions, carbon pricing instruments and reporting obligation strengthened energy efficiency, increased the use of renewable energy sources, promoted new carbon emission rules and introduced the Social Climate Fund.

Additionally, EU member states vowed to lessen dependence on foreign energy sources, enhance energy efficiency, reduce environmental pollution and pressures on natural resources, improve health and well-being, and foster new opportunities for innovation, investment and employment. Additionally, aside from multilateral alliances of nations like the OECD, the EU emerges as a global leader in the 'green growth' initiative. It is meant to facilitate economic development and growth while preserving natural resources and ecosystem services within secure ecological bounds (EC, 2019; OECD, 2012). These principles served as the cornerstone for EU's green and digital transition. Its successful implementation is proof that economic growth and environmental sustainability can be mutually reinforcing.

3.2. The Policy Initiatives and Regulations for Net-Zero Carbon Future of Tourism

It seems that the tourism industry was not explicitly targeted by climate and energy regulations until recently. According to scientific and professional sources, it can be concluded that the key challenges for defining viable policies related to ensuring net-zero carbon future of tourism were its complexity in terms of activities, goods and services, as well as the difficulties in assessing its overall carbon footprint. These challenges have been successfully answered with strongest low-carbon initiatives in the last decade (UNWTO, 2021). It appears that approaches that are more systematic are being taken to address the issues arising from the complexity of the tourism value chain and the fragmentation of the GHG measuring landscape (UNWTO, 2023).

As one of the outcomes of COP 26, The Glasgow Declaration coordinates climate actions among various tourism stakeholders, including international organisations, government and institutional agencies, donors and financial institutions, civil society, the private sector, academia and the general public (UNWTO, 2021) aimed at halving emissions by 2030 and achieving net zero by 2050. It is an integral part of the United Nations World Tourism Organization's One Planet Sustainable Tourism Agenda.

With the primary objective of maintaining Europe as a top travel destination in the world, the European Parliament adopted the Resolution on establishing the EU Strategy for Sustainable Tourism in 2021 (EC, 2021e) in line with the

EU Green Deal, the EU Digital Strategy, and the UN Sustainable Development Goals. It was adopted with the aim to prevent carbon-intensive tourism and to promote travel and travel activities with a minimal impact on the environment, such as ecotourism, cultural tourism, and agro-tourism. It urges the governments of EU member states to base their tourism strategies and plans on environmentally friendly, fiscally responsible, resilient, and climate-neutral solutions. The resolution gaining access to certain EU funds and announces the role of the European Investment Bank in promoting tourism decarbonisation. The recently published EC's report (2022) Transition Pathway for Tourism outlines the components of sustainable tourism as follows: infrastructure, social dimension of skills, investment and financing, research and innovation, green and digital technological solutions, and research and innovation. The aforementioned components are combined with horizontal policies in Europe to steer the growth of its tourism sector, with a focus on environmental sustainability, the digital transition, climate neutrality, and increased tourist community resilience. As a followup to this report, the European Agenda for Tourism 2030 was adopted in 2022. It supports digital transformation, more sustainable development, and the restoration of the tourism industry following the pandemic crisis (EU, 2022). It calls on Europeans to change their travel and tourism habits, and tourism stakeholders to assist decarbonisation of travel-related mobility. EU member states are advised to raise the energy efficiency of tourism and lessen its adverse effects on ecosystems by low-carbon technological innovations. This document highlighted the importance of achieving the growth of multimodal travel with 'smart' and sustainable modes of transportation. It is expected that the EC synergistically complement the architecture of EU decarbonisation management with new documents on tourism policy and its instruments, instead of fundamentally changing it.

3.3. Nexus Between Tourism and Innovation

Reducing carbon emissions throughout the energy sector requires a green and digital transition. This trajectory implies a significant reduction in the total use of fossil fuels, the transition to clean energy and a higher degree of energy efficiency with inevitable innovative 'smart' solutions (Jahanger et al., 2022; Wen et al., 2022). Successful application of low-carbon innovations in the technical and technological sense as well as in the field of innovative business operations are more visible in the tourism industry.

It seems that energy use in tourist facilities relies on three aspects: technological solutions implemented (Cingoski & Petrevska, 2018; López-Bernabé et al., 2021), the perspectives and choices of executives and staff members (Chou, 2014; Wang et al., 2023b) and the potential for guest participation in energy savings (Ali et al., 2008; Gössling et al., 2019). The tourism industry is increasingly implementing renewable energy sources, energy-efficient measures and clean energy for transportation, including innovative approaches for low-carbon business processes. Additionally, the gradual implementation of digital solutions on physical equipment, which lowers energy consumption and GHG emissions, is supporting the low-carbon transformation efforts of tourism. The use of light, heat and cooling sensors, networked devices, energy data analytics and digitised services for customised experiences are dramatically changing and improving the comfort of low-carbon tourism facilities (Youssef & Zeqiri, 2022). Owners and managers may be more interested in building low-energy accommodations with eco-design (passive heating and cooling) if they have access to energy consultancy and incentive programs. Increased energy awareness, along with changes in service design, particularly in food preparation and serving, can lead to further decreases in carbon emissions. Finally, behavioural changes aimed at reducing the carbon footprint suggest that all tourism stakeholders are developing a greater awareness of their travel habits and the consequences of energy-intensive tourism.

There are evidences that decarbonisation is a driver of added value in terms of increased financial resources that could be directed towards sustainable-oriented operations and increased productivity (Cadarso et al., 2016; Gössling et al., 2023). According to several authors (Gössling & Lund-Durlacher, 2021; Versteijlen et al., 2017), climate-focused strategies and staff training on low-carbon operations could considerably contribute to operational energy savings and have a favourable impact on behavioural changes. Gössling and Lund-Durlacher (2021) stated that accommodation has the potential for total decarbonisation by 2040. To reduce carbon emissions and the price of carbon removal technologies it is equally vital to preserve and enhance natural carbon sinks like wetlands, soil, agricultural lands, and forests. Even while it involves a variety of anthropogenic activities and services, such as food preparation, laundry rooms and wellness, it appears that decarbonising tourist accommodation is far more achievable than the decarbonisation of passenger transportation.

By increasing production and markets for environmentally friendly technologies and goods, the green and digital transition represents a significant opportunity for tourism business. It can be said that digitialisation is now considered a critical factor in the decarbonisation of the travel and tourism industry. Nevertheless, regulatory, infrastructural, financial and security barriers need to be overcome (Ye, 2021).

3.4. The Challenges in Assessing Tourism's Carbon Emissions

As previously mentioned, heterogeneity in the emission profiles of the tourist offer is a distinct challenge to calculate the carbon footprint of tourism. Individual indicators could be used to track GHG emissions from the tourism industry, but only to a limited extent. Thus, within the EU Nomenclature of Economic Activities (NACE rev2), the indicator Air emissions accounts for GHG emissions is available for the sectors Accommodation and food services (I) and Travel agencies, tour operators and other reservation services and related activities (N79) (Eurostat, 2023). Comprehensive indicators are available on the EC platform EU Tourism Dashboard, according to the Nomenclature of Territorial Units for Statistics (NUTS) at the national and regional level (EC, 2023). The EC has created six indicators for environmental impact on tourism, and three of them are climate-related: Tourism GHG intensity, Tourism energy intensity and Air travel emission intensity.

For the development of tourism products that prioritise sustainability and calculate their carbon footprint, a number of sustainability indicator systems are available. The most important are the UNWTO framework for sustainability assessment and the European Tourism Indicators System (ETIS) of the European Commission (Marković Vukadin et al., 2020). It is also possible to use some models to investigate the impacts (I) of population (P), affluence (A) and technology (T) on the environment (Ehrlich & Holdren, 1971). According to this IPAT model, Japanese economists developed the Kaya identity, which applies specifically to GHG emissions (Kaya & Yokoburi, 1997). It is a specific form of a more general IPAT model, where emission scenarios cover a wide range of driving forces – from demographic, to technological and economic developments. It consists of four main drivers of GHG emission: population growth, GDP per capita, energy intensity (energy consumed per unit of GDP) and carbon intensity (emissions per unit of energy consumed). For detecting GHG emissions resulting from essential socio-economic patterns the Kaya identity could be implemented in the tourism industry to a higher extent (Robaina-Alves et al., 2016). Accordingly, economic scale and energy savings serve as the primary causes of change in GHG emissions, whilst technological advancements in energy efficiency are the key drivers of emission control.

4. Conclusion

Energy consumption is directly correlated to economic growth (GDP). Generated from non-renewable sources it is strongly contributing to the inventory of GHG emissions. Nevertheless, the slow transition from fossil fuels to clean energy has exposed the global economy and population to the greatest challenge facing humanity so far – climate change. It is a systematic threat that affects all aspects of the economy and life on Earth.

To ensure the long-term economic stability and human well-being, the international community has directed efforts on green energy transition towards net-zero carbon future and particularly towards decoupling of economic growth from GHG emissions. Targeted international agreements and binding legislation, efficient economic and fiscal policies including innovative technologies and solutions are cornerstones of tourism decarbonisation. In addition, a unified framework for measuring and reporting GHG emissions and educational initiatives are equally important prerequisites for making informed decisions and raising awareness of the path towards a net zero carbon future. Moreover, the window for addressing the global warming crisis is rapidly shrinking, thus linking all industries in coordinated and timely action towards a net zero carbon future should be of outmost importance.

Tourism is a sophisticated industry as it encompasses a wide range of sectors and activities with different energy consumption demands. As it mainly relies on fossil fuels, tourism part in climate neutrality efforts is quite challenging. The effort aimed at the reduction of carbon emissions requires the close cooperation of numerous tourism stakeholders and related sectors to support and accelerate tourism decarbonisation. It is evident that the tourism industry can no longer depend only on the decarbonisation strategies of other economic sectors but should additionally determine its energy transition on the decoupling of economic growth from carbon emissions. On the other hand, climate determines the length and cycles of tourist seasons, the suitability of the specific type of destination for a wide range of activities and has a significant impact on business costs. It seems that the actual implications of climate change cause a kind of uncertainty on the geographical and seasonal redistribution of visitor flows, but also significant changes in existing business models.

Today, the tourism industry has taken a more serious approach towards decarbonisation. It adopts new concepts of long-term profitability due to the growing implications of climate change, an increase in energy costs and energy uncertainty. It is obvious that new climate and energy initiatives, regulatory provisions and carbon pricing instruments encourage the design of innovative products and services. In this sense, low-carbon tourism offers a significant opportunity to boost economic benefits resulting from reduced energy consumption and lower costs associated with carbon pricing. Decreasing operational costs boosts revenue and makes it possible to encourage pro-environmental behaviour while increasing the attractiveness of the tourist market.

References

Adriaanse, A., Bringezu, S., Hammond, S., Moriguchi, Y., Rodenburg, E., Rogich, D., & Schuetz, H. (1997). *Resource flows: The material basis of industrial economies*. World Resources Institute.

Ali, Y., Mustafa, M., Al-Mashaqbah, S., Mashal, K., & Mohsen, M. (2008). Potential of energy savings in the hotel sector in Jordan. *Energy Conversion and Management*, *49*(11), 3391–3397. https://doi.org/10.1016/j.enconman.2007.09.036

Aviation Transport Action Group (ATAG). (2021). *Waypoint 2050. Balancing growth in connectivity with a comprehensive global air transport response to the climate emergency: A vision of net-zero aviation by mid-century* (2nd ed.). https://www.atag.org/our-publications/latest-publications.html

Cadarso, M., Gómez, N., López, L. A., & Tobarra, M. (2016). Calculating tourism's carbon footprint: Measuring the impact of investments. *Journal of Cleaner Production*, *111*(part b), 529–537. https://doi.org/10.1016/j.jclepro.2014.09.019

Chou, C. J. (2014). Hotels' environmental policies and employee personal environmental beliefs: Interactions and outcomes. *Tourism Management*, *40*, 436–446. https://ideas.repec.org/a/eee/touman/v40y2014icp436-446.html

Cingoski, V., & Petrevska, B. (2018). Making hotels more energy efficient: the managerial perception. *Economic Research*, *31*(1), 87–101. https://doi.org/10.1080/1331677X.2017.1421994

Cruise Lines International Association. (2020). *State of the cruise industry outlook 2020*. https://cruising.org/-/media/research-updates/research/state-of-the-cruise-industry.pdf

Deng, S. (2023). Energy and water uses and their performance explanatory indicators in hotels in Hong Kong. *Energy and Buildings*, *35*(8), 775–784. https://doi.org/10.1016/S0378-7788(02)00238-4

Ehrlich, P. R., & Holdren, J. P. (1971). Impact of population growth. *Science*, *171*(3977), 1212–1217. https://www.jstor.org/stable/1731166

Eurocontrol. (2022). *Objective Skygreen 2022–2030: The economics of aviation decarbonization towards the European Union 2030 Green Deal milestone.* https://www.eurocontrol.int/publication/objective-skygreen-2022-2030

Eurostat. (2023). *Greenhouse gas emission statistics – Emission inventories.* https://ec.europa.eu/eurostat/statistics-explained/index.php?title=Greenhouse_gas_emission_statistics_-_emission_inventories

European Commission (EC). (2019, December 11). *Communication from The Commission to The European Parliament, The European Council, The Council, The European Economic and Social Committee and the Committee of the regions. The European Green Deal (COM 640 final).* https://eur-lex.europa.eu/legal-content/EN/TXT/?uri=COM%3A2019%3A640%3AFIN

European Commission (EC). (2020, September 17). *Communication from the Commission to the Parliament, the Council, the European Economics and Social Committee and the Committee of the Regions: Stepping up Europe's 2030 climate ambition Investing in a climate-neutral future for the benefit of our people (COM 562 final).* https://eur-lex.europa.eu/legal-content/EN/TXT/?uri=CELEX:52020DC0562

European Commission (EC). (2021a, September 16). *Commission Notice – Technical guidance on the climate proofing of infrastructure in the period 2021-2027 (C 373).* https://eur-lex.europa.eu/legal-content/EN/TXT/?uri=CELEX:52021XC0916(03)

European Commission (EC). (2021b, May 5). *Annual Single Market Report 2021 Accompanying the Communication from the Commission to the European Parliament, the Council, the European Economic and Social Committee and the Committee of the regions updating the 2020 new industrial strategy: Building a stronger single market for Europe's recovery.* https://eur-lex.europa.eu/legal-content/en/TXT/?uri=CELEX%3A52021SC0351

European Commission (EC). (2021c, June 30). *Regulation (EU) 2021/1119 of the European Parliament and of the Council of 30 June 2021 establishing the framework for achieving climate neutrality and amending Regulations (EC) No 401/2009 and (EU) 2018/1999 (European Climate Law) (L 243/1).* https://eur-lex.europa.eu/legal-content/EN/TXT/?uri=celex%3A32021R1119

European Commission (EC). (2021d, July 14). *Communication from the Commission to the European Parliament, the Council, the Europe am Economic and social committee and Committee of the Regions Empty "Fit for 55": delivering the EU's 2030 Climate Target on the way to climate neutrality (COM 550 final).* https://eur-lex.europa.eu/legal-content/EN/TXT/?uri=CELEX%3A52021DC0550

European Commission (EC). (2021e, March 25). *European Parliament of 25 March 2021 on Establishing an EU Strategy for Sustainable Tourism (C 494/106).* https://eur-lex.europa.eu/legal-content/EN/TXT/?uri=CELEX%3A52021IP0109

European Commission (EC). (2022, March 10). *European Commission, Directorate-General for Internal Market, Industry, Entrepreneurship and SMEs: Transition Pathway for Tourism (Report of the European Union).* https://op.europa.eu/en/publication-detail/-/publication/404a8144-8892-11ec-8c40-01aa75ed71a1/language-en

European Commission (EC). (2023). *EU Tourism Dashboard – Indicator Map view.* https://tourism-dashboard.ec.europa.eu/?lng=en&ctx=tourism

European Commission & Joint Research Centre (EC & JRC). (2023). *Regional impact of climate change on European tourism demand.* Publications Office of the European Union. https://data.europa.eu/doi/10.2760/899611

European Environment Agency (EEA). (2019). *Trends and projections in Europe 2019: Tracking progress towards Europe's climate and energy targets, Technical report 15/2019, Luxembourg.* https://dio.org/10.2800/51114

European Travel Commission (ETC). (2018, March 18). *Tourism and Climate Change Mitigation – Embracing the Paris Agreement.* https://etc-corporate.org/reports/tourism-and-climate-change-mitigation-embracing-the-paris-agreement/

European Union (EU). (2022, December 1). *Council conclusions on "European Agenda for Tourism 2030".* https://data.consilium.europa.eu/doc/document/ST-15441-2022-INIT/en/pdf

Gössling, S., Araña, J. E., & Aguiar-Quintana, J. T. (2019). Towel reuse in hotels: Importance of normative appeal designs. *Tourism Management, 70,* 273–283. https://doi.org/10.1016/j.tourman.2018.08.027

Gössling, S., & Lund-Durlacher, D. (2021). Tourist accommodation, climate change and mitigation: An assessment for Austria. *Journal of Outdoor Recreation and Tourism, 34,* 100367. https://doi.org/10.1016/j.jort.2021.100367

Gössling, S., Balas, M., Mayer, M., & Sun, Y. (2023). A review of tourism and climate change mitigation: The scales, scopes, stakeholders and strategies of carbon management. *Tourism Management, 95,* 104681. https://doi.org/10.1016/j.tourman.2022.104681

Haberl, H., Wiedenhofer, D., Virág, D., Kalt, G., Plank, B., Brockway, P., Fishman, T., Hausknost, D., Krausmann, F., Leon-Gruchalski, B., Mayer, A., Pichler, M., Schaffartzik, A., Sousa, T., Streeck, J., & Creutzig, F. (2020). A systematic review of the evidence on decoupling of GDP, resource use and GHG emissions, part II: Synthesizing the insights. *Environmental Research Letters, 15*(6), 65003. https://dx.doi.org/10.1088/1748-9326/ab842a

Howitt, O. J. A., Revol, V. G. N., Smith, I. J., & Rodger, C. J. (2010). Carbon emissions from international cruise ship passengers' travel to and from New Zealand. *Energy Policy, 38*(5), 2552–2560. https://doi.org/10.1016/j.enpol.2009.12.050

International Civil Aviation Organization (ICAO). (2020). *Economic impacts of COVID-19 on Civil aviation.* https://www.icao.int/sustainability/Pages/Economic-Impacts-of-COVID-19.aspx

International Energy Agency (IEA). (2023). *CO_2 Emissions in 2022.* https://www.iea.org/reports/co2-emissions-in-2022

Intergovernmental Panel on Climate Change (IPCC). (2014). *Climate Change 2014: Synthesis Report. Contribution of Working Groups I, II and III to the Fifth Assessment Report of the Intergovernmental Panel on Climate Change.* IPCC. http://www.ipcc.ch/report/ar5/index.shtml

Intergovernmental Panel on Climate Change (IPCC). (2022a). In H.-O. Pörtner, D.C. Roberts, M. Tignor, E.S. Poloczanska, K. Mintenbeck, A. Alegría, M. Craig, S. Langsdorf, S. Löschke, V., Möller, A., & Okem, B. Rama (Eds.), *Climate change 2022: Impacts, adaptation, and vulnerability. Contribution of working group ii to the sixth assessment report of the intergovernmental panel on climate change.* Cambridge University Press. https://doi.org/10.1017/9781009325844

Intergovernmental Panel on Climate Change (IPCC). (2022b). M. Pathak, R. Slade, P. R. Shukla, J. Skea, R. Pichs-Madruga, D. Ürge-Vorsatz, 2022: Technical summary. In P. R. Shukla, J. Skea, R. Slade, A. Al Khourdajie, R. van Diemen, D. McCollum, M. Pathak, S. Some, P. Vyas, R. Fradera, M. Belkacemi, A. Hasija, G. Lisboa, S. Luz, & J. Malley (Eds.), *Climate change 2022: Mitigation of climate change. Contribution of working group iii to the sixth assessment report of the intergovernmental panel on climate change.* Cambridge University Press. https://doi.org/10.1017/9781009157926.002

Jahanger, A., Usman, M., Murshed, M., Mahmood, H., & Balsalobre-Lorente, D. (2022). The linkages between natural resources, human capital, globalization, economic growth, financial development, and ecological footprint: The moderating role of technological innovations. *Resources Policy, 76,* 102569. https://doi.org/10.1016/j.resourpol.2022.102569

Jiaqi, Y., Yang, S., Ziqi, Y., Tingting, L., & Teo, B. S. X. (2022). The spillover of tourism development on CO_2 emissions: A spatial econometric analysis. *Environmental Science and Pollution Research International, 29,* 26759–26774. https://doi.org/10.1007/s11356-021-17026-z

Kaya, Y., & Yokoburi, K. (1997). *Environment, energy, and economy: Strategies for sustainability*. United Nations University Press.

Lawal, A. I., Asaleye, A. J., Iseolorunkanmi, J., & Popoola, O. R. (2018). Economic growth, agricultural output and tourism development in Nigeria: An application of the ARDL bound testing approach. *Journal of Environmental Management and Tourism, 9*(4), 786–794. https://doi.org/10.14505//jemt.v9.4(28).12

Lenzen, M., Sun, Y. Y., Faturay, F., Ting, Y. P., Geschke, A., & Malik, A. (2018). The carbon footprint of global tourism. *Nature Climate Change, 8*, 522–528. https://doi.org/10.1038/s41558-018-0141-x

López-Bernabé, E., Foudi, S., Linares, P., & Galarraga, I. (2021). Factors affecting energy-efficiency investment in the hotel industry: Survey results from Spain. *Energy Efficiency, 14*(41), 1–22. https://doi.org/10.1007/s12053-021-09936-1

Marković Vukadin, I., Zovko, M., & Krešić, D. (2020). Review and evaluation of existing international systems of tourism sustainability indicators. *Croatian Geographical Bulletin, 82*, 85–110. https://dio.org/10.21861/HGG.2020.82.01.04

Matthews, E., Amann, C., Bringezu, S., Fischer-Kowalski, M., Huettler, W., Kleijn, R., & Moriguchi, Y. (2000). *The weight of nations: Material outflows from industrial economies*. World Resources Institute.

Organization for Economic Co-operation and Development (OECD). (2012). *Green growth and developing countries: A summary for policy makers*. https://www.oecd.org/green-growth/green-development/50526354.pdf

Page, S. J., & Duignan, M. (2023). Progress in tourism management: Is urban tourism a paradoxical research domain? Progress since 2011 and prospects for the future. *Tourism Management, 98*, 104737. https://doi.org/10.1016/j.tourman.2023.104737

Perera, F. (2017). Pollution from fossil-fuel combustion is the leading environmental threat to global pediatric health and equity: Solutions exist. *International Journal of Environmental Research and Public Health, 15*(1), 16. https://doi.org/10.3390/ijerph15010016

Robaina-Alves, M., Moutinho, V., Costa, R., & Robaina, M. (2016). Change in energy-related CO_2 (carbon dioxide) emissions in Portuguese tourism: A decomposition analysis from 2000 to 2008. *Journal of Cleaner Production, 11*(part B), 520–528. https://doi.org/10.1016/j.jclepro.2015.03.023

Statista. (2023). *Travel & Tourism – Worldwide*. https://www.statista.com/outlook/mmo/travel-tourism/worldwide

Tian, Y. (2023). Study on the impact of carbon emission pollution on urban tourism environment. *Engineering Reports, 5*(8), e12641. https://doi.org/10.1002/eng2.12641

Umpfenbach, K. (2015). *How will we know if absolute decoupling has been achieved and will it be enough? – Common Approach for DYNAMIX, Deliverable D.1.3*. Ecologic Institute. https://www.ecologic.eu/10254

United Nations (UN). (1992, May 9). *United Nations Framework Convention on Climate Change (UNFCCC)*. UN New York Press.

United Nations (UN). (2016, January 29). *Adoption of the Paris Agreement, Decision 1/ CP.21, in COP Report No. 21, Addendum, at 2, U.N. Doc. FCCC/CP/2015/10/Add.1*.

United Nations Environmental Programme (UNEP). (2011). *Decoupling natural resource use and environmental impacts from economic growth: A Report of the Working Group on Decoupling to the International Resource Panel*. https://wedocs.unep.org/handle/20.500.11822/9816;jsessionid=4FB823A7BFB866A51B495E52D09E6B26

United Nations Environment Programme (UNEP). (2022). *Emissions gap report 2022*. https://www.unep.org/emissions-gap-report-2022

United Nations Framework on Climate Change (UNFCCC). (1992, May 9). *United Nations Framework Convention on Climate Change*. United Nations, FCCC/INFORMAL/84 GE.05-62220 (E) 200705, Secretariat of the United Nations Framework Convention on Climate Change, Bonn, Germany.

United Nations Framework on Climate Change (UNFCC). (2021, November 13). *Glasgow climate pact, Decision 1/CMA.3.* United Nations, FCCC/PA/CMA/2021/L.16, Conference of the Parties serving as the meeting of the Parties to the Paris Agreement (CMA), Glasgow, United Kingdom.

United Nations World Tourism Organization (UNWTO). (2021). *One planet sustainable tourism programme – Glasgow Declaration: A commitment to a decade of climate action.* https://www.oneplanetnetwork.org/programmes/sustainable-tourism/glasgow-declaration

United Nations World Tourism Organization (UNWTO). (2023). *Climate action in tourism – An overview of methodologies and tools to measure greenhouse gas emissions.* https://doi.org/10.18111/9789284423927

United Nations World Tourism Organization & International Transport Forum (UNWTO & ITF). (2019). *Transport-related CO_2 emissions of the tourism sector – Modelling results.* https://doi.org/10.18111/9789284416660

United Nations World Tourism Organization, United Nations Environment Program & World Meteorological Organization (UNWTO, UNEP & WMO). (2008). *Climate change and tourism: Responding to global challenges.* https://www.e-unwto.org/doi/book/10.18111/9789284412341

United Nations World Tourism Organization & World Tourism Cities Federation (UNWTO & WTCF). (2018). *UNWTO/WTCF city tourism performance research.* https://doi.org/10.18111/9789284419616

Versteijlen, M., Salgado, F. P., Janssen Groesbeek, M., & Counotte, A. (2017). Pros and cons of online education as a measure to reduce carbon emissions in higher education in the Netherlands. *Current Opinion in Environmental Sustainability, 28,* 80–89. https://doi.org/10.1016/j.cosust.2017.09.004

Volpi, Y. D., & Paulino, S. R. (2018). The sustainability of services: Considerations on the materiality of accommodation services from the concept of life cycle thinking. *Journal of Cleaner Production, 192,* 327–334. https://doi.org/10.1016/j.jclepro.2018.04.166

Wang, Q., Zhang, H., Huang, J., & Zhang, P. (2023a). The use of alternative fuels for maritime decarbonization: Special marine environmental risks and solutions from an international law perspective. *Frontiers in Marine Science, 9.* https://doi.org/10.3389/fmars.2022.1082453

Wang, Q., Ren, Y., Liu, X., Chang, R., & Zuo, J. (2023b). Exploring the heterogeneity in drivers of energy-saving behaviours among hotel guests: Insights from the theory of planned behaviour and personality profiles. *Environmental Impact Assessment Review, 99,* 107012. https://doi.org/10.1016/j.eiar.2022.107012

Ward, J. D., Sutton, P. C., Werner, A. D., Costanza, R., Mohr, S. H., Simmons, C. T. (2016). Is Decoupling GDP Growth from Environmental Impact Possible? *PloS one, 11*(10), e0164733. https://doi.org/10.1371/journal.pone.0164733.

Wen, J., Okolo, C. V., Ugwuoke, I. C., & Kolani, K. (2022). Research on influencing factors of renewable energy, energy efficiency, on technological innovation. Does trade, investment and human capital development matter? *Energy Policy, 160,* 112718. https://doi.org/10.1016/j.enpol.2021.112718

World Economic Forum (WEF). (2023). *The global risk report 2023. 18th Edition – insight report.* https://www3.weforum.org/docs/WEF_Global_Risks_Report_2023.pdf

World Travel and Tourism Council, United Nations Environment Programme & United Nations Framework Convention on Climate Change (WTTC, UNEP & UNFCCC). (2021). *Driving climate action: A net zero roadmap for travel & tourism.* https://action.wttc.org/climate-environment

World Travel and Tourism Council (WTTC). (2021). *A net zero roadmap for travel & tourism: Proposing a new target framework for the travel & tourism sector.* WTTC London. https://action.wttc.org/climate-environment

Youssef, B., & Zeqiri, A. (2022). A hospitality industry 4.0 and climate change. *Circular Economy and Sustainability*, *2*, 1043–1063. https://doi.org/10.1007/s43615-021-00141-x

Ye, J. (2021). Using digitalization to achieve decarbonization goals. *Centre for Climate and Energy Solutions*. https://www.c2es.org/wp-content/uploads/2021/09/C2ES_Digitalization-to-Achieve-Decarbonization-Goals_FINAL_PH.pdf

Zervas, G., Proserpio, D., & Byers, J. W. (2017). The rise of the sharing economy: Estimating the impact of Airbnb on the hotel industry. *Journal of Marketing Research*, *54*(5), 687–705. https://hdl.handle.net/2144/40311

Zhang, J., & Zhang, Y. (2020). Low-carbon tourism system in an urban destination. *Current Issues in Tourism*, *23*(13), 1688–1704. https://doi.org/10.1080/13683500.2019.1641473

Zovko, V., & Zovko, M. (2020). Decoupling economic growth from natural resource use and environmental impacts in Croatia. In G. Družić & T. Gelo (Eds.), *Conference proceedings of the international conference on the economics of decoupling (ICED)* (pp. 69–84). https://iced.net.efzg.hr/conferences/proceedings

Chapter 4

Capacities of Adaptation and Mitigation Measures in Tourism to Answer Challenges of the Climate Crisis

Izidora Marković Vukadin[a], Naser Ul Islam[b], Diana Baus[a] and Damir Krešić[a]

[a]*Institute for Tourism, Zagreb, Croatia*
[b]*Tata Institute of Social Sciences, Mumbai, India*

Abstract

This chapter explores the reciprocal dynamics between climate change and tourism, underlining the imperative to comprehend this connection for effective mitigation strategies and sustainable practices. It focuses on two contrasting regions, the Mediterranean and Himalayan, elucidating their geographical and economic disparities. The Mediterranean, known for its coastal and marine attractions, faces high vulnerability to climate change, impacting outdoor recreation and tourism activities. This region experiences a Mediterranean climate characterised by distinct seasonal patterns, but it also grapples with high-impact atmospheric events like floods and droughts, while the Himalayan region is experiencing more untimely rain and snowfall, erratic monsoons, and decreased snowfall. These climatic challenges, coupled with a growing population and dependence on imported resources, necessitate adaptation strategies for the agricultural and food production sectors. This chapter evaluates climate anomalies and impacts in both the Indian Himalayan and the Adriatic region, with a particular focus on the tourism industry's adaptation and mitigation capacities.

In addition to vulnerabilities resulting from climate change, it also analysed existing measures and documents related to climate change, as well

Tourism in a VUCA World: Managing the Future of Tourism, 43–63
doi:10.1108/978-1-83753-674-020241004

as their effectiveness based on the expert opinion of the focus groups. The findings reveal that both regions experience shared and region-specific climate change impacts, affecting agriculture, water resources, human health, and infrastructure. Further research opportunities are identified, including the study of ecosystem resilience, biodiversity preservation, sustainable water resource management, and long-term public health implications of changing climatic conditions. This chapter underscores the urgency of climate action and the imperative for adaptive strategies in a complex and uncertain landscape.

Keywords: Tourism; climatic change; adaptation and mitigation strategies; Adriatic region; Indian Himalayan region

Introduction

Contemporary tourism demand is increasingly influenced by external factors, one of the most important of which is undoubtedly the effect of climate change. Climate change is a pressing global issue with far-reaching implications for various sectors, including tourism. Tourism depends on environmental resources, while climate defines the length and quality of tourism seasons; thus, the climate is a factor that is a prerequisite for staying in the destination (Bhuiyan et al., 2023). Therefore, accelerating climate action in tourism is of utmost importance for the sector's resilience (Agulles et al., 2022). Understanding the reciprocal relationship between climate change and tourism is crucial for developing effective strategies to mitigate negative impacts and promote sustainable practices. In the scientific literature, there is a great deal of heterogeneity in estimates of the physical and socio-economic impacts of climate change, which vary by destination and methodology (Arabadzhyan et al., 2021).

This chapter focuses on two very different regions of the world, the Mediterranean and Himalayan. Both regions differ according to their geographical and economic aspects (Paramati et al., 2016). Mediterranean coastal and marine environments are the most popular and visited destinations worldwide. The wide range of outdoor recreation and tourism activities makes the Mediterranean the most vulnerable to climate change, and it devises appropriate adaptations in habits. The Mediterranean climate is characterised by mild, wet winters, and hot, dry summers but also by a large spectrum of high-impact atmospheric processes, such as floods, droughts, and cyclogenetic patterns (Michaelides et al., 2018; Satta et al., 2017). However, the severe weather, draughts, and wildfires cause adverse effects, substantially decreasing the region's quality of life. Moreover, the Mediterranean basin has a growing population projected to reach 529 million by 2025 (Grid-Arendal, UNEP, 2014), and its agriculture strongly depends on imported resources (Sanz-Cobena, 2017). Adaptation is a crucial factor that will determine the future severity of the impacts of climate changes on agriculture and food production in the Mediterranean (Iglesias et al., 2011).

In the past decades, climate change in the Himalayan region has degraded the quality of life for residents on a socio-economic scale. According to the research of Scott et al. (2019), South Asia (including India) has a high Climate Change Vulnerability Index for Tourism (2019). Therefore, the Himalayan Climate Change Adaptation Programme (2012–2017) was developed, which focused on the following three steps: (1) reduction of uncertainty through downscaling and customising global climate change scenarios, and developing water availability and demand scenarios for parts of major river basins; (2) increase of knowledge and enhance capacities to assess, monitor, and communicate the impacts of and responses to climate change (compounded with other drivers of change) on natural and socioeconomic environments at the local, national, and regional levels; (3) making of concrete and actionable proposals for strategies and policies considering vulnerabilities, opportunities and potentials for adaptation.

Therefore, this chapter examines the existing climate anomalies and impacts occurring in the Indian Himalayan region and the Adriatic Sea and the capacities of adaptation and mitigation measures in the tourism industry to respond effectively to the challenges posed by the climate crisis. This paper intends to explore the strategies, policies, and actions that enable the tourism industry to adapt to and mitigate the impacts of climate change. By understanding and assessing these capacities, this study seeks to contribute to developing sustainable practices and policies for a more resilient and climate-conscious tourism sector.

Dichotomy of Climate Change and Tourism Impacts

Climate change is recognised as one of our most critical global challenges. It has caused widespread adverse impacts and related losses and damages to nature and people unequally distributed across systems, regions, and sectors, including tourism (IPCC, 2023). The relationship between climate change and tourism is complex and multidimensional, involving direct and indirect effects (Arabadzhyan et al., 2021; Carrillo et al., 2022). Tourism is one of the significant contributors to greenhouse gas (GHG) emissions (Becken & Simmons, 2008; Russo et al., 2020; Sun et al., 2022) and is in constant conflict with the global climate policy which seeks to mitigate and adopt climate change through sustainable projects under the umbrella of sustainable tourism. Therefore, societies can pursue sustainable development in two ways. Either adapt to specific climate changes (Kaján et al., 2015) or enhance existing present capacities (Scott et al., 2010). Both actions serve to diminish GHGs and their consequential impacts.

Each region in the world differs geographically and, therefore, is exposed to climate change differently. Some regions are more vulnerable than others, mostly in regions with poor economies and social infrastructure. These regions are in more trouble resisting climate occurrences as they cannot adapt quickly. The first step to developing a response to this vulnerability is to assess the existing macro state caused by tourism emissions (Becken & Patterson, 2006) and then evaluate micro-level impacts (Dorgu et al., 2019). Only after looking at the situation, the connection with the vulnerability of the space and the existing impacts and hazards (Arabadzhyan et al., 2021; Hein et al., 2009) should one approach the formation of measures, which, depending on the existing situation, represent a meaningful reaction. Therefore, the vulnerability and resilience of a country in general, or the tourism industry, must be assessed prior to developing climate change mitigation and adaptation measures (Ford et al., 2012; Fuessel & Hilden, 2014) in a cyclical, systematic approach (Dorgu et al., 2019). Dorgu et al. (2019) discussed the methods of detecting potential impacts of climate change and developing feasible mitigation and adaptation strategies as step-by-step processes such as vulnerability and resilience assessment (macro scale), the effect of vulnerability and economic activities (macro scale), feasible mitigation and adaptation strategies (macro scale), vulnerability and resilience assessment (micro scale), feasible mitigation and adaptation strategies (micro scale), and creating climate models and scenarios.

In research conducted by Agulles et al. (2021, 2022), it was concluded that exposure and vulnerability in all the tourist destinations in the region are very similar, and the hazard will vastly increase in the following decades. Therefore, the capacity to implement adaptation strategies would be more important than the projected change in the hazard (Agulles et al., 2022). Therefore, the main question arises: What are those measures and their capacity?

In a 'VUCA' context, climate change poses several significant challenges and impacts (Sempiga & Van Liedekerke, 2023). Climate change leads to increased weather volatility. Rising global temperatures result in more frequent and severe weather events, such as hurricanes, droughts, floods, and wildfires. These events can disrupt economies, infrastructure, and communities. Additionally, climate change introduces uncertainty in various aspects of life. This includes uncertainty in agricultural production due to shifting growing seasons, uncertainty in water resource availability, and uncertainty in the resilience of ecosystems. This all adds complexity to a range of global challenges. For instance, it exacerbates food security issues (El Hathat et al., 2023), triggers migration due to environmental factors, and influences geopolitical dynamics (Miska et al., 2020). Understanding and addressing these interrelated challenges require complex solutions for different economic sectors (Ross et al., 2022). The impacts of climate change are often ambiguous in terms of timing and specific outcomes. While the long-term trends are clear, the exact impacts on a regional or local scale can be challenging to predict. This ambiguity necessitates a cautious and proactive approach to risk management.

Adaptation Measures Overview

Adaptation to climate change refers to adjusting natural or human systems in response to actual or expected climatic stimuli or their effects, which moderates harm or exploits beneficial opportunities (UNEP, 2008). Similarly, the European Environment Agency defines adaptation as an appropriate action to prevent or minimise the damage they can cause or take advantage of possible opportunities. Examples of good adaptation practices to climate change include various possible changes (Bujosa et al., 2015). These can be minor changes, such as behavioural shifts among tourists and residents towards nature, food, or water. The change in behaviour does not always consider renunciation of previous activities and habits.

Moreover, it enables sectors and institutions to take advantage of climate change, such as extending the season or shifting it to another part of the year. Also, it considers the ultimate growth of the personnel working in tourism, as adaptation often means dissemination of knowledge and personal upgrade. Therefore, it develops the tourism sector. Likewise, adaptation can refer to significant infrastructural changes, such as the construction of defences against the rise of the sea (León et al., 2021). In essence, adaptation to climate change is necessary and specific in its form in each region globally. Considering everything mentioned, adaptation is a necessary precondition to sustainable tourism.

Societies, institutions, individuals, and governments can pursue adaptation. It can be motivated by economic, social, or environmental drivers through many mechanisms, such as social activities, market activities, and local or global interventions (Adger et al., 2007). When discussing adaption to global climate changes, this embraces adjustment in technologies, resources, and foremost, human behaviour towards nature (Hu et al., 2022).

Climate change adaptation depends on three essential resources: money, knowledge, and time (UNEP, 2008). Different tourism suppliers have different adaptability capacities. Tourism service suppliers and operators at specific destinations have less adaptive capacity than large tour operators, who do not own the infrastructure. They are better positioned to adapt to changes at destinations because they can respond to clients' demands and provide information to influence clients' travel choices. Destination communities and tourism operators with significant investments in immobile capital assets (e.g. hotels, resort complexes, marinas, or casinos) have the least adaptive capacity (UNEP, 2008). Therefore, some adaptations take decades to be implemented and often cannot be fully implemented, but only partially, because otherwise, they would cause significant costs that tourism stakeholders are unwilling to bear.

Many studies and proposals for adaptive measures have been suggested for both regions. For the potential local adaptations in mountain tourism and coastal tourism, it is principal that measures are grounded and practical. Practical examples of local-level adaptive responses include locating new tourist facilities or relocating old ones to low-risk areas. Mountain tourism destinations must develop their capacity to respond to sudden catastrophic events and disasters, for example, by installing early warning systems and search and rescue stations, and they must be able to adapt to rapidly changing ground conditions. That also holds for the coastal Mediterranean regions, where severe storms can occur unpredictably and cause potentially life-threatening situations and environmental damage. Preserving buffer forests, parks, and other protective land use features is equally important to reduce underlying exposure and vulnerability.

Adaptation to climate change is based on the following steps, which need to be satisfied: (1) establishment of institutional stakeholders (decision-making bodies) who can define climate-related effects, (2) stable income sources and employment, (3) strong partnership between private and public entities; mutual support and development of support mechanisms at the local level, and (4) identification and prioritisation of local adaptation measures, based on adequate provision of knowledge, technology, policy, and financial support.

Considering tourism in the adaptation process, national and regional level climate adaptation should be focused on strengthening and creating an enabling environment for adaptation of the tourism sector, diversifying tourism products and services, and disaster management and adaptive responses in tourism training curricula.

Mitigation Measures Overview

Compared to adaptation, mitigation refers to actions that reduce the impacts of climate change by preventing or reducing the emission of GHGs into the atmosphere (Abbass et al., 2022). It is achieved by enhancing technological, economic, and social infrastructure (Michailidou et al., 2016). Mitigation proposes more drastic changes and substitutions that can reduce emissions.

Even though mitigation can be realised through technological innovation and market mechanisms, a significant reduction in GHG emissions can be achieved through behavioural change, given an ever-increasing number of human beings participating in tourism (UNEP, 2008). Many researchers state that adaptation and mitigation can be complementary, substitutable, or independent (Bogner et al., 2008). If complementary, adaptation reduces the costs of climate change impacts and thus reduces the need for mitigation (Le, 2020). Adaptation and mitigation are substitutable up to a point. However, mitigation will always be required to avoid irreversible changes to the climate system, and adaptation will still be necessary due to the irreversible climate change resulting from current and historic rises in GHG and the inertia in the climate system (UNEP, 2008). Ideally, mitigation and adaptation should simultaneously be included in tourism planning (Spandre et al., 2019) so that GHG emissions are entirely diminished.

Climate mitigation is deliverable through national policies that serve as a roadmap for carbon reduction (Becken & Whittlesea, 2020). Mickwitz (2009) noted that national policies often constitute roadmaps for carbon reduction, especially in the aviation industry (Leal Filho et al., 2023). National mitigation policies are driven by international agreements, which provide frameworks and critical objectives for national emission reductions (e.g. the Paris Agreement, UNFCCC, 2015). The national policy translates these into strategies and actions, where the implications for individual sectors should be considered. However, policies often remain generic, such as establishing emission reduction pathways or high-level strategies, such as investment in renewable energy (Becken & Whittlesea, 2020).

Becken and Whittlesea (2020) researched policy documents with the framework for climate mitigation. They defined three categories of documents: (1) dedicated tourism and climate change policies, (2) tourism policies that included climate change, and (3) climate change policies that included tourism. They concluded that mitigation is less proposed as a solution to navigate tourism and climate changes together. They consider that mitigation measures are only sometimes feasible in the scientific world. Adaptation and mitigation strategies will likely fail when vulnerability and resilience assessments are missing (Fuessel & Hilden, 2014).

Methodology

This section outlines the methodology employed to gather qualitative data through focus group discussions as part of this research on the capacities of adaptation and mitigation measures in tourism to answer climate crisis challenges. The primary objective of the focus group discussions was to explore and understand the attitudes, beliefs, and perceptions of experts in the areas of tourism management and climate action in tourism. Specific research topics included official sources (climate change adaptation strategy, tourism adaptation/mitigation action plan, etc.) that are used to estimate climatic risk to tourism and the contribution of tourism to climate change, meteorological anomalies, and related implications and challenges, main impacts of tourism on the climate in Adriatic and Indian Himalayan region. The second part of the focus group was focused on mitigation and adaptation measures, emphasising the examples, challenges, practical and related partnerships, and policies included in its implementation.

Participants for the focus group discussions were recruited using purposive sampling. Eligibility criteria included professionals and academics included in tourism management, environmental topics, climate action implementation, and tourism monitoring. Potential participants were contacted via email and telephone, where an introductory email explained the purpose of the study and invited eligible participants to join the focus group discussions. Before participating in the focus group discussions, participants were provided with informed consent forms explaining the purpose of the study, the voluntary nature of their participation, and the assurance of confidentiality. A chapter author with expertise in qualitative research methodologies moderated focus group discussions.

A total of two focus group sessions were conducted, each with six participants. Each session lasted approximately 90 minutes and was held via Zoom platform. Sessions were audio-recorded, and notes were taken to capture non-verbal cues. These recordings and notes served as the primary sources of qualitative data for analysis. A semi-structured discussion guide in the form of a PPT presentation was developed to facilitate the focus group discussions. The guide included open-ended questions and prompts related to impacts, anomalies, policies, measures, and challenges. Qualitative data collected from the focus group discussions were transcribed verbatim and analysed using thematic analysis. Data were coded and categorised into themes and sub-themes related to the research objectives. The analysis process involved iterative reviews of transcripts and discussions among the research team to ensure the validity and reliability of the findings. Ethical considerations were paramount throughout the research process. Participants were informed of their right to withdraw from the study at any point without consequence.

Also, an analysis of strategic and action plans, policies, and initiatives for both regions (Adriatic and Indian Himalayan) was carried out, with the primary aim of determining the current situation at the supranational, national, and regional level in terms of planning and implementation of mitigation and adaptation measures.

Research Area

Two geographical, developmental, and touristic regions were chosen for the research. The Adriatic region, part of the world's most important tourist region (the Mediterranean), and the Indian Himalayan region, part of the enormous mountain massif, are areas of proactive development for winter and mountain tourism (Fig. 1). Although these are very different regions at first glance, they are united by at least two characteristics: intensive tourism development and the significant impacts of climate change on the region.

The Adriatic region is composed of the countries surrounding the Adriatic Sea, namely Italy, Slovenia, Croatia, Bosnia and Herzegovina, Montenegro, and Albania. It is essential to note that Slovenia, Bosnia, and Herzegovina have very short coastlines. Adriatic region is of immense importance in the tourism industry due to its natural beauty, historical and cultural significance, diverse destinations, and wide range of activities that cater to different types of travellers. The region's unique blend of offerings makes it a desirable and attractive destination for tourists worldwide. Tourism brings a range of economic benefits to the Adriatic region, contributing to the economic development of the countries along its coastline. These benefits include job creation, revenue generation, and the stimulation of various economic sectors. According to a report from the World Travel & Tourism Council (WTTC), the travel and tourism sector supported approximately 11% of total employment in the Mediterranean region, which

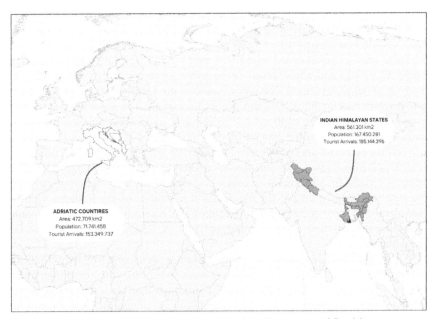

Fig. 1.   Adriatic and Indian Himalayan Region Features and Position.
Source: Authors.

includes parts of the Adriatic coast (Bloomberg, 2019). The demand for tourism leads to investments in infrastructure development, including roads, airports, ports, and public transportation, which can have a positive impact on the overall economy and help spread economic benefits to less-developed regions along the Adriatic coast (Marković & Klarić, n.d.). Finally, the region increasingly focuses on sustainable and eco-friendly tourism practices, which protect the environment and attract environmentally conscious travellers (Arih & Korošec, 2015; Cocco, 2021). However, some have concluded that the Mediterranean region will become 'too hot' for tourist comfort in the peak summer season by the 2030s (Rutty & Scott, n.d.). In addition, permanent coastal flooding is expected due to the mean sea level rise in the Mediterranean (Agulles et al., 2021; Hochman et al., 2022), and the coastal zone is severely impacted by extreme climatic events (e.g. storm surges) coupled with human-induced pressures (e.g. uncontrolled building on coasts), resulting in a growing vulnerability (Satta et al., 2017).

Tourism in the Indian Himalayan brings various benefits to the region, including economic, social, and environmental advantages. In rural areas where agriculture may be the primary occupation, tourism offers an additional source of income, helping to diversify livelihoods and reduce dependency on a single sector (Bhalla et al., 2016). Furthermore, tourism has contributed to cultural preservation and exchange (Chettry, 2013) and the conservation of nature areas, raising awareness about the importance of environmental protection and wildlife conservation among visitors and locals (UNDP India, 2019). Finally, tourism brought opportunities for residents to engage in education and training in the hospitality and tourism sectors (Gupta & Singh, 2015).

It is important to note that while tourism brings many benefits to the Indian Himalayan region, it also poses challenges, including environmental degradation, cultural changes, and social issues (Chaudhary & Angmo, 2021). Sustainable tourism practices and responsible tourism management are crucial to maximising positive impacts while minimising negative consequences. Additionally, the benefits and impacts of tourism vary from region to region within the Indian Himalayan region.

Strategies, Policies, and Measures in the Adriatic and Indian Himalayan Region

Climate change is a global issue; however, measures to address it in both the Adriatic region and the Indian Himalayan region involve a combination of national and regional efforts (Table 1). These measures include policies, strategies, and initiatives aimed at mitigating the impacts of climate change and adapting to its effects in various macro and micro-level aspects. In terms of the Adriatic region, it is essential to point out that the necessity of integration is recognised through numerous initiatives (such as the Adriatic-Ionian initiative) to integrate interstate efforts and achieve a synergistic impact of state policies and measures. All the countries of the Adriatic are either members of the EU or are in pre-accession negotiations, which makes it easier to monitor progress or harmonise state policies with a common goal.

Table 1. Measures and Documents Related to Climate Change in the Adriatic and Indian Himalayan Region.

Factor	Adriatic Region	Indian Himalayan Region
Climate law	Some EU countries have adopted Climate laws, such as climate change and Ozone Protection Act (Croatia)[1]	Climatic change and environmental protection are dealt with by a set of existing laws and act at the national level by the Indian government, such as the Environmental Protection Act of 1986, the Air (Prevention and Control of Pollution) Act of 1981, Water (Prevention and Control of Pollution) Act of 1974, Forest Conservation Act of 1980, National Action Plan on Climate Change (NAPCC) (2008)
National climate action plans/strategy	Each country bordering the Adriatic Sea (Italy, Croatia, Slovenia, Montenegro, Albania, and Greece)[2] has its national climate action plan. These plans outline strategies and actions for reducing GHG emissions, transitioning to renewable energy sources, and adapting to the impacts of climate change	National Action Plan on Climate Change (NAPCC): The NAPCC, launched in 2008, outlines India's comprehensive strategy for addressing climate change. It includes eight national missions, one of which is the National Mission for Sustaining the Himalayan Ecosystem (NMSHE), aimed at conserving and sustaining the fragile Himalayan ecosystem[3]
Regional cooperation agreements	Regional organisations, such as the Adriatic-Ionian Initiative,[4] play a role in coordinating climate change measures among Adriatic countries. Agreements and strategies may be developed through these forums to address shared challenges like sea-level rise, extreme weather events, and coastal erosion	SAARC Environment and Climate Change Centre (SECC) and International Centre for Integrated Mountain Development (ICIMOD) are regional organisations playing crucial roles in combating climate change and protecting the environment in the Himalayan region, such as 'The Himalayan Climate Change Adaptation Programme'

		At the regional level, India partnered with Bhutan, Nepal, and Bangladesh to address the adverse effects of climate change through adaptation actions in the four thematic areas of Food, Water, Energy, and Biodiversity[5]
Coastal zone management plans	Due to the vulnerability of coastal areas in the Adriatic region, countries often develop coastal zone management plans. These plans aim to protect and manage coastal ecosystems while considering the effects of climate change, such as rising sea levels and increased storm events	Not applicable
Environmental Impact Assessments (EIAs)	EIAs are required for significant development projects in all EU countries. These assessments evaluate projects' potential environmental and climate impacts and propose mitigation measures	EIAs in India are required for projects with environmental and climatic change requirements. It falls under the Environment Act, 1986, Forest Act, 1980, and other relevant laws laid by the Ministry of Environment, Forest and Climate Change (MoEFCC) that apply to projects in the Indian Himalayan
Renewable energy development plans	Transitioning to renewable energy sources is a critical component of addressing climate change. Countries in the Adriatic region plan to increase wind, solar, and hydropower use in their energy mix	India has set ambitious targets for renewable energy development, including solar and wind power. Promoting renewable energy sources can help reduce the region's carbon footprint and decrease reliance on fossil fuels

(Continued)

Table 1. *(Continued)*

Factor	Adriatic Region	Indian Himalayan Region
Climate adaptation strategies	These documents outline measures to adapt to the changing climate. This includes strategies for managing water resources, protecting biodiversity, and enhancing disaster preparedness in the Adriatic region	Indian government launched Eight National Missions under NAPCC, 2008, representing multi-pronged, long-term term, and integrated strategies for achieving critical goals in climate change
Climate action monitoring and reporting	All EU countries have mechanisms to monitor progress towards their climate goals. These include GHG inventories, climate action reports, and regular updates on adaptation efforts	Indian Government reconstituted the Prime Minister's Council on Climate Change (PMCCC) in 2014 (initially constituted in 2007).[6] The functions of the council are to evolve a coordinated response to issues relating to climate change at the national level, to provide oversight for the formulation of action plans in the area of assessment, adaptation, and mitigation of climate change, and to monitor critical policy decisions periodically
Research and scientific reports	Scientific organisations and research institutions in the Adriatic region contribute to understanding the impacts and solutions of climate change. Their reports and studies inform policy decisions	Various scientific organisations and institutions, such as the Geological Survey of India and G.B. Pant Institute of Himalayan Environment and Development (GBHED), are actively involved in scientific studies in Indian Himalayan region[7]
Public awareness campaigns	Public engagement is critical for successful climate action. Governments and NGOs may run awareness campaigns to educate the public about climate change and encourage sustainable practices	Public awareness is essential for achieving eight national missions under NAPCC

International agreements	The Adriatic region is part of international agreements like the Paris Agreement under the United Nations Framework Convention on Climate Change. These agreements set global targets for reducing GHG emissions and are integrated into national and regional climate strategies. Also, it is managed by the EU Strategy on Adaptation to Climate Change (EU, 2022)	India collaborates with neighboring countries in the Himalayan region on various climate change initiatives and programs, recognising that climate change is a transboundary issue[8]

[1] https://narodne-novine.nn.hr/clanci/sluzbeni/2019_12_127_2554.html
[2] https://climate-adapt.eea.europa.eu/en/countries-regions/countries/greece
[3] https://archivepmo.nic.in/drmanmohansingh/climate_change_english.pdf
[4] https://eur-lex.europa.eu/legal-content/EN/TXT/?uri=COM:2021:82:FIN
[5] https://loksabhadocs.nic.in/Refinput/New_Reference_Notes/English/climate_I.pdf
[6] https://loksabhadocs.nic.in/Refinput/New_Reference_Notes/English/climate_I.pdf
[7] https://dst.gov.in/sites/default/files/NMSHE_Mission_document.pdf
[8] https://loksabhadocs.nic.in/Refinput/New_Reference_Notes/English/climate_I.pdf

On the other hand, the Himalayan, as a vast area, also include many countries (India, China, Pakistan, Nepal, and Bhutan). However, the level of policy integration is significantly lower due to the lower level of state relations. India has implemented various climate change mitigation policies and initiatives to address the impacts of climate change in the Indian Himalayan region. These policies aim to reduce GHG emissions, promote sustainable development, and enhance resilience to climate change. These policies and initiatives are part of India's commitment to addressing climate change and its impacts on vulnerable regions like the Himalayas. The government continues to refine and expand its strategies to mitigate climate change while promoting sustainable development in the region.

Among the most critical measures in the National Action Plan on Climate Change (NAPCC), stress out initiatives to increase forest and tree cover in the Himalayan region are essential for carbon sequestration and biodiversity conservation, hydropower projects which are designed and managed sustainably to minimise environmental impacts, biodiversity conservation: to contribute to carbon sequestration and ecosystem resilience, climate-resilient agricultural practices. Finally, for all the stated measures, umbrella measures accessing climate finance mechanisms, including international climate funds, are crucial for implementing climate mitigation projects in the Himalayan region.

Adriatic region has long been exposed to the adverse effects of climate change, resulting in significant economic losses. According to the European Environment Agency (EEA) report, Italy is in second place in the number of fatalities caused by weather – and climate-related extreme events (1980–2022), while Italy, Greece, and Croatia are all in the top 10 countries considered economic losses and fatalities caused by weather- and climate-related extreme events (1980–2022) (EEA, n.d.).

Focus Group Results and Discussion

Climate Change Impacts and Hazards

Experts in the panel have various meteorological anomalies and impacts of climate change. Some central meteorological anomalies and climate change impacts are similar for both regions, but most are specific. Among those common are temperature increases, changing precipitation patterns and increased frequency of extreme weather events. It was stated that both the Adriatic and Indian Himalayan regions are experiencing a rise in average temperatures and are warming faster than the global average, leading to warmer summers and milder winters.

Climate change leads to altered precipitation patterns, resulting in more erratic rain and snowfall, a decrease in snowfall, floods, and, at times, extended periods of drought. These changes can affect ecosystems, agriculture, and human health and increase the risk of heatwaves, floods, landslides, and forest fires in both regions. Warming temperatures and changing precipitation patterns increase the risk of forest fires, threatening biodiversity and releasing carbon stored in forests. Furthermore, it was stressed that both regions are experiencing increased frequency of extreme weather events, such as heavy rainfall, rising temperatures, storms, extreme winds flash floods, and decreased snowfall. These events can significantly damage infrastructure and agriculture and affect the safety of tourism destinations.

Since the primary driver of all nature and most of the economic processes in the Adriatic region is the Adriatic Sea, it was emphasised that the rising global sea levels impact the entire Adriatic coast, causing increased coastal erosion, inundation of low-lying areas and damage to infrastructure. This poses a threat to coastal communities and ecosystems. Likewise, elevated atmospheric carbon dioxide levels lead to increased sea acidification. This can harm marine ecosystems, particularly coral reefs (Croatia and Montenegro) and shellfish populations., threatening the biodiversity of the Adriatic region, including its unique marine life.

Impacts on anthropogenic activity in the Adriatic region have also been emphasised, where impacts on crop yields, agricultural practices, and tourism vulnerability were pointed out. Also, higher temperatures can lead to heat-related illnesses and vector-borne diseases. Changes in precipitation patterns affect water quality and availability (mostly on islands), posing risks to public health. Finally, as a last hazard, infrastructure vulnerability was highlighted, where rising sea levels and extreme weather events can damage infrastructure along the coast (Italy), including ports, roads, and buildings (Albania).

Due to different geographical and climatological characteristics, the hazards arising from the climate change in the Himalayas are significantly different from those in the Adriatic region. The Indian Himalayan region is home to numerous glaciers, and many retreat due to rising temperatures. This has far-reaching consequences, including reduced water availability in downstream areas. Similarly, decreasing snowpack and earlier snowmelt can affect water availability for agriculture, hydropower, and drinking water, particularly in the downstream regions of significant rivers. Ice melting and increased frequency of extreme rainfall can trigger landslides and soil erosion, posing risks to infrastructure and human settlements in hilly and mountainous areas. As glaciers retreat, they often leave behind glacial lakes. The rapid melting of glaciers can increase the risk of Glacial Lake Outburst Floods, which result in devastating downstream flooding.

The broader regional consequences for the entire Indian subcontinent were also emphasised: the Indian Himalayan are the source of major rivers, including the Ganges, Brahmaputra, and Indus. Climate change can impact the quantity and quality of water flowing into these rivers, affecting millions downstream.

Experts have recognised changes in biodiversity as one of the essential hazards; the Himalayas' unique biodiversity is at risk due to habitat loss, shifting ecosystems, and the spread of invasive species. Species that are adapted to cold climates are particularly vulnerable. Related to the aforementioned is the disruption in agriculture, where temperature and precipitation patterns can affect agricultural practices and crop yields, leading to shifts in what can be cultivated in the region. Finally, it was recognised that increased temperatures can lead to heat-related illnesses, and changes in precipitation patterns can impact water quality and availability, potentially leading to health risks. This ultimately causes vulnerability of indigenous communities, which often have a deep connection with the land and are disproportionately affected by climate change impacts, including changing patterns of traditional livelihoods.

Adaptation and Mitigation Measure Capacities

Most experts state that implementing climate adaptation measures can be complex and face various challenges and issues. These challenges can vary depending on the specific measures, geographical location, and political and socioeconomic context. Some challenges were typical for the Adriatic and Indian Himalayan regions, such as institutional capacity, coordinating multiple stakeholders and lack of political will and/or leadership.

It was stated that many governments and organisations lack the institutional capacity to plan and execute climate adaptation measures effectively. This includes a lack of skilled personnel, technical expertise, and organisational structures. Furthermore, climate adaptation and mitigation often involve multiple stakeholders, including government agencies, NGOs, local communities, and private sector actors. Coordinating and aligning the efforts of these diverse groups can be challenging, as a lack of political will, leadership, and strong commitment highlights the most difficult bridging challenge. Without the will to act, measures may not be implemented effectively or may be delayed. All experts, those from India and those from EU and non-EU countries, emphasised this.

There are diverse challenges for recognition for the Himalayan region and non-EU countries in the Adriatic region, such as lack of funding and resource constraints. Securing funding is a significant challenge, especially for developing countries or local communities with limited financial resources. Furthermore, climate adaptation and mitigation are often intertwined with other challenges like poverty, health, and food security. Addressing climate adaptation without considering these interconnected issues can lead to suboptimal outcomes. Similarly, community acceptance and willingness to participate in adaptation measures are crucial. Resistance or cultural barriers can impede implementation. In line with the previous conclusion, it was recognised that climate adaptation can have differential impacts on vulnerable and marginalised communities. Ensuring that adaptation measures do not exacerbate existing inequalities is a challenge of utmost importance. Finally, it was addressed that many measures require new technologies or infrastructure, which may not be readily available or affordable. Developing, implementing, and maintaining these technologies can be a significant challenge.

Some other challenges in efficiency and capacities of measures were recognised for the Adriatic region, where it must be emphasised that there were quite a lot of diverse challenges recognised by experts from EU countries (Italy, Slovenia, and Croatia) and those from non-EU countries (B&H, Montenegro, and Albania). Especially in non-EU countries, a lack of awareness and understanding was emphasised. Many people, including policymakers, may not fully understand the importance of climate adaptation or the specific measures to take. Raising awareness and building consensus can be difficult.

In EU countries, otherwise, the most common objections have been recognised as regulatory and policy barriers, where existing policies and regulations may hinder the implementation of climate adaptation and mitigation measures. Adapting or changing these policies can be a lengthy and bureaucratic process, insufficiently adapted to extreme weather events that are becoming more frequent. The region prioritises short-term economic and political considerations over long-term climate adaptation goals, especially in the post-COVID period. This can hinder the implementation of necessary measures.

Data and information gaps were addressed in non-EU countries as essential challenges, where measures often rely on accurate climate data and projections. Data may be scarce or unreliable in some regions, making planning and implementing effective measures difficult.

In Italy, environmental and ecological concerns caused by measures were highlighted, where some adaptation measures have unintended ecological consequences. For example, building seawalls to protect against sea-level rise may disrupt coastal ecosystems (e.g. in Venice).

Finally, in the Adriatic region, there is a challenge/question of legal and liability issues. Implementing climate adaptation and mitigation measures can raise legal and liability concerns. As was stated by one of the experts:

> *If measures fail to protect against climate impacts, who is responsible for the resulting damages?*

In both regions, the following challenges were emphasised: the lack of implementation of strategies/plans and actions on the ground and the lack of information about their success. According to focus groups, the solution for increasing capacities of measures is not technological innovation but careful planning, multisectoral collaboration, public engagement, and a long-term perspective. Climate adaptation is an ongoing process that may need to evolve as the climate changes.

Research Implications and Conclusions

The results indicate that both the Adriatic and Indian Himalayan regions are experiencing the impacts of climate change. Warming temperatures and changing precipitation patterns are shared across both regions, leading to altered agricultural practices, water resource management challenges, and increased risks of floods, landslides, and forest fires. These changes also affect human health, particularly heat-related illnesses and vector-borne diseases. While some meteorological anomalies and climate change effects are common, many are region-specific, emphasising the need for tailored adaptation strategies. Based on the analysis of the available documents, as well as the conducted focus groups, is the fact that on a global level, there is frequent application of copy-paste adaptation and mitigation practices, which, given the specificities of individual regions and hazards, are ultimately not sufficiently focused and aimed at solving problems, as was previously stated by Scott et al. (2010). What is common are activities aimed at reducing emissions from transport (and specifically from tourism). However, the diversity of levels of economic development, emission markets and the like are often not considered (Ross et al., 2022). Various impacts and hazards emphasised by experts can result in a loss of touristic attractiveness due to climate change in destinations. However, if measures increase the level of resilience of destinations, the attractiveness of destinations in tourism will stay similar or the same (Agulles et al., 2022).

Climate change has diverse and far-reaching impacts on both regions, affecting ecosystems, agriculture, human health, and infrastructure. The specific effects in each region are driven by their unique geographical and climatological characteristics, highlighting the importance of understanding local vulnerabilities and downstream consequences. In the Himalayas, the impacts on glaciers and water sources have downstream consequences for significant rivers, affecting more than 300 million people.

Based on the literature review and primary research, few important further research objectives have emerged. Further research into the resilience of ecosystems in the face of climate change is critical. Understanding how biodiversity can be preserved or restored is vital. Given the dependence of both regions on water resources, in-depth studies on sustainable water resource management in the face of changing precipitation patterns are crucial. Furthermore, due to the huge local population and enormous number of tourism arrivals, investigating the long-term public health implications of changing temperatures and precipitation patterns, including heat-related illnesses and vector-borne diseases, is essential. Finally, due to the global nature of climate change, considering the broader regional consequences, such as the downstream impacts on major rivers, is essential to inform policies at larger scales.

Finally, in a VUCA context, addressing climate change requires adaptive strategies, resilience building, and a willingness to embrace innovation and technology. It also calls for global collaboration and recognising that climate change exacerbates vulnerabilities and inequalities. Organisations, governments, and communities must adapt to the realities of climate change in this complex and uncertain landscape.

Acknowledgements

We would like to express our sincere appreciation to the participants of the focus group discussion on the Adriatic and Indian Himalayan regions. Your contributions have been invaluable in shaping the outcomes of this research.

References

Abbass, K., Qasim, M. Z., Song, H., Murshed, M., Mahmood, H., & Younis, I. (2022). A review of the global climate change impacts, adaptation, and sustainable mitigation measures. *Environmental Science and Pollution Research, 29*, 42539–42559. https://doi.org/10.1007/s11356-022-19718-6

Adger, W. N., Agrawala, S., Mirza, M. et al. (2007) Assessment of adaptation practices, options, constraints and capacity. In M. L. Parry, O. F. Canziani, J. P. Palutikof, C. E. Hanson and P. J. van der Linden (Eds.), *Climate Change 2007: Impacts, Adaptation and Vulnerabiliy*, (pp. 719–743). Contribution of Working Group II to the Fourth Assessment Report of the Intergovernmental Panel on Climate Change. Cambridge: Cambridge University Press.

Agulles, M., Jordà, G., & Lionello, P. (2021). Flooding of sandy beaches in a changing climate. The case of the Balearic Islands (NW Mediterranean). *Frontiers in Marine Science, 8*, 60725.

Agulles, M., Melo-Aguilar, C., & Jordà, G. (2022). Risk of loss of tourism attractiveness in the Western Mediterranean under climate change. *Frontiers in Climate, 4*. https://doi.org/10.3389/fclim.2022.1019892

Arabadzhyan, A., Figini, P., García, C., González, M. M., Lam-González, Y. E., & León, C. J. (2021). Climate change, coastal tourism, and impact chains – A literature review. *Current Issues in Tourism, 24*(16), 2233–2268. https://doi.org/10.1080/13683500.202

Arih, I., & Korošec, T. (2015). Api-tourism: Transforming Slovenia's apicultural traditions into a unique travel experience. *WIT Transactions on Ecology and the Environment, 193*, 963–974.

Becken, S., & Patterson, M. (2006). Measuring national carbon dioxide emissions from tourism as a key step towards achieving sustainable tourism. *Journal of Sustainable Tourism, 14*(4), 323–338. https://doi.org/10.2167/jost547.0

Becken, S., & Simmons, D. (2008). Using the concept of yield to assess the sustainability of different tourist types. *Ecological Economics, 67*(3), 420–429.

Becken, S., & Whittlesea, E. L. (2020). Tourism and climate change: Evaluating the extent of policy integration. *Journal of Sustainable Tourism, 28*, 1603–1624.

Bhalla, P., Coghlan, A., & Bhattach, P. (2016). Homestays' contribution to community-based ecotourism in the Himalayan region of India. *Tourism Recreation Research, 41*(2), 213–228.

Bhuiyan, M. A., Zhang, Q., Xuan, W., Rahman, M. K., & Khare, V. (2023). Does good governance promote sustainable tourism? A systematic review of PESTEL analysis. *SN Business & Economics, 3*(33). https://doi.org/10.1007/s43546-022-00408-x

Bloomberg, W. T. (2019). *World, transformed: Megatrends and their implications for travel & tourism.* World Travel & Tourism Council (WTTC) & Bloomberg.

Bogner, J., Pipatti, R., & Hashimoto, S. (2008). *Mitigation of global greenhouse gas emissions from waste: Conclusions and strategies from the Intergovernmental Panel on Climate Change (IPCC) Fourth Assessment Report.* Working Group III (Mitigation).

Bujosa, A., Riera, A., & Torres, C. M. (2015). Valuing tourism demand attributes to guide climate change adaptation measures efficiently: The case of the Spanish domestic travel market. *Tourism Management, 47*, 233–239. https://doi.org/10.1016/j.tourman.2014.09

Carrillo, J., González, A., Pérez, J. C., Expósito, F. J., & Díaz, J. P. (2022). Projected impacts of climate change on tourism in the Canary Islands. *Regional Environmental Change, 12*, 8093. https://doi.org/10.1038/s41598-022-12132-5

Chaudhary, M., & Angmo, S. (2021). Developing tourism impact index: A measure of tourism suppliers' perceptions in Leh. *International Journal of Tourism Policy, 11*(3), 289–308.

Chettry, A. (2013). Preserving cultural identity through tribal self-governance: The Lachenpa and Lachungpa Tribes of Sikkim Himalaya (India). *American International Journal of Research in Humanities, Arts and Social Sciences, 3*.

Cocco, E. (2021). Towards an open, relational and community based regeneration of the waterfront: Turning the ancient harbors of the Adriatic into eco-tourist destinations. *Adrion, 84*.

Dorgu, T., Marchio, E., Bulut, A., & Suess, C. (2019). Climate change: Vulnerability and resilience of tourism and the entire economy. *Tourism Management, 72*, 292–305.

El Hathat, Z., Sreedharan, R., Venkatesh, G., Zouadi, T., Arunmozhui, M., & Shi, Y. (2023). Modelling and analysing the GHG emissions in the VUCA world: Evidence from tomato production in Morocco. *Journal of Cleaner Production, 382*.

European Environment Agency (EEA). (n.d.). *What is the difference between adaptation and mitigation.* European Environment Agency. https://www.eea.europa.eu/help/faq/what-is-the-difference-between

Ford, J., Bolton, K., Shirley, J., Pearce, T., & Westlake, M. (2012). Mapping human dimensions of climate change research in the Canadian Arctic. *Ambio, 41*(8), 808–822.

Fuessel, H., & Hilden, M. (2014). How is uncertainty addressed in the knowledge base for national adaptation planning? In *Adapting to an uncertain climate* (pp. 41–66). https://doi.org/10.1007/978-3-319-04876-5_3

Grid-Arendal, UNEP. (2014). *Board Report* 2013.

Gupta, S., & Singh, A. (2015). Potential and performance of rural tourism in India: Assessing IntraState Variations. *International Journal of Research in Management & Business Studies, 2*(4), 9–16.

Hein, L., Metzger, M. J., & Moreno, A. (2009). Potential impacts of climate change on tourism: A case study for Spain. *Current Opinion in Environmental Sustainability, 1*(2), 170.

Hochman, A., Marra, F., Messori, G., Pinto, G., Yosef, Y., Zittis, G., & Raveh-Rubin, S. (2022). Extreme weather and societal impacts in the eastern Mediterranean. *Earth System Dynamics, 13*(3), 749–777.

Hu, Q., Becken, S., & He, X. (2022). Climate risk perception and adaptation of tourism sector in China. *Journal of Destination Marketing & Management, 23*, 100675. https://doi.org/10.1016/j.jdmm.2021.100675

ICIMOD, CICERO & GRID. (2012–2017). *Adaptation in the Himalayas: Knowledge, action and results: Highlights from the Himalayan Climate Change, Adaptation Programme (HICAP), 2012–2017* (pp. 3–28). https://gridarendal-website-live.s3 .amazonaws.com/production/documents/:s_document/39

Iglesias, A., Mougou, R., Moneo, M., & Quiroga, S. (2011). Towards adaptation of agriculture to climate change in the Mediterranean. *Regional Environmental Change, 11*, 159–166.

Intergovernmental Panel on Climate Change (IPCC). (2023). Summary for policymakers climate change 2023: Synthesis report. Contribution of Working Groups I, II and III to the Sixth Assessment Report of the Intergovernmental Panel on Climate Change. IPCC.

Kaján, E., Tervo-Kankare, K., & Saarinen, J. (2015). Cost of adaptation to climate change in tourism: Methodological challenges and trends for future studies in adaptation. *Scandinavian Journal of Hospitality and Tourism, 15*(3), 311–317. https://doi.org/ 10.1080/15022250.2014.970665

Le, T. D. N. (2020). Climate change adaptation in coastal cities of developing countries: Characterising types of vulnerability and adaptation options. *Mitigation and Adaptation Strategies for Global Change, 25*, 739–761. https://doi.org/10.1007/ s11027-019-09888-z

Leal Filho, W., Ng, A. W., Sharifi, A., Janová, J., Özuyar, P. G., Hemani, C., Heyes, G., Njau, D., & Rampasso, I. (2023). Global tourism, climate change and energy sustainability: Assessing carbon reduction mitigating measures from the aviation industry. *Sustainability Science, 18*, 983–996. https://doi.org/10.1007/s11625-022-01207-x

León, C. J., Giannakis, E., Zittis, G., Serghides, D., Lam-González, Y. E., & García, C. (2021). Tourists' preferences for adaptation measures to build climate resilience at coastal destinations. Evidence from Cyprus. *Tourism Planning and Development, 20*(9), 1–27.

Lionello, P., Jordà, G., & Lionello, P. (2021). Flooding of sandy beaches in a changing climate. *The Case of the Balearic Islands (NW Mediterranean), 4*, 1–15. https://doi. org/10.3389/fmars.2021.760725

Marković, V. I., & Klarić, Z. (n.d.). Attitudes of the local population of tourism impacts on destination sustainability: Case of Croatia. *Tourism, 19*(3), 98–110. https://doi. org/10.5937/Turizam1503098M

Michaelides, S., Karacostas, T., Sánchez, J. L., Retalis, A., Pytharoulis, I., Homar, V., Romero, R., Zanis, P., Giannakopoulos, C., Bühl, J., Ansmann, A., Merino, A., &

Melcón, P. (2018). Reviews and perspectives of high impact atmospheric processes in the Mediterranean. *Atmospheric Research, 208*, 4–44. https://www.sciencedirect.com/science/article/abs/pii/S0169809517310700?via%3Dihub

Michailidou, A. V., Vlachokostas, C., & Moussipoulos, N. (2016). Interactions between climate change and the tourism sector: Multiple-criteria decision analysis to assess mitigation and adaptation options in tourism areas. *Tourism Management, 55*, 1–12.

Mickwitz, P. A. (2009). *Climate policy integration, coherence and governance*. Technical Report.

Miska, C., Economou, V., & Stahl, K. (2020). Responsible leadership in a VUCA world. In *Responsible global leadership: Dilemmas, paradoxes, and opportunities* (pp. 11–28).

Paramati, S. R., Alam, M. S., & Chen, C.-F. (2016). The effects of tourism on economic growth and CO2 emissions: A comparison between developed and developing economies. *Journal of Travel Research, 56*(6), 712–724.

Ross, D., Leonard, B., & Inayatullah, S. (2022). Leadership beyond the great pause: Climate change and other wicked problems. *Journal of Futures Studies, 26*, 15–22.

Russo, M. A., Relvas, H., Gama, C., Lopes, M., Borrego, C., & Rodrigues, V. (2020). Estimating emissions from tourism activities. *Atmospheric Environment, 220*. https://doi.org/10.1016/j.atmosenv.2019.117048

Rutty, M., & Scott, D. (n.d.). Will the Mediterranean become "Too Hot" for tourism? A reassessment. *Tourism and Hospitality Planning & Development, 7*, 267–281. https://doi.org/10.1080/1479053X.2010.502386

Sanz-Cobena, A. (2017). Strategies for greenhouse gas emissions mitigation in Mediterranean agriculture: A review. *Agriculture, Ecosystems & Environment, 238*, 5–24.

Satta, A., Puddu, M., Venturini, S., & Giupponi, C. (2017). Assessment of coastal risks to climate change related impacts at the regional scale: The case of the Mediterranean region. *International Journal of Disaster Risk Reduction, 24*, 284–296.

Scott, D., Hall, C., & Gössling, S. (2019). Global tourism vulnerability to climate change. *Annals of Tourism Research, 77*, 49–61.

Scott, D., Peeters, P., & Gössling, S. (2010). Can tourism deliver its "aspirational" greenhouse gas emission reduction targets? *Journal of Sustainable Tourism, 18*(3), 393–408. https://doi.org/10.1080/09669581003653542

Sempiga, O., & Van Liedekerke, L. (2023). Investing in sustainable development goals: Opportunities for private and public institutions to solve wicked problems characterising a VUCA world. In G. Prelipcean & M. Boscoianu (Eds.), *Investment strategies: New advances and challenges*. IntechOpen.

Spandre, P., Francois. H., Verfaillie, D., Pons, M., Vernay, M., Lafaysse, M., George, E., & Morin, S. (2019). Winter tourism under climate change in the Pyrenees and the French Alps: Relevance of snowmaking as a technical adaptation. *Cryosphere, 13*(4), 1325–1347.

Sun, Y., Gossling, S., & Zhou, W. (2022). Does tourism increase or decrease carbon emissions? A systematic review. *Annals of Tourism Research, 97*, 103502. https://doi.org/10.1016/j.annals.2022.103502

UNEP. (2008). *Climate change:* Adaptation and Mitigation in the Tourism Sector: Frameworks, Tools and Practices. https://www.unep.org/resources/report/climate-change-adaptation-and-mitigation-tourism-sector-frameworks-tools-and

UNDP India. (2019). Assessment of conservation, livelihoods and economic development values of Indian himalayan protected areas.

UNWTO. (n.d.). *Sustainable development*. https://www.unwto.org/sustainable-development

Chapter 5

The Impact of Technologies as an Alternative Reality on Business in Hotel Industry: Virtual, Augmented, and Artificial

Ana Portolan and Marino Stanković

Department of Economics and Business, University of Dubrovnik, 20000 Dubrovnik, Croatia

Abstract

Technologies like virtual reality (VR), augmented reality (AR), and artificial intelligence (AI) impact the decision-making process related to the creation of tourist offers. The aim of this chapter is to analyse the exigency of application technologies in the tourism industry from the aspect of business, in order to demonstrate the readiness of certain organisations to apply alternative reality technologies. This chapter analyses the attitudes of top, middle, and operational managers in 3-star, 4-star, and 5-star hotels at the regional level of Dubrovnik-Neretva county in order to assess the necessity for businesses in the hotel industry to adopt alternative reality technologies as well as the key benefits and opportunities that come with it. Empirical research was conducted using a convenience purposive sample of managers in order to determine the relationship between the application of specific technologies and tourism organisations. Statistical methods were used to evaluate the data in order to test the importance of the respondent's examination attitudes. The results reflect the state of hotel organisations in terms of the usefulness that technologies as alternative forms of reality can provide them in business and point to the increasing adaptation of the tourist sector for the application of such technologies.

Keywords: Virtual reality; augmented reality; artificial intelligence; implementation technologies; hotel organisations

Tourism in a VUCA World: Managing the Future of Tourism, 65–76
Copyright © 2024 by Ana Portolan and Marino Stanković
Published under exclusive licence by Emerald Publishing Limited
doi:10.1108/978-1-83753-674-020241005

Introduction

The dynamism of everyday life and numerous circumstances that took place due to various crisis situations such as the COVID-19 pandemic directed the world to greater development, usage of technologies and people to adapt to such trends. These cases accelerated the digitisation of customers and the business supply chain last years. Research by executives at a major corporation points out that there has been a 7-year acceleration in the share of digitally enabled products (McKinsey & Company, n.d.). With regard to the aforementioned crisis, one of the most affected sectors is a hospitality sector; hence, this precise sector is expected to accept digitisation and transform its layout. There are different types of technologies that are predicted to be suitable for implementation in the service sector; some of their characteristics of use in the said sector are explained in this research, as well as the potential implementation effect that is tried to be presented (Gursoy & Chi, 2020).

In today's accommodation sector, especially in the post-pandemic era, technical advancement and digital transformation are significant factors. To stay competitive, hospitality firms must adapt their services and products to the most recent technological advancements in order to meet the difficulties of workforce shortages, rising labour costs and changes in consumer needs and behaviour (Zeqiri et al., 2020). However, there is also worry that the increasing trend of implementing digital technologies in the service sector is the main reason for the decrease in employment opportunities, as human resources are the foundation of catering services and the lever for higher quality tourism products and greater consumer satisfaction.

Primarily, the technologies described in this research are virtual reality (VR), augmented reality (AR), and artificial intelligence (AI) systems. The mentioned technologies belong to the secondary type of ICTs and digital technologies (Spremić, 2017). VR represents a simulation of an experience in which a person is given the possibility of communication within an environment conceived in an artificial way. On the other hand, AR is a technology that adds digital elements to an environment that is realistic and real human environment (Ramos & Brito, 2020). These two technologies have especially grown in popularity in the hotel industry as a solution for certain intangible services that the hotel offers and provides to users in its business, and the AR market is predicted to increase to almost 200 billion US dollars in 2025 (Statista Content Marketing Trend Study, 2022). The main reason why VR and AR have emerged as an important turning point in business is the tendency of hotel organisations to emphasise the physical component offered as a service to guests (Gursoy & Chi, 2020; Wynn & Jones, 2022). However, guests mostly rely heavily on the opinions and comments of other guests, and it is difficult to present a realistic hotel product. Based on this, VR and AR enable hotels to target a wider segment of guests and more efficiently align with the market, and it has a strong role as a marketing tool because it promotes the product in an interactive and unique way. Regardless of the fact that, fortunately, the pandemic is behind us, there is an understanding that the effect of corona has remained on the guests and that they are becoming more and more careful in the process of consuming services, and thus hospitality businesses can have great benefits in connection with digital menus and contactless food ordering and payment (Ball & Taleb, 2011; Gursoy & Chi, 2020; Nikopoulou et al., 2023).

The high reliability of computer programs and lightning-fast disruptive effects on the market have caused the integration of AI technology and robotic interfaces. The basic function of AI technology is to perform tasks like a human in a real situation; hence, the purpose of such technology is manifested in the automation of human activities in business processes. However, in the service sector, it is necessary to carefully determine the balance between the automatic effect of AI and the provision of a specific experience for the guest. There are three main components of AI technology that can most often be used in the tourism sector and therefore in the hotel business: chatbots, data analysis, and voice control (Alotaibi, 2020; Lukanova & Ilieva, 2019). Chatbots are intelligent programming software that creates a simulated interaction in the desired language during the stay of the guests in the hotel, answering the questions asked mainly regarding the conditions of reservations, hotel content, attractions of the destination, and the like. These seeking technologies to automate business processes in an efficient, consistent, and personalised way so that hotel employees can devote themselves more to more complex tasks (Skift Megatrends 2020; Medallia, n.d.).

Hotel organisations often tend to provide as much personalised service as possible during their guests' stay, giving them a special feeling of attention and respect. This is why they are increasingly implementing a voice search and control system in order to strengthen the interaction between guests and hotel rooms. In this way, AI technology in the form of voice control provides guests with the possibility of reserving a table, room service without physical activity (Sharma & Gupta, 2021). This is the direction in which the hotel can approach the label of a smart hotel by focusing on energy efficiency and sustainable development and a way to minimise the operating costs of the business. In addition, hotels use AI as a kind of Big Day system to be able to manage data in business. Such systems collect relevant data about guests, their habits, behaviour, and the like, in order to crystallise the true profile of the market segment of a certain hotel and accelerate the revenue and cost management system in real time. VR hospitality strategies can help improve the quality of experience delivered at almost every stage of the customer journey (Limna, 2022; Ramos & Brito, 2020). While AI cannot replace the human touch in the hospitality industry, AI-powered tools can handle many tasks that would traditionally be performed by staff. Many office tasks can be automated, reducing human error, increasing efficiency and freeing up staff for more important work.

The aim of this research is to analyse the relationship of strategic initiatives of hotel organisations in the form of business readiness for the implementation of VR, AR, and AI technologies. An attempt is made to answer certain research questions in this case. What is the intensity of the connection between the strategic activities of the hotel management and the application of the aforementioned digital technologies? What is the climate within the hotel system regarding the effort to implement VR, AR, or AI? Are the conditions developed for the implementation of digital technologies in the hotel? On the basis of the transitional research presented in the research review, one gets an insight into the implications that can potentially provide an answer to the research questions and a certain contribution to this topic. Also, the created survey questionnaire is abstracted on statements that have proven to be trustworthy and important when examining the attitudes and thoughts of hotel managers, on the top, middle, and operational levels of management, about the VR, AR, and AI implementation. The variables in the research were conceived to form a model that combines the hotel's strategy and the tendency to implement the aforementioned technologies, so the statement from the survey questionnaire, measured on a Likert scale, was transformed into a variable needed to test the model. Data processing from surveyed respondents yields data (for one dependent variable and three independent variables) which are presented as research results with relevant explanations and final findings through statistical analysis of descriptive statistics and correlation by Pearson's coefficient.

A Literature Review

Some authors believe that the application of digital technologies such as VR in the service sector, including in the hotel, is the most useful for simulating certain tourist activities and experiences. One of the most common uses of VR in the hospitality sector has been the creation of virtual travel experiences, using 360-degree video technology (Ben Youssef & Zeqiri, 2022; Kattara & El-Said, 2013). Through this, users can experience a virtual recreation of different aspects of travel, from the flight, to arrival, to some of the key sights. People can experience virtual tours, 360-degree films, or the operation of authentic processes in a virtual environment by employing VR headsets. Some hotels also provide a tour of the hotel structure to give guests an overview of the amenities and facilities (Iranmanesh et al., 2022; Martínez-Ros & Orfila-Sintes, 2009; Nikopoulou et al., 2023). This is especially well-liked with visitors who have reserved accommodation at a hotel and want to learn more about it. As a result, such virtual experiences are accessible to customers on the hotel's website, enabling them to explore accommodation units and other hotel areas before making a reservation or physically checking into the hotel. Among the interesting things about the use of virtual reality technology, there is a case recently started by companies, which is about the creation of VR booking processes in a way that allows users to search for hotel prices, flights and book a hotel room using VR headsets (Suárez-Cebador et al., 2018).

Hotel owners are increasingly trying to use AR technology in order to improve the offer by means of interactive elements inside the hotel rooms. By combining AR with wall maps that are placed in certain hotel rooms and by pointing a smartphone at the placed map, guests are provided with additional information about their destinations (Thakur, 2022; Tong-On et al., 2021). Here, guests can get information about local gastronomy, tourist attractions, and individual destinations that make your stay more pleasant and practical. The above features represent a clear way and advantages that hotels can develop their own hotel applications to create a more pleasant hotel environment for their guests to spend their time (Wynn & Jones, 2022).

AI for the hotel represents a very significant technology because for business activities such as reconciliation of revenue from multiple different sources that would take several days, AI can complete in minutes, with highlighted shortcomings that could be further refined. Certainly, the transformation of complex tasks into automated processes executed faster and with fewer errors can ensure cost reduction for hotel organisations (Alotaibi, 2020; Iranmanesh et al., 2022). The best example of this is robots that provide information to guests and are able to adapt to situations based on the guests' habits because they respond to the guests' questions and requests. Direct customer service is integrated and programmed into the robot interface and has proven to be one of the most effective ways to automate business tasks based on direct messages and online chat exchanges (Lukanova & Ilieva, 2019; Lai & Hung, 2018; Limna, 2022). AI chatbots are used on social networks so that they are available to everyone at any time, quickly and efficiently, which is often impossible for hotels to do due to the impossibility of constantly maintaining interaction with guests. An even more dominant way of recognising guest needs than chatbots is the digital concierge. It is a digital communication system that has the programming power of understanding context loops, matching, and keywords. This system differentiates the requirements that guests need to fullfill instantly, so they get immediate help without engaging hotel employees (Lai & Hung, 2018; Sharma & Gupta, 2021). In addition, what hotels like to pay attention to when it comes to the character of guests is the personalisation of services. In the hotel industry, an important role is played by loyalty programs that are offered to attract regular customers and create a circle of trust. Personalised offers for guests aim to strengthen the loyal base of loyal guests by simultaneously eliminating potential churn. AI solutions make it easier to record and update user data and potential preferences in order to keep more detailed notes, to track the past patterns of guest habits, such as what they were satisfied with and what services they consumed (Pelet et al., 2019). All of this helps to arrange the personal experience of the guests so that their stay in the hotel remains the best memory. An important role for AI is in operational efficiency because of how hotels can manage guests. Throughout the hotel building, data is collected in many ways and for many different things such as reviews, orders, transactions, and the like. Certain AI tools generate and compare all the data obtained in the hotel and transform them in a meaningful and efficient way into recommendations and possible conclusions about current or potential guests in order to improve certain activities of the hotel departments, to more easily overlook the needs of the guests and to simplify the hotel's operations globally (Manigandan & Raghuram, 2022; Nam et al., 2021). Given the aforementioned benefits, AI can help analyse consumer attitudes towards hotel products and services. By monitoring and analysing the mood of the guests, conversations with employees, an assessment of the guests' reaction to the consumption of the service is ensured.

As for the reservation system in hotels, the prices are mostly formed at the optimal level that the hotel would satisfy, ensuring the realisation of the expected income. In this segment, AI technology combines tools that can process large amounts of data on trends in the local market, occupancy, expected demand, and by using them, a dynamic price structure is developed that will strongly suit the hotel's needs. In this way, it will be difficult for the hotel to fail to reduce the price if it has an opportunity for a potential guest because it is recognised how to bring the product to the segment that wants to consume it, while at the same time avoiding the sale of cheap accommodation capacities, so revenues are optimised (Keating & Harrington, 2003). Also, technology is used to filter those distribution channels that are more affordable and most effective for a specific group of customers. In every large business, there is a certain degree of wastage of resources, but in this case, it is necessary to have a tendency to reduce such a trend. Food waste is a big problem in the service sector and in hotels in general (Maier & Edwards, 2020). AI can put an end to this situation, because with the help of the tools of the mentioned technology, it is possible for hotels to monitor the quantities and types of purchased and consumed goods, which realises the forecasting of the hotel's needs, avoiding the wastage of food and supplies, and thus this model is also applied to communal services (electricity, water, and heating).

Methodology

For the purpose of this investigation, a systematised survey questionnaire in the Croatian language was utilised as the major data source for the population of managers working in categorised hotels in the Dubrovnik-Neretva County in the Republic of Croatia at the top, middle, and operational levels of management. The service industry, which is connected to tourism and hospitality, is the focus of the chosen research area. The research was carried out in March 2023, and the sample technique used was systematic purposive. In order to gather managers' opinions and attitudes about how ready hotel organisations are to implement technologies like VR, AR, and AI, the research process is performed with a data selection of a questionnaire formatted into statements using the Likert scale of agreement in Google Forms.

The questionnaire consisted of 34 questions, from which, for the purposes of this research, those questions that exclusively refer to the mentioned technologies were extracted. A selected question and the data obtained by the questionnaire belong to the construct related to hotel technology, which in the best way describes the hotel's organisations readiness for VR, AR, and AI.

The method of filling out the survey questionnaire by managers from different levels of management in the hotel took place via e-mail in February 2023.

There are 83 hotels registered in the Dubrovnik-Neretva County: 6 hotels have two stars (**), 31 have three stars (***), 28 have four stars (****), and 18 have five stars (*****), in terms of that case were collected 64 responses from managers. The variables in the research were formed as statements that were measured according to the Likert scale of agreement with the thesis on a scale of values from 1 to 5, where 1 marks the lowest degree of agreement and 5 represents the highest degree of agreement with a certain statement.

The observed variables are the part of two constructs selected from the questionnaire survey for the purpose of this research. The dependent variable is included in the construct related to strategy, while the three independent variables are part of the construct related to the implementation of different forms of digital technologies. The selected variables for this research reflect on strict statements that explain the attitudes of hotel managers at different management levels about the readiness to implement specific technologies. For the independent variables, the claims are represented in the construct related to the hotel's digital technological equipment and explain the intensity of the hotel's readiness to introduce VR, AR, and AI technologies, respectively.

The coding of variables according to the statements in the survey questionnaire is processed according to the model of certain reviewed articles that investigated similar problems and cases. The three independent variables that appear in the model are coded with respect to the form of digital technology being examined, so it is for the independent variable of VR technology implementation at TEC1. For testing the implementation of AR technology, the dependent variable is written as TEC2, while for AI the independent variable is TEC3. A dependent variable reflects the statement about the existence of strategic initiatives of the administration for the implementation of digital technologies in hotel organisations and belongs to the construct related to the hotel's organisation business strategy. As it is the only dependent variable related to the hotel's strategy, the specified variable is written as STR. All independent variables and the dependent variable are expressed in the rating of agreement with the respondent's statement of the hotel manager at a certain level in the management of the organisation.

Regarding the collected data and set variables, this research tries to analyse the relations between the strategic initiatives of the hotel management and the potential implementation of digital technologies. In the research, descriptive statistics analysis, correlation analysis with Pearson's coefficient to present the strength and direction in a relationship between the dependent variable of the hotel's strategic initiative for digital technologies application and the independent variables of the hotel's readiness to implement technologies such as VR, AR, and AI.

Results

The results of this research are first based on the analysis of descriptive statistics, where the observed variables in the model were analysed both for the independent and for the dependent variable. The total number of respondents or managers at the top, middle, and operational level of hotel management is 64, which makes up the total number of respondents' answers for substantiated claims. In Table 1, according to the average values (MEAN) of the observed independent variables (TEC1, TEC2, and TEC3) and dependent variable (STR), all values exceed the middle, hence determining that the hotel manners mostly rated the statements with a higher degree of agreement. While the dependent variable STR has a value of the Variation Coefficient lower than 30%, the values disperse more around the mean value. The variation coefficients for the independent variables of the construct TEC are less than 30%, which explains the level of dispersion around the MEAN is higher. In this study, the data are consistent and closely interrelated, and the values of Cronbach Alpha – a measure of internal consistency for the observed variables are higher than the test reliability limit of 0.50. The Kolmogorov–Smirnov Z test (K-S test), which assesses whether the acquired data deviate significantly, was applied to test for normal distribution. The study's findings demonstrate that the Kolmogorov–Smirnov Z test is more significant than the critical value of 0.17 for 64 observations ($N = 64$) and a significance level of 5% ($\alpha = 0.05$), the data deviate from the normal distribution cause of in the series are thus not normally distributed.

A series of distribution data is not random for the observed series of individual independent variables TEC1, TEC2, TEC3, and dependent variable STR. The independent variables TEC1 and TEC2 related to readiness for implementing VR and AR in the construct TEC display significance lower than alpha ($\alpha = 0.05$) level of 5% significance, while the variable TEC3 is not significant, cause of p-value is higher than 5% of the alpha level. It proves a greater degree of differentiation of hotel managers' attitudes, cause of readiness for implementation AI is not significant. In the case of the dependent variable STR, which refers to the existence of strategic initiatives for implementation technologies in the hotel organisation, its p-value is lower than the 0.05 (5%) level of significance.

For analysing the correlation between the observed variables, Pearson's correlation coefficient analysis was performed to determine the direction and strength between the manifested variables (Table 2). All values of the Pearson correlation coefficient are positive, which indicates a positive direction between the observed variables. The correlation coefficient values range mostly between 0.5 and 0.9. The relationship between the dependent variable STR expressed in the rating of hotel managers' agreement that the hotel has strategic technology implementation initiatives and the independent variables TEC1, TEC2, and TEC3 expressed

Table 1.   Descriptive Statistics and Test Normality Analysis of Observed Data.

	STR	TEC1	TEC2	TEC3
Mean	4.2581	3.6129	3.5484	3.5968
Std.Dev	0.9221	1.2194	1.2633	1.2605
Cronbach Alpha	0.894	0.9595	0.959	0.959
p-value	0.0000	0.0302	0.0000	0.0580
Kolmogorov–Smirnov Z test	0.833	0.810	0.746	0.738
Var. Coeff	21.66%	33.75%	35.60%	35.05%
N	64	64	64	64

Table 2.   Correlation Matrix.

	STR	TEC1	TEC2	TEC3
STR	1			
TEC1	0.590867	1		
TEC2	0.564138	0.900576	1	
TEC3	0.566631	0.877422	0.892249	1

in the rating of hotel managers' agreement with statements about readiness to apply VR and AR technology, and AI varies between 0.5 and 0.6. Values within this interval prove that there is a moderately strong connection between the strategic hotel initiative and the implementation of the mentioned technologies. The most pronounced relationship between the dependent variable STR and some dependent variable occurs with TEC1, the implementation of VR technology.

Conclusion

This research presents an analysis of the connection between the strategic initiatives of hotel organisations and the readiness to implement digital technologies such as VR, AR, and AI. The research was carried out on the basis of surveyed hotel managers at the top, middle, and operational levels of management who expressed their agreement with the statements made on a Likert scale with grades from 1 to 5 in the survey questionnaire. It is a primary survey, which was conducted in February 2023, and 64 respondents' answers were collected. In the model that seeks to investigate the strength and direction of the connection between the variables, the dependent variable STR is the existence of a strategic initiative in hotels, measured in the ratings of hotel managers' agreement with the statement, while the independent variables are the willingness to implement VR, AR, and AI technologies, respectively, TEC1, TEC2, and TEC3 also measured in ratings of hotel managers' agreement with the statement. Looking at the average agreement with the statements by hotel managers, it can be seen that the ratings are higher than the average, and therefore managers of hotel organisations mostly agree that there are certain strategic initiatives in hotels and the readiness to introduce VR, AR, and AI technologies.

According to the *p*-values, the independent variables TEC1 and TEC2 and the dependent variable STR are significant at a significance level of 5%, and it can be concluded that the hotel's strategic initiatives and readiness to implement VR and AR technologies as such can be taken into account when developing the research model. The independent variable TEC3, which refers to the readiness to implement AI technology in hotel organisations, is not statistically significant at a significance level of 5%, and it is better not to include it in the model. Correlation analysis using the Pearson correlation coefficient concludes that in the model there is a moderately strong and positive relationship between the dependent variable STR and the independent variables TEC1, TEC2, and TEC3. This proves that the more hotel managers agree that the hotel is ready to implement VR, AR, and AI technologies, the better and more focused strategic initiatives are on the implementation of these technologies in hotel organisations. When there is a more pronounced tendency of the hotel to implement the mentioned technologies, the hotel management will focus more on such activities in strategies and projects.

The Correlation analysis using the Pearson correlation coefficient established a positive and moderately strong relationship between the dependent variable of strategic initiatives of the hotel STR and the independent variables TEC1, TEC2, and TEC3 – readiness of implementing technologies such as VR, AR, and

AI. Based on these results, it can be implied that hotel management will have stronger strategic initiatives regarding the implementation of the mentioned technologies, and the greater the readiness of the hotel for such activities. The most pronounced connection was established between the hotel's strategic initiative (STR) and the organisation's readiness to implement VR technology (TEC1). Specifically, a climate that strengthens the tendency to implement VR will influence hotel management to develop certain strategies and plans and focus more on such possible outcomes. This confirms certain research by the authors mentioned in the literature review, that the implementation of VR technologies for the hotel represents an important role, especially in the virtual presentation of the contents and services offered by the hotel, the authentic way of providing services, and the possibility of insight into the characteristics of certain hotel services before the reservation itself and the potential number of guests in hotel (Ben Youssef & Zeqiri, 2022; Iranmanesh et al., 2022; Nikopoulou et al., 2023; Suárez-Cebador et al., 2018).

Furthermore, a moderately strong relationship was established between the implementation of AR and AI technologies and the hotel's strategic initiatives, but the independent variable TEC3, which refers to the readiness of the hotel to implement AI technology, is not statistically significant at the significance level of 5% in this model, does not provide a statement for that case. The existence of a moderately strong and positive relationship between the dependent variable of the hotel's strategic initiative and the willingness to implement AR technology proves that the hotel management will be more strategically active in the matter of AR implementation if the hotel's readiness for its implementation is stronger. Some authors mentioned about numerous benefits provided by AR technology for hotel business, and among the most recognisable are cases of interaction between guests and intelligent tools for providing information about the hotel, destination, tourist attractions, etc. (Thakur, 2022; Tong-On et al., 2021; Wynn & Jones, 2022). This research presents a certain indication that hotels increasingly use manual strategies in their programs and focus their business on the possible implementation of digital technologies as a possible competitive advantage and thus strive to improve their business through recognition in the service provision process, work productivity, and especially more innovative and high-quality approaches in interaction with market segments.

The limitations of research are related to the finding the best analysis to examine the relationship between variables. In addition, there is often a level of subjectivity when filling out questionnaires by hotel managers, hence certain indicators and variables with regard to the degree of agreement with the statement do not seem realistic. The sample of 64 surveyed hotel managers is potentially not sufficient to give general conclusions about the readiness of hotel organisations to implement technologies such as VR, AR, and AI, but this research aims to provide insight into the case for a specific tourist region and provide opportunities for further research. For future research, it would be useful to investigate which categories of hotels with regard to the number of stars display higher relationships in process of digital technologies implementation. This type of research can be applied to smaller hotels or themed hotels such as: green hotels, hotels in rural areas, heritage hotels, because this type of hotel relies on sustainable development. Future research should upgrade the model with multiple regression – OLS and to apply this kind of research to organisations operating in other sectors of the economy.

References

Alotaibi, E. (2020). Application of machine learning in the hotel industry: A critical review. *Journal of Association of Arab Universities for Tourism and Hospitality, 18*(3), 78–96. https://doi.org/10.21608/jaauth.2020.38784.1060

Ball, S., & Taleb, M. A. (2011). Benchmarking waste disposal in the Egyptian hotel industry. *Tourism and Hospitality Research, 11*(1), 1–18. https://doi.org/10.1057/thr.2010.16

Ben Youssef, A., & Zeqiri, A. (2022). Hospitality industry 4.0 and climate change. *Circular Economy and Sustainability, 2*(3), 1043–1063. https://doi.org/10.1007/s43615-021-00141-x

Gursoy, D., & Chi, C. G. (2020). Effects of COVID-19 pandemic on hospitality industry: Review of the current situations and a research agenda. *Journal of Hospitality Marketing & Management, 29*(5), 527–529. https://doi.org/10.1080/19368623.2020.1788231

Iranmanesh, M., Ghobakhloo, M., Nilashi, M., Tseng, M.-L., Yadegaridehkordi, E., & Leung, N. K. Y. (2022). Applications of disruptive digital technologies in hotel industry: A systematic review. *International Journal of Hospitality Management, 107*, 103304. https://doi.org/10.1016/j.ijhm.2022.103304

Kattara, H. S., & El-Said, O. A. (2013). Innovation strategies: The implementation of creativity principles in Egyptian hotels. *Tourism and Hospitality Research, 13*(3), 140–148. https://doi.org/10.1177/1467358414522053

Keating, M., & Harrington, D. (2003). The challenges of implementing quality in the Irish hotel industry. *Journal of European Industrial Training, 27*(9), 441–453. https://doi.org/10.1108/03090590310506450

Lai, W.-C., & Hung, W.-H. (2018). A framework of cloud and AI based intelligent hotel. *ICEB 2018 Proceedings* (Guilin, China). https://aisel.aisnet.org/iceb2018/99

Limna, P. (2022). Artificial intelligence (AI) in the hospitality industry: A review article. *International Journal of Computing Sciences Research, 6*, 1–12. https://doi.org/10.25147/ijcsr.2017.001.1.103

Lukanova, G., & Ilieva, G. (2019). *Robots, artificial intelligence and service automation in hotels* (pp. 157–183). Emerald Publishing Limited. https://doi.org/10.1108/978-1-78756-687-320191009

Maier, T., & Edwards, K. (2020). Service system design and automation in the hospitality sector. *Journal of Hospitality, 2*(1–2), Article 1–2.

Manigandan, R., & Raghuram, D. N. V. (2022). Artificial intelligence (AI) in hotel industry and future development: An extensive in-depth literature review and bibliometric analysis. *International Journal of Intelligent Systems and Applications in Engineering, 10*(4), Article 4.

Martínez-Ros, E., & Orfila-Sintes, F. (2009). Innovation activity in the hotel industry. *Technovation, 29*(9), 632–641. https://doi.org/10.1016/j.technovation.2009.02.004

McKinsey & Company. (n.d.). *McKinsey 2020 business articles: The year in review.* Retrieved May 1, 2023, from https://www.mckinsey.com/featured-insights/2020-year-in-review

Medallia. (n.d.). *Medallia reports record fourth quarter fiscal 2020 financial results.* Medallia. Retrieved May 1, 2023, from https://www.medallia.com

Nam, K., Dutt, C. S., Chathoth, P., Daghfous, A., & Khan, M. S. (2021). The adoption of artificial intelligence and robotics in the hotel industry: Prospects and challenges. *Electronic Markets, 31*(3), 553–574. https://doi.org/10.1007/s12525-020-00442-3

Nikopoulou, M., Kourouthanassis, P., Chasapi, G., Pateli, A., & Mylonas, N. (2023). Determinants of digital transformation in the hospitality industry: Technological, organizational, and environmental drivers. *Sustainability, 15*(3), Article 3. https://doi.org/10.3390/su15032736

Pelet, J.-E., Lick, E., & Taieb, B. (2019). Internet of things and artificial intelligence in the hotel industry: Which opportunities and threats for sensory marketing? In F. J. Martínez-López, J. C. Gázquez-Abad, & A. Roggeveen (Eds.), *Advances in national brand and private label marketing* (pp. 154–164). Springer International Publishing. https://doi.org/10.1007/978-3-030-18911-2_20

Ramos, C. M. Q., & Brito, I. S. (2020). The effects of Industry 4.0 in tourism and hospitality and future trends in Portugal. In A. Hassan & A. Sharma (Eds.), *The Emerald handbook of ICT in tourism and hospitality* (pp. 367–378). Emerald Publishing Limited. https://doi.org/10.1108/978-1-83982-688-720201023

Sharma, K., Dhir, S., & Ongsakul, V. (2022). Artificial intelligence and hospitality industry: Systematic review using TCCM and bibliometric analysis. *Journal for International Business and Entrepreneurship Development, 14*(1), 48–71. https://doi.org/10.1504/JIBED.2022.124245

Sharma, U., & Gupta, D. (2021). Analyzing the applications of the Internet of things in the hotel industry. *Journal of Physics: Conference Series, 1969*(1), 012041. https://doi.org/10.1088/1742-6596/1969/1/012041

Skift Megatrends. (2020). Skift. https://skift.com/megatrends-2020/

Spremić, M. (2017). *Digitalna transformacija poslovanja.* https://www.bib.irb.hr/934725

Statista Content Marketing Trend Study. (2022). Statista content & design. Retrieved May 1, 2023, from https://statista.design/en/statista-content-marketing-trend-study-2022/

Suárez-Cebador, M., Rubio-Romero, J. C., Pinto-Contreiras, J., & Gemar, G. (2018). A model to measure sustainable development in the hotel industry: A comparative study. *Corporate Social Responsibility and Environmental Management, 25*(5), 722–732. https://doi.org/10.1002/csr.1489

Thakur, A. (2022). Sensor-based technology in the hospitality industry. In *Mobile computing and technology applications in tourism and hospitality* (pp. 24–43). IGI Global. https://doi.org/10.4018/978-1-7998-6904-7.ch002

Tong-On, P., Siripipatthanakul, S., & Phayaphrom, B. (2021). *The implementation of business intelligence using data analytics and its effects towards on performance in the hotel industry in Thailand* (SSRN Scholarly Paper No. 3944077). https://papers.ssrn.com/abstract=3944077

Wynn, M., & Jones, P. (2022). IT strategy in the hotel industry in the digital era. *Sustainability, 14*(17), Article 17. https://doi.org/10.3390/su141710705

Zeqiri, A., Dahmani, M., & Youssef, A. B. (2020). Digitalization of the tourism industry: What are the impacts of the new wave of technologies. *Balkan Economic Review, 2*, 63.

Part II

Community Perspectives and Tourist Behaviour in VUCA

Chapter 6

Nudging: A Possible Solution for a More Successful Destination Management

Snježana Boranić Živoder

Institute for Tourism, Zagreb, Croatia

Abstract

When tourists visit new destinations, they often bring their own values and cultural system, their behaviours, and ways of relaxing, which sometimes do not coincide with the host's expectations. Holidays are usually associated with relaxation and fun, so tourists are not inclined to think about the norms of behaviour or environmental issues or any other concerns that worry the society today. Tourist destinations face numerous problems related to their sustainability and try to achieve a balance between economic development, environmental protection, and satisfaction of residents' guests. Sometimes even small changes in behaviour could contribute to sustainability. In this chapter, an attempt will be made to identify the problems related to the behaviour of tourists in destinations, the reasons for such behaviour, and the potential for using the nudging approach to elicit different behaviour. Qualitative research methodology was used to gather the opinion of destination managers about the use of a nudge. For research purposes, a workshop was held with stakeholders in the destination on the possibilities of using nudging to solve problems in the destination concerning tourist behaviour. The results have shown that destination managers were not familiar with nudging. Therefore, the theoretical framework with examples of Croatian destination managers and their views on the possibilities of using nudging will be presented. The managers were positive about the use of nudging as a tool in destination management. With regards to the specificities of their destinations and bad tourist

Tourism in a VUCA World: Managing the Future of Tourism, 79–91
Copyright © 2024 by Emerald Publishing Limited
All rights of reproduction in any form reserved
doi:10.1108/978-1-83753-674-020241006

behaviour with which they are faced, they mentioned different possibilities for applying nudging.

Keywords: Sustainability; destination management; nudging; tourist behaviour; destination

1. Introduction

'The father' of the nudge theory is Richard Thaler, a Nobel Prize-winning economist, and the first application of the theory was in the field of economics. Recently, numerous possibilities for the application of this theory have been recognised in tourism, many of them in the field of sustainable tourism (Bar et al., 2022; Benner, 2019, 2020; Dolničar, 2020; Juvan & Dolničar, 2014; Souza-Neto et al., 2022).

Popular tourist destinations are visited by large numbers of tourists who can, in a short period, create possibly dramatic changes in the 'everyday life' of these destinations. Crowds in destinations created by too many tourists often lead to numerous social problems and the dissatisfaction of some groups of tourists, as well as the local community. For this reason, it is necessary to encourage certain changes in the behaviour of visitors. World Tourism Organization (UNWTO, 2019) acknowledges that addressing visitor behaviour is a subject of tourism policy by referring to measures such as awareness raising or education on regulations and norms. To address the gap between deeply embedded attitudes regarding social desirability and individual action, behavioural economics offers possible solutions (Benner, 2019). Behavioural patterns and decision-making are often the result of cognitive boundaries, biases, or habits and this pattern may be 'nudged' to better options. 'A nudge is any aspect of the choice architecture that alters people's behaviour in a predictable way without forbidding any options or significantly changing their economic incentives' (Thaler & Sunstein, 2008, p. 6). Nudging plays a crucial role in the context of tourism within a VUCA environment. In such unpredictable conditions, where travellers face numerous uncertainties and rapidly changing circumstances, nudging can serve as a powerful tool for guiding tourist behaviour. By designing subtle yet influential interventions, such as personalised recommendations or incentives for sustainable choices, destinations, and tourism stakeholders can encourage responsible and adaptive behaviour. Nudging not only enhances the overall tourist experience but also promotes sustainable practices, helps manage overcrowding, and contributes to the resilience of the tourism industry in the face of unexpected challenges, ultimately ensuring a more enjoyable and responsible travel experience for tourists and a more sustainable future for destinations.

This chapter is divided into several thematic units. It starts with an overview of tourism and tourist trends with an emphasis on the consequences of its continuous growth in the number of arrivals and overnight stays. By arriving at a destination, tourists bring many changes to the environment of the destination and the lives of its residents. Destination managers are faced with numerous challenges to reconcile the negative impact of tourism with the need of economic growth and the needs of residents for a better life. This is why sustainability appears as the only development possibility, and at its core, it implies a balance between the economy, people, and the environment. Behavioural economics and nudging as one of the possible tools for better destination management in the function of sustainable tourism is the next topic. Since nudging in tourism is a relatively new topic, an overview of several topics with which professional and scientific circles deal is given considering the possibility of its application in tourism. Finally, the results of a workshop held with destination managers in Croatia, with the aim of researching their attitudes and opinions on the possibilities of applying nudging in solving specific problems related to the behaviour of tourists in their destinations, are presented.

2. Tourism and Sustainability

The United Nations Brundtland Commission defined sustainability as 'meeting the needs of the present without compromising the ability of future generations to meet their own needs (World Commission on Environment and Development [WCED], 1987)'. That was in 1987, and since then, sustainability has become the main principle of development in almost all countries of the world that are developing tourism. In 2015, the United Nations adopted a plan for sustainability entitled 'Transforming our World: The 2030 Agenda for Sustainable Development' (United Nations, 2015) in which tourism directly or indirectly impacts all of the 17 development goals. Tourism is one of the largest and fastest-growing economic sectors in the world and a key economic sector in many advanced and emerging economies. In addition, after fuels and chemicals, and ahead of automotive products and food, tourism is the world's third-largest export category (UNWTO, 2019). Most tourism enterprises (around 80%) are micro-, small-, and medium-sized enterprises (UNWTO, 2019), which is very important for the economies of many destinations.

According to the UNWTO, sustainable tourism should: (1) make optimal use of environmental resources that constitute a key element in tourism development, maintaining essential ecological processes and helping to conserve natural heritage and biodiversity; (2) respect the socio-cultural authenticity of host communities, conserve their built and living cultural heritage and traditional values, and contribute to inter-cultural understanding and tolerance; and (3) ensure viable, long-term economic operations, providing socio-economic benefits to all stakeholders that are fairly distributed, including stable employment and income-earning opportunities and social services to host communities, and contributing to poverty alleviation.

Although sustainable development is a mission of most destinations, it is still rarely measured, monitored, and implemented. The European Commission has launched (European Commission, 2016) the European Tourism Indicator System (ETIS), a voluntary tool to manage, inform, and monitor the sustainability performance of tourist destinations. The indicators are structured in four categories: destination management, social and cultural impact, economic value, and environmental impact. The intention was to encourage destination managers to establish their own sustainability indicator systems, regarding specific characteristics of each destination. Destination management organisations should be able to incorporate these indicators into their policies and encourage other stakeholders to adopt sustainability. Unfortunately, these processes are often slow and have limitations. Font et al. (2023) evaluated the absorptive capacity of destination management organisations (DMOs) to implement and use the sustainable tourism indicators in making policy decisions and showed that the European Commission had unrealistic expectations. Their results showed that, at the European and global levels, the completeness and comparability of tourism data is still poor.

However, the health crisis caused by the COVID-19 pandemic further highlighted the sensitivity of tourism and additionally emphasised the need to apply sustainable principles for its development. This implies tourism that will not harm nature or introduce an imbalance in the social and economic development. During the crisis, numerous discussions were held in the professional and scientific community with the aim of finding a better and more balanced model of tourism development. On the other hand, the economies of numerous countries around the world are extremely dependent on tourism and strive for fast tourism growth. Having this in mind, tourism stakeholders and destination managers have a great responsibility to find ways to implement sustainability principles and at the same time protect natural and cultural heritage as the basis for future tourism development.

The development of tourism is balanced if it offers a satisfying experience for guests in destinations, favourable business results for those who invest, and all the while improves the quality of life for local residents. Interestingly, new terminology is being introduced today in scientific discussions on tourism – sustainable, responsible, transformative, or regenerative tourism. Sustainable tourism is about the long-term viability of travel and tourism, about positive change, and about supporting our planet, responsible tourism focuses on the accountability of each actor and regenerative tourism seeks to not just maintain, but also improve a destination (Sustainability Leaders United, 2021).

When it comes to the social dimension of sustainability, it mostly refers to the quality of life of the local population. There are various positive and negative impacts of tourism on the local population. The positively perceived social impacts of tourism include community benefits, increased community pride and value, community participation, cultural exchanges, and sharing cultural knowledge, while some common negative impacts are increased vandalism and crime, alcohol abuse, noise, prostitution, etc. (Ramkkisson, 2020). Besides that, when it comes to sustainability, the literature suggests that although travellers express positive evaluations for pro-environmental options, they tend to go for economically better but less sustainable options when they make actual choices (Kim et al., 2019, pp. 1–2). This phenomenon, called moral hypocrisy, was investigated by Batson and Thompson (2001). They talked about the inconsistency between attitude and actual behaviour of intention which occurs when people want to appear moral but tend to avoid the cost of being moral.

3. Behaviour Economics and the Nudge Theory

The history of behavioural economics research is more than half a century long (Kahneman, 2011; Simon, 1978; Thaler & Sunstein, 2008; etc.). During the last several decades, behavioural economics has become an important and integrated component of modern economic thought. Traditional economics implies models that derive from the assumption that consumers make reasonable and rational decisions when purchasing and that these decisions are defined by the utility that the customer expects from the product (Kahneman, 2011). In contrast, behavioural economics, as a branch of economics, talks about the consumer with virtues, flaws, and emotions. Such an imperfect consumer makes decisions that are not perfect. They are not logical and rational as traditional economists believe. Behavioural economics is an interdisciplinary field that investigates the effect of human psychology on economic decision-making, and the importance of this field has been proven as the Nobel Prize was awarded to psychologist Daniel Kaheneman and economist Vemon Lomax-Smith in 2002.

Behavioural economics deals with questions such as how people try to pick the best feasible options and why, despite their best feasible efforts, they make mistakes. It can be said that today behavioural economics has become an important and integrated component of modern economic thought. Liabson and List (2015) talk about complementarities between traditional and behavioural economics and state that behavioural economics uses variants of traditional economy assumptions (often with a psychological motivation) to explain and predict behaviour, and to provide policy prescriptions. Behavioural economics explores the effects of emotional, social, and cognitive factors on economic behaviour and consumer decision-making (Šarganović, 2020). Unlike the neoclassical economic theory, which believes that consumers behave rationally, behavioural economics deals with deviations from rational consumer behaviour. In other words, behavioural economics deals with the observation of human behaviour, which often shows that people do not make rational and optimal decisions, regardless of the information and knowledge they possess.

Human behaviour is complicated and very often unpredictable. The nudge theory is based on behavioural economics that combines elements of economics and psychology to understand how and why people behave the way they do. Thaler and Sunstein (2008, p. 6) defined nudge as 'any aspect of choice architecture that alters people's behaviour in a predictable way without forbidding any options or significantly changing their economic incentives. To count as a merge nudge, the intervention must be easy to avoid'. The main idea of nudging is to facilitate or recommend a certain behaviour without removing options or the freedom to choose, which means the elimination of any kind of manipulation. Hansen (2016) defined nudge as

> a function of any attempt at influencing people's judgment, choice
> or behaviour in a predictable way (1) that is made possible because
> of cognitive boundaries, biases, routines, and habits in individual
> and social decision-making posing barriers for people to perform

rationally in their own declared self-interests and which (2) works by making use of those boundaries, biases, routines, and habits as integral parts of such attempts.

For the use of behavioural sciences in public policies, Pelle Guldborg Hansen and Organisation for Economic Co-operation and Development (OECD) have developed 'The BASIC toolkit' (BASIC is an acronym for 'Behaviour', 'Analysis', 'Strategies', 'Intervention', and 'Change'). Behavioural insights (BI) help understand how context and other influences can impact decision-making and inform the actual behaviour of people and organisations (OECD, 2019). BASIC encompasses the whole process involved in BI-projects and could help destination managers in management processes.

4. Application of Nudging in Tourism

Generally, the application of nudging in tourism is a relatively new scientific topic that has elicited greater interest in research in the last ten years. The implementation of nudges in the tourism industry is considered a "win-win" situation because they can influence people's behaviour in the right direction while reducing operation expenditures and, many times, enhancing the tourist experience (Souza-Neto et al., 2020). That is highlighted by Dolničar et al. (2017, p. 241) 'The hedonistic nature of tourism and lack of economic incentive make tourist behaviour particularly hard to change'. This emphasises two important components. First, during the trip, tourists want to relax, enjoy, and not think too much about the rules and restrictions they are exposed to in their everyday life. Second, behaviours are generally difficult to change, and people are not inclined to do so.

The application of behavioural insights is still relatively unexplored in the tourism sector, but there is a growing interest in it mainly due to the increasingly promoted need for sustainability. In the travel cycle, which includes planning, booking, travelling, staying in the destination, and returning home, tourists make numerous decisions that can either positively or negatively affect the sustainability of destinations. While staying in hotels, eating in restaurants, visiting attractions, or just walking around destinations, several points of contact can be found to encourage tourists to make better decisions and behave more responsibly. Some of the areas that have captured the interest of researchers in the last 10 years are the following: hotel management, food waste, hotel reservations, transportation choices, tourism flows, and visitor management.

Hotel management and energy conservation: For many years, the hotel industry has been looking for ways to encourage guests to behave more responsibly when it comes to energy consumption. Through some research, interesting results were obtained regarding the possibilities of using nudging. Knežević Cvelbar et al. (2021) deal with the influence of default setting on consumer decisions on the example of daily room cleaning. Results of the study conducted in a three-star city hotel suggest that a change in default settings significantly reduces room cleaning and affects certain segments of hotel guests. The results also showed that changing defaults from 'grey' to 'green' in the hotel room cleaning context represents a promising strategy for reducing the environmental harm resulting from accommodation service provision without reducing guest satisfaction (Dolničar et al., 2019; Knežević Cvelbar et al., 2021).

Food waste: Some parts of the world today face enormous amounts of food waste which, in addition to being an ethical issue, also has a great impact on the environment. Kallbekken and Saelen (2013) showed that reducing plate size and providing social cues reduces the amount of food waste in hotel restaurants by around 20% and introducing a sign that encourages guests to help themselves more than once reduces food waste by 20.5%. The topic of food and nudging, which has been addressed by several authors recently (Chang, 2022; Dolničar et al., 2020; Hansen et al., 2019; Saulais et al., 2019), is also interesting due to the growing popularity of various aspects of gastronomy in tourism.

Travel booking and transportation: There are several interesting studies that illustrate travel decision-making (Arana & Leon, 2016; Jin et al., 2012; Kim & Hyun, 2020; Kim et al., 2017, 2019) focusing on the choice architecture. Opperwal et al. (2015, p. 467) deal with destination choice and in their study, they compared two choice tasks that have the same instructions and attributes but differ with respect to which attribute is exposed first and used to label the choice options: the destination name or the experience type. Their results are interesting to everyone involved in the promotion of tourist destinations because they showed that early exposure to either attribute enhances the importance of the attribute, although the effect is less pronounced for experiences than for destinations.

Tourist flow and overtourism: Numerous attractive and well-known destinations, tourist attractions, airports, beaches, etc., due to the increase in the number of tourists, face crowds that demand better management of their flows. Hulgaard et al. (2016) showed on the example of the CHT airport in Copenhagen that flow problems can sometimes be reduced easily by simple yet effective means. They identified that the bottleneck problem was the exit located in the customs area. Most people preferred to use the right door, and the solution was an intervention which led to more people using the left door. They noticed that 90 per cent of passengers used the right door.

Overtourism has received more and more attention in recent years and encourages numerous discussions among the scientific community and the public (UNWTO, 2019). Many European tourist destinations, such as Barcelona, Venice, Dubrovnik, etc., have become the subject of a public debate on overtourism (Benner, 2019).

> Overtourism occurs when there are too many visitors to a particular destination. 'Too many' is a subjective term, of course, but it is defined in each destination by local residents, hosts, business owners and tourists. When rent prices push out local tenants to make way for holiday rentals, that can be characterized as overtourism. When narrow roads become jammed with tourist vehicles, that is also an aspect of overtourism. When wildlife is scared away, when

tourists cannot view landmarks because of the crowds, when fragile environments become degraded – these are all signs of overtourism. (Justin, n.d.)

Benner (2019, p. 1) suggests strategies that can be grouped in four dimensions
of polices, organisation, institutions, and behaviour and pointed out that

Pure qualitative growth, measured in terms of tourist arrivals to
a destination and overnight stays in it, does not appear to be a
sustainable model in the long run, and the public in overcrowded
destinations seems to become aware of the underlying dilemma...
overtourism is not only a matter of numbers but also of tourist
behaviour, visitor management and further factors going beyond
a purely qualitative perspective of carrying capacity.

Many European tourist destinations have become the subject of a public and
scientific debate on overtourism, especially when it comes to protected areas or
cities under UNESCO protection. Overtourism causes social, cultural, and environmental problems not only because of the high number of tourist arrivals but
also because of tourists' behaviour (Muler Gonzalez et al., 2018). The behaviour of tourists in Amsterdam, Dubrovnik, Rome, Venice, and other cities that
attract large numbers of tourists often causes resentment from the local population. However, 'residents play a vital role in developing sustainable tourism, as
they are the cultural agents and the social group in which tourism is delivered'
(Muler Gonzalez et al., 2018). Unacceptable social behaviour in the destination
visited is the subject of more and more discussions in the scientific and professional community. Visitors are sometimes rude and insensitive to the people and
the destination in which they are staying, and this is no longer due just to differences stemming from culture and history. Instead of using the opportunity to
have a cultural experience, learn something new and different and meet the hosts,
tourists sometimes just want to 'have a good time'.

Souza-Neto et al. (2022) reviewed literature on nudges and their results highlight the applications of nudges in numerous domains, predominantly in hotels
and restaurants and they proposed a conceptual model that will guide the design
of nudges in tourism settings. In that model, they proposed several stages, with
the first one being the exploratory stage in which problems and desired behaviour
are identified as well as the reasons for the problem. Second comes the planning
stage describing the design and testing of the intervention. Third comes the testing stage including both a pre-test in a randomised environment and a test in a
real-life environment. The fourth and the last stage is nudge validation.

5. Nudge and Tourism Destinations

In recent years, there have been more and more discussions about excessive tourism and sustainability as well as about the behaviour of tourists in destinations.
Given that sustainable tourism encompasses the social and environmental effects

of tourism in addition to economic aspects, it is the topic that will require even more attention, especially from destination managers. Some destinations have already started applying certain measures – the 'stay away' campaign in Amsterdam, codes of conduct in nature-protected areas, group size restrictions in tourist attractions, etc. Changing behaviour is also possible in the following ways – agencies can lead groups outside the main tourist streams, awareness can be raised through campaigns with positive examples – use of natural straws, repeated use of some equipment, agencies can play films and videos to show tourists what they expect from them and what norms of behaviour exist in the destination, etc. Behavioural nudges are also one of those possibilities. Since tourism as an economic activity encompasses various activities and sectors, there are numerous areas of application of nudging for the sustainability of destinations.

Tourists are exposed to a lot of information and should be encouraged to make decisions that are good both for them and the community. This information has to be simple to understand, available, and encouraging sustainable behaviour (Fig. 1). In doing so, information must not be withheld, but rather the advantages and benefits of individual options should be clearly pointed out, feedback should be given on the activities and behaviours of others, the importance of sustainability should be emphasised and the role and the possible contribution of each individual communicated.

6. Possibilities of Using a Nudge as a Tool for DMOs: The Case of Croatia

Tourist boards are organisations that operate according to the principles of destination management and are established to promote and develop tourism in the Republic of Croatia. They perform activities directly related to tourism in such a way as to manage the destination on the level for which they were established. Through their plans and activities, destination managements promote sustainability and stimulate the positive impact of tourism in their destinations. At the same time, they warn about the problems arising from tourism development and try to solve the negative impacts. Their ability in implementing, managing, and controlling the development is relatively limited, but they can point out to problems, bring together stakeholders, such as the local tourism industry, residents,

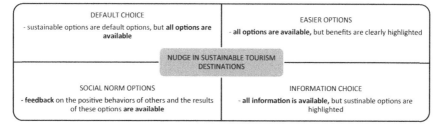

Fig. 1.   Nudges and Destination Sustainability. *Source*: Author.

travel agencies, public institutions, etc., and encourage problem-solving. Regarding seasonality and overtourism in many Croatian destinations, one of the problems is tourism flows. Destination managers have been trying to take measures such as to promote tourism products outside the main season (cycling, hiking, cultural tourism, etc.), stimulate events in off-peak months, promote new itineraries, stimulate the development of guided tours with less popular attractions, etc.

Representatives of destination management organisations in municipalities in Croatia, from the continental and the Adriatic regions alike, met at a workshop with the aim of testing 'nudging' as a suitable tool for solving some of the problems related to tourism flows, alongside general problems with tourist behaviour that appear in their destinations. The question was whether it would be possible to find new solutions outside the usual (mainstream) plans and activities undertaken. The workshop started with a presentation on nudging and the possibilities of applying it in tourist destinations. Possible conflicts within the destination between inhabitants, tourists, tourism companies and the public sector were discussed. To check if the participants understood the 'nudging approach', several questions were asked: Can you list challenges/problems in your destination which, in your opinion, can be improved or solved by using 'nudging'? The answers were as follows: too many birds in the town park; use of public toilettes (vs. non-use); rubbish disposal (putting rubbish in rubbish bins instead of beside them); drawing graffiti on facades; attract tourists to spend more time in nature and not only in the city centre; promotion of a healthy life through tourism; better use of bicycles for rent; promote less use of plastic bottles and PVC in general; connecting the urban and the rural 'part of the city'; pollution of public spaces with signage and advertisements; better promotion of local products; use of alternative routes and transport; public spaces for children (and not for dogs).

All participants said they were not aware of the possible use of nudging nor of the fact that it could work better than the bans they usually had in their destinations. They were going to think about how and where to use nudging. Although we presented a lot of practical examples, they would like to have more examples adapted to problems seen in their destinations. One of the participants from a destination with a long-term problem with young tourists who come for music events pointed out that nudging should be an important component of the new destination communication strategy.

7. Conclusions

Tourism brings numerous economic benefits, but at the same time, it affects the life of local population and the 'life of destinations' in numerous ways. Due to the constant growth of tourism, the question of how to ensure the sustainable development of tourist destinations has become a global issue. When tourists travel and visit destinations, they make numerous decisions based on the information to which they are exposed. They often tend to behave in a way that allows them to relax, and they do not tend to research and compare information or think too much about their decisions. Because of this, there are opportunities to encourage tourists to engage in certain behaviours that would be beneficial for them and for the community and destination they are visiting, without giving them orders or denying them certain information.

Destination managers are faced with numerous problems concerning the behaviour of tourists in their destination. Sometimes these problems are not excessively pronounced, and local population is willing to tolerate them because of economic benefits; other times they cause a more serious damage that could threaten the sustainability of the destination. Various tools are used to solve problems in destinations, from adopting regulations and promoting sustainable behaviour to providing information, etc. The issue of sustainability is becoming a major development challenge, and especially so in destinations exposed to large numbers of tourists. Numerous activities are undertaken at different levels, from macro to micro, so that the idea of sustainability is better recognised and adopted as a fundamental norm of development. However, sustainability is still too little and too slowly implemented in development policies and practices. Can nudging offer some solutions? Can it become an effective tool for encouraging behaviours that are better for the individual and for the community? Nudging has already shown results in certain areas of human activities, as well as in tourism, especially in the hotel industry. The question is what can be done at the level of destinations where there is no default system of responsibility and management like in other organisations and businesses.

There are no universal solutions because each destination has its own specificities. Destination sustainability can be monitored through sustainability indicators which indicate critical areas of sustainability and the need to undertake certain activities. It is in this part that behavioural sciences can offer certain solutions and provide tools. With forecasts of further growth in tourist trends and an increase in the number of tourists, the number of destinations that will face these problems can also be expected to grow. Therefore, it is important that destination managers undertake concrete activities and implement them in practice. As shown from the research in Croatia, nudging is still a relatively new and unknown topic, but one certainly deserves more attention. Good practice examples, already implemented by some destinations, could be useful to others. In this sense, designing educational modules and spreading the idea of nudging among the professional and scientific community would be extremely useful.

References

Arana, J. E., & Leon, C. J. (2013). Can defaults save the climate? Evidence from a field experiment on carbon offsetting programs. *Environmental and Resource Economics*, *54*, 613–626. https://doi.org/10.1007/s10640-012-9615-x

Bar, S., Korrmann, L., & Kursheidt, M. (2022). How nudging inspires sustainable behavior among event attendees: A qualitative analysis of selected music festivals. *Sustainability*, *14*, Article 6321. https://doi.org/10.3390/su14106321

Batson, C. D., & Thompson, E. R. (2001). Why Don't Moral People Act Morally? Motivational Considerations. *Current Directions in Psychological Science, 10*(2), 54–57. https://doi.org/10.1111/1467-8721.00114

Benner, M. (2019). *From overtourism to sustainability: A research agenda for qualitative tourism development in the Adriatic.* [MPRA Paper, 92213. University Library of Munich, Germany].

Benner, M. (2020). Overcoming overtourism in Europe: Towards an institutional-behavioral research agenda. *Zeitschrift für Wirtschaftsgeographie, 64*(2), 74–87. https://doi.org/10.1515/zfw-2019-0016

Chang, Y. Y. (2022). All you can eat or all you can waste? Effects of alternate serving styles and inducements on food waste in buffet restaurants. *Current Issues in Tourism, 25*(5), 727–744. https://doi.org/10.1080/13683500.2020.1870939

Dolničar, S. (2020). Designing for more environmentally friendly tourism. *Annals of Tourism Research, 84*, Article 102933.

Dolničar, S., Juvan, E., & Grun, B. (2020). Reducing the plate waste of families at hotel buffets. *Tourism Management, 80*, Article 10410. https://doi.org/10.1016/j.tourman.2020.104103

Dolničar, S., Knežević Cvelbar, L., & Grun, B. (2017). A sharing-based approach to enticing tourists to behave more environmentaly friendly. *Journal of Travel Research, 58*(2), 241–252. https://doi.org/10.1177/0047287517746013

Dolničar, S., Knežević Cvelbar, L., & Grun, B. (2019). Changing service settings for the environment – How to reduce negative environmental impact without sacrificing tourist satisfaction. *Annals of Tourism Research, 76*, 301–304. https://doi.org/10.1016/j.annals.2018.08.003

European Commission. (2016). *The European tourism indicator system ETIS toolkit for sustainable destination management.* http://doi.org/10.18111/wtobarometereng

Font, X., Torres-Delgado, A., & Crabolu, G. (2023). The impact of sustainably tourism indicators on destination competitiveness: The European tourism indicator system. *Journal of Sustainable Tourism, 31*(7), 1608–1630. https://doi.org/10.1080/09669582.2021.1910281

Hansen, P. G. (2016). The definition of nudge and libertarian paternalism: Does the hand fit the glove? *European Journal of Risk Regulation, 7*(1), 155–174. https://doi.org/10.1017/S1867299X00005468

Hansen, P. G., Schilling, M., & Malthesen, M. S. (2019). Nudging healthy and sustainable food choices: Three randomized controlled field experiments using a vegetarian lunch–default as a normative signal. *Journal of Public Health, 43*(2), 392–397. https://doi.org/10.1093/pubmed/fdz154

Hulgaard, K., Herrik, E., Koster Madsen, T., Schuldt-Jensen, J., Maltesen, M., & Hansen, P. G. (2016). *Nudging passenger flow in CPH airports.* I Nudge You. https://inudgeyou.com/wp-content/uploads/2017/08/OP-ENG-Passenger_Flow.pdf

Jin, L., He, Y., & Song, H. (2012). Service custamization: To upgrade or to downgrade? An investigation of how option framing affects tourists' choice of package-tour services. *Tourism Management, 33*(2), 266–275. https://doi.org/10.1016/j.tourman.2011.03.005

Justin, F. (n.d.). *Overtourism – What is it, and how can we avoid it?* Responsible Travel. https://www.responsibletravel.com/copy/what-is-overtourism

Juvan, E., & Dolničar, S. (2014). The attitude-behaviour gap in sustainable tourism. *Annals of Tourism Research, 48*, 76–95. https://doi.org/10.1016/j.annals.2014.05.012

Kahneman, D. (2011). *Thinking, fast and slow.* Penguin Books.

Kallbekken, S., & Saelen, H. (2013). 'Nudging' hotels guests to reduce food waste as a win-win environmental measure. *Economics Letters, 119*(3), 325–327. https://doi.org/10.1016/j.econlet.2013.03.019

Kim, H., & Hyun, S. (2020). The anchoring effect of aviation green tax for sustainable tourism, based on the nudge theory. *Journal of Sustainable Tourism, 29*(7), 1082–1097. https://doi.org/10.1080/09669582.2020.1820017

Kim, J., Kim, P. B., & Kim, J. (2017). Different or similar choices: The effect of decision framing on variety seeking in travel bundle packages. *Journal of Travel Research*, *57*(1). https://doi.org/10.1177/0047287516684977

Kim, J., Kim, S., Lee, J., Kim, P., & Cui, Y. (2019). Influence of choice architecture on the preference for a pro-environmental hotel. *Journal of Travel Research*, *59*(3), 512–527. https://doi.org/10.1177/0047287519841718

Knežević Cvelbar, Lj., Grun, B., & Dolničar, S. (2021). "To clean or not to clean?" Reducing daily routine hotel room cleaning by letting tourist answer this question for themselves. *Journal of Travel Research*, *60*(1), 220–229. https://doi.org/10.1177/0047287519879779

Liabson, D., & List, J. A. (2015). Principles of (behavioral) economics. *American Economic Review*, *105*(5), 385–390. http://dx.doi.org/10.1257/aer.p20151047

Muler Gonzalez, V., Coromina, L., & Gali, N. (2018). Overtourism: Residents' perceptions of tourism impact as an indicator of resident social caring capacity – Case of a Spanish heritage town. *Tourism Review*, *73*(3), 277–296. https://doi.org/10.1108/TR-08-2017-0138

Opperwal, H., Huybers, T., & Crouch, G. (2015). Tourist destination and experience choice: A choice experimental analysis of decision sequence effects. *Tourism Management*, *48*, 467–476. https://doi.org/10.1016/j.tourman.2014.12.016

Organisation for Economic Co-operation and Development (OECD). (2019). *The BASIC toolkit – Tools and ethics for applied behavioural insights*. https://www.oecd.org/gov/regulatory-policy/BASIC-Toolkit-web.pdf

Ramkkisson, H. (2020). Perceived social impact of tourism and quality life: A new conceptual model. *Journal of Sustainable Tourism*, *31*(2), 442–459. https://doi.org/10.1080/09669582.2020.1858091

Šarganović, H. (2020). Bihevioralna ekonomija i psihologija ekonomskog ponašanja i odlučivanja potrošača na tržištu [Behavioral economics and psychology of economic behavior and consumer decision-making in the market]. *Društvena i tehnička istraživanja*, 162–175.

Saulais, L, Massey, C., Perez-Cueto, F. J. A., Appleton, K. M., Dinnella, C., Monteleone, E., Depezay, L., Hartwell, H., & Giboreau, A. (2019). When are "Dish of the day" nudges most effective to increase vegetable selection? *Food Policy*, *85*, 15–27. https://doi.org/10.1016/j.foodpol.2019.04.003

Simon, H. A. (1978). Information-processing theory of human problem solving. In W. K. Estes (Ed.), *Handbook of learning and cognitive processes* (pp. 271–295). Erlbaum.

Souza-Neto, V., Marques, O., Mayer, V. F., & Lohmann, G. (2022). Lowering the harm of tourist activities: A systematic literature review on nudges. *Journal of Sustainable Tourism*, *31*(9), 2173–2194. https://doi.org/10.1080/09669582.2022.2036170

Souza-Neto, V. R., Marquez, O. R. B., Mayer, V. F., & Lohmann, G. (2020). *An overview of Nudge Theory on tourism research: Some insight from a systematic literature review*. [Paper presentation]. XVII Annual Seminar of the National Association for Research and Postgraduate Studies in Tourism, Sao Paulo, Brazil.

Sustainability Leaders United. (2021, October 13). *Sustainable, responsible, transformative, or regenerative tourism: Where Is the difference?* https://sustainability-leaders.com/sustainable-responsible-regenerative-tourism-explained/

Thaler, R. H., & Sunstein, D. R. (2008). *Nudge: Improving decisions about health, wealth, and happiness*. Yale University Press.

United Nations. (2015). *Transforming our world: The 2030 Agenda for sustainable development*. https://sdgs.un.org/2030agenda

World Commission on Environment and Development. (1987). *Our common future*. United Nations. https://sustainabledevelopment.un.org/content/documents/5987our-common-future.pdf

World Tourism Organization. (2019). *"Overtourism"? Understanding and managing urban tourism growth beyond perceptions: Executive summary*. World Tourism Organization.

Chapter 7

Cruise Tourism, Local Life, and Rhythms in Pre-, During, and Post-Pandemic Times

Allegra Celine Baumann

TU Darmstadt, Germany

Abstract

This chapter focuses on cruise tourism and its impact on cities and local life in relation to the COVID-19 pandemic. Three-time phases will be analysed: pre-, during, and past the main phase of the pandemic. Before the outbreak of COVID-19, a lot of cities, especially in the Mediterranean, were struggling with the amount of cruise tourists in the context of overtourism. During the travel restrictions due to the pandemic, cruise tourism almost came to a total stillstand. Using Dubrovnik, Croatia, as a case study, this chapter reflects on strategies of cruise companies and city governments to deal with the pandemic situation and the comeback of cruise tourism afterwards. Moreover, the impact of cruise tourism on local life and citizens during these three phases will be analysed. Unpredictable risks like pandemics change the tourist world and require solutions to deal with risks to overcome critical situations and phases. Analysing these situations generates knowledge, which can be used for the further development of solutions in the VUCA world.

Keywords: Cruise tourism; overtourism; rhythmanalysis; rhythm; local life; Dubrovnik

1. Introduction

The COVID-19 pandemic brought huge changes to everyday life, as well as to other areas, such as tourism. Nowadays, tourism is a central part in human lives. Some even declare that we are living in the 'age of tourism' (D'Eramo, 2018).

Tourism in a VUCA World: Managing the Future of Tourism, 93–103
Copyright © 2024 by Emerald Publishing Limited
All rights of reproduction in any form reserved
doi:10.1108/978-1-83753-674-020241007

Before the outbreak of COVID-19, the term 'overtourism' was part of nearly every discussion related to tourism. The term refers to mass tourism which is perceived in a negative way by locals and/or tourists themselves (UNWTO, 2018). Cruise tourism was considered by the media to be the symbol of overtourism due to the spatial and temporal concentration of cruise passengers in cities (Baumann, 2021c). City governments were searching for and implementing solutions to deal with huge amounts of cruise tourists. Whereas a lot of cities, especially in the Mediterranean, were struggling with the number of cruise tourists in the context of overtourism from 2017 to 2019, the COVID-19 pandemic at the beginning of 2020 and travel restrictions brought this to an end. At this time, solutions like sea-only cruises were established by cruise companies. However, port cities in the Mediterranean were struggling again this time, due to their economic dependency on tourism. After the loosening of travel restrictions, cruise tourism came back. Thereby, city governments had the chance – up to a certain point – to begin with their handling of cruise tourism from a new starting point.

The tourist season and the everyday flow of tourists show that everyday life and tourism are deeply connected to rhythms of movement. Rhythms of everyday life were examined by Henri Lefebvre (2021), who states that there are linear and circular rhythms, which consist of short and long intervals. In tourism, Endensor researched rhythms, for example, in his work about a coach tour in Ireland (Edensor & Holloway, 2008). In the city, especially the local transportation infrastructure is affected by tourist rhythms (Baumann, 2021b). Besides small rhythms with relatively short intervals, there are rhythms with long intervals, such as the tourist season. The COVID-19 pandemic interrupted these rhythms and brought tourism to a complete stillstand.

Using Dubrovnik, Croatia, as a case study, this chapter reflects on strategies of cruise companies and city governments to deal with the pandemic situation and the handling of the coming back of cruise tourism afterwards. Moreover, it will analyse how the impact of cruise tourism on local life and local citizens changed during these three phases and which kind of interaction between cruise tourists and locals took place. Unpredictable risks like pandemics change the tourist world and, moreover, require solutions to deal with these risks and to overcome critical situations and phases. Analysing these situations and solutions generates knowledge, which can be used for the further development of solutions and can be applied in future situations in the VUCA world.

2. Methods

The concept, which forms the basis of this study, is Henri Lefebvre's rhythmanalysis. Lefebvre's aim was to connect his understanding of time and space with everyday life through the idea of rhythm. Lefebvre's work about rhythmanalysis, which was published after his death, provides a concept and terms, but not the empirical tools to analyse rhythms. In the past years, scholars from different disciplines in the field of tourism studies started to use Lefebvre's concepts to analyse movement (Edensor, 2000; Edensor & Holloway, 2008; Flemsaeter et al., 2020).

In this chapter, two methods were chosen to translate Lefebvre's concept into empirical research: expert interviews and observations (participating and non-participating). Expert interviews allow deriving data from experts' evaluations of rhythms in a city, whereas observations give the researcher the possibility to experience city rhythms themselves. Therefore, the data were derived from 17 interviews with experts from different branches (e.g. city government, engineers, journalists, and political activists) as well as from several observations (Baumann, 2021a). The data collection took place in three phases in 2019, before, during, and after the cruise tourist season, and followed the methodology of grounded theory. Hence, data collection and evaluation took place in a circular process until theoretical saturation was achieved.

3. Case Study: Dubrovnik, Croatia

Dubrovnik was chosen as a case study. Dubrovnik is situated at the southern end of Croatia and is famous for its historic city centre, called Old Town (in Croatian: Grad), which has a size of approximately one square kilometre and is surrounded by the city walls. The UNESCO World Heritage city is an important cruise tourism destination in the Mediterranean and therefore was one of the main cities struggling with overtourism before the COVID-19 pandemic. Dubrovnik was paid a visit by UNESCO due to the impact of mass tourism, which resulted in requirements given by UNESCO to keep the status as a World Heritage. In 2017, Dubrovnik was rated one of the 'Destinations not to visit' by Cable News Network (CNN) (Minihane, 2018).

The city is of geographical interest as it is surrounded by mountains on one side and the sea on the other side. Due to its geographic shape and its historical structure, built improvements to fit the huge number of tourists are rarely possible. Hence, measures implemented by the city government during the high tides of mass tourism mostly focused on management solutions.

4. Rhythms of Local Life in Pre-Pandemic Times

Tourism and cruise tourism had their peaks before the COVID-19 pandemic. In media as well as in academia, there was a huge discussion going on around the topic of 'overtourism' as lots of European cities were struggling with the massive numbers of tourists (Dodds & Butler, 2019; Galloway, 2019; Koens et al., 2018; Milano, 2017; Raab, 2019). The United World Tourism Organisation counted 1.5 billion tourists worldwide in 2019 – 4% more than in the year before (UNWTO, 2020). In particular, cruise tourism was considered by the media to be the symbol of overtourism, because huge amounts of cruise passengers were flooding historic city centres at the same time (Connolly, 2019; Gibson, 2012). Hence, cruise tourism contributed to 'overcrowding' as a relevant cause of overtourism (Freytag & Kagermeier, 2019; Milano, 2017). The rhythms of local life in pre-pandemic times serve as a kind of starting point for this analysis, as these times are often referred to as the 'old normal'.

According to Lefebvre and Régulier (2021), Mediterranean cities have their own, specific rhythms, which differ from cities in the north. Following this argumentation, local life in pre-pandemic times can be characterised by two main rhythms:

- Seasonal.
- Daily.

Seasonal rhythms are mainly influenced by the tourist season with the cruise tourist season being a main driver. The tourist season in Dubrovnik starts with Eastern in April and ends in October with the main season for cruise tourism from May to September.

As Dubrovnik's main income is derived from tourism, most of the citizens are working in tourism or in branches related to tourism. Hence, during the tourist season, the main activities of locals are connected to tourism. Locals themselves experienced their life during tourist season to be mainly affected by tourist rhythms. One expert from a political activists group states it as follows:

> We don't have the programme in the theatre. Even if we had one, we are pressed to work so hard during the high season that we don't have time for anything. Not even to spend the money that we earn. That's how hard that pressure is.

Hence, during the tourist season, locals are working in or for tourism. During the off-season, the preparation for tourist season takes place or businesses like restaurants are closed. One expert working in a local garbage company puts the dilemma into words:

> Today we have that high pressure period of nine months. Our tourist season is not from 1st or 15th of June until the end of September, maybe half of October. Now we start in March and end in November. So, a way longer period of working on that high level. And then, we don't have a lot of time to deal with our equipment, to make repairs, to get all people to rest. We have to employ people only for tourist season. Because there is more work in the tourist season than in winter. In winter you don't have lots of tourists.

Besides these seasonal rhythms, there are daily rhythms, which are mostly characterised by the difference between day and night. During daytime, the Old Town belongs to the tourists. Guided tours and cruise ship tourists find their way through the small streets of the historical city centre. One of the findings of the study is that local rhythms are relocated to other times of the day, due to the impact of cruise tourism rhythms. As an example, children can only play soccer in the streets of the Old Town during nighttime, when cruise tourists already went back to the ship (Fig. 1).

Fig. 1.   Children Playing Soccer in the Tourist Season During Nighttime.
Source: Author.

Concluding, for pre-pandemic times, it can be said that local rhythms adapted to cruise tourist rhythms by 'synchronisation' (Baumann, 2021a; Lefebvre, 2021). This leads to the conclusion that cruise tourist rhythms were more assertive – probably due to the high economic importance of tourism for the city and its inhabitants, which may have partly led to a voluntary adaption of local rhythms to cruise tourism rhythms.

The city government's measures to handle the high number of tourists are another factor that affected the adaption of local rhythms to cruise tourism rhythms. Due to the predictability of cruise tourism and the requirements of UNESCO, the city government's measures mainly focused on cruise tourism. Following Baumann (2021a), the measures can be labelled as 'forced synchronisation' as they are implemented to willingly synchronise the rhythms of people in the city. The measures can be differentiated into four categories. First, regarding the way synchronisation takes place: 'ad hoc', meaning at the place and time of a potential 'rhythm conflict' (Baumann, 2021a) or 'ex ante', meaning at a different place or before a rhythm conflict takes place. Second, regarding their form of implementation ('human-controlled', 'material-controlled', 'decreed-regulated', 'informative-requested', 'financial stimulus', and 'structuring'). Third, if there is a spatial setup. And fourth, regarding the form of a spatial setup ('continuous', 'punctual', and 'spontaneous').

As an example, a spatial setup consisting of a rope, piles, and signs was put at the main entrance of the Old Town, the Pile Gate, to direct visitors to enter the city on the right side of the rope and leave it on the left side (Fig. 2). This measure was an 'ad hoc', material-controlled, continuous, spatial setup. The measure of stewards checking the traffic at the main node point at Pile Gate and, in the case of a potential traffic jam, communicating with their colleagues in the port to order the cruise ship excursion busses to wait there until the situation in the city is more relaxed, can be defined as an 'ex ante', human-controlled, punctual measure.

Fig. 2.   Spatial Setup at Pile Gate. *Source*: Author.

Analysing the measures implemented by the city government, it becomes obvious that all these measures aim at solving or avoiding rhythm conflicts by focusing on cruise tourism rhythms. The term 'rhythm conflict' was introduced by Baumann (2021a) to describe and analyse potentially colliding rhythms of movement. Overall, it can be stated that the city government's measures do not focus on strengthening local rhythms. Moreover, they contribute to the adaptation of local rhythms to cruise tourist rhythms by prioritising the latter.

5. Rhythms of Local Life During Pandemic Times

The COVID-19 pandemic had a huge influence on tourism (Arora & Sharma, 2021; Ito & Kawasaki, 2020). During the COVID-19 pandemic, from 2020 until 2022, cruise tourism slowed down. At one point, cruise companies had to be creative and developed new forms of cruise travels, for example, sea-only cruises, when cruise ships were not allowed to enter ports. For locals, this development meant less income from tourism. However, they could enjoy their cities almost without tourists.

Hence, the pandemic gave cities (with their inhabitants and city governments), which were before struggling with overtourism, the chance to breathe – and to think about new ways to deal with tourism (Koh, 2020; Rosin & Gombault, 2021). Before the pandemic, it often seemed like city governments were only dealing with the symptoms of overtourism and trying to minimise negative side effects as much as possible. This forced break due to the pandemic was the possibility to start from a new point and not only to deal with the symptoms, but also with the causes.

Moreover, the pandemic and the lack of tourists had enormous effects on local life. In Eastern 2020 local newspaper in Dubrovnik printed a photograph of a traditional Easter egg placed on a piece of grass which was growing on Stradun, the main street of the Old Town. Usually, Stradun is shining bright with its white stones, polished by thousands of feet passing by – not a single plant is able to survive in the small gaps between the stones on the Old Town's main street. However, due to the pandemic and the lack of visitors, nature came back and conquered its part. Nevertheless, not only nature, also locals were able to take a stroll in the Old Town during any time of the day. An expert from the Port Authority in Gruž, the main cruise port of Dubrovnik, expressed the connected feeling with the phrase: 'Finally, the city belongs to us'. Taking a stroll down the streets of the Old Town and playing football during daytime was something, most locals enjoyed – even though, of course, local rhythms were affected by pandemic-related rules and locals were facing the economic consequences related to the pandemic.

6. Rhythms of Local Life in Post-Pandemic Times

In 2022, cruise travel started slowly to come back. Even before the pandemic, locals in Dubrovnik had two different, ambivalent opinions towards cruise tourism. On one hand, it is a 'symbol of hope' and on the other hand, because local rhythms adapt to cruise tourist rhythms, some say cruise tourism ruined local life (Baumann, 2021a). In the context of local rhythms in post-pandemic times, the cruise ship as a symbol of hope is of main interest, because it is a recurring concept in Dubrovnik's local narrative. After the Homeland War in the early 1990s, the Greek cruise ship 'La Palma', which was the last to leave before the attack on the city, was the first one to come back 4 years later. Thereby, it brought 'the new light', as an expert on the cruise history of Dubrovnik states it (Baumann, 2021a). The coming back of tourism was perceived as a rebirth:

> Because, you know, war is war and when you have seen the first ship, the first plane, the first tourist, you have just been born once again. (Baumann, 2021a, p. 239)

A similar experience can be seen in local narratives connected to the First and the Second World Wars. After the Second World War, it was the Norwegian ship 'Den norske Amerikalinje', which came back as the first cruise ship to Dubrovnik in 1953 and was a symbol of 'the breaking of the isolation of the Yugoslavia on the West, from the west side' as the historian expert said (Baumann, 2021a). The expert for Dubrovnik's cruise history summarises it as follows:

> We had several times, after the First World War, after the Second World War and after our domestic war here, the Homeland War, that – again – the ships brought back life. (Baumann, 2021a, p. 239)

Interestingly, the cruise ship as a symbol of a 'light of hope' in Dubrovnik's narrative is mainly connected to traumatically historical events such as wars – and parallels can be drawn to post-pandemic times. Dubrovnik's mayor, Mato Franković, commented on the return of the first cruise ship after the pandemic on his social media channel with the following words:

> After more than a year and a half, the first ship of the Viking com-
> pany sailed into Dubrovnik. This continues the tourist recovery
> of our city. In the coming weeks, we expect new ships from other
> companies. (Thomas, 2021)

Hence, Dubrovnik's mayor values the first cruise ship after the pandemic as a symbol of 'the tourist recovery' of the city. A phrase that can also be translated as a 'symbol of hope for economic recovery'.

Even though tourism is Dubrovnik's main economy, the city struggled with the impact of overtourism in pre-pandemic times. Politicians worldwide demanded that the COVID-19 pandemic should be used as a break to end overtourism. In Dubrovnik, the mayor and the city government took this advice by heart. Franković said in an interview: 'The time of the COVID-19 crisis for us was a period of restart, which gave us time to rearrange, to rethink' (Trkanjec, 2022). Franković continued by saying that Dubrovnik 'aims to push forward diversified forms of tourism and support local gastronomy through family farming to adjust to the post-pandemic reality' (Trkanjec, 2022). Moreover, the city government planned to focus on diversified forms of tourism, such as film tourism (which in this case should be better called 'filmmakers' tourism') and digital nomads.

For filmmakers' tourism, the pandemic was not too bad as film crews were able to shoot in the Old Town at any time of the day without any concerns regarding regular tourism. Therefore, three productions were screened in Dubrovnik during the pandemic in autumn 2020, and in 2021, 25 film teams were hosted in Dubrovnik (Trkanjec, 2022).

As the second main tourist group in post-pandemic times, Dubrovnik's government plans to focus on digital nomads. As Dubrovnik's mayor pointed out, the city government already organised a conference as well as other events for digital nomads and made efforts to be listed in the 'Top 10 Savills Real Estate Executive Nomads List' (Trkanjec, 2022). One of the main goals of strengthening digital nomadism is to spread tourism throughout the whole year and thereby prolong the tourist season.

Regarding local rhythms, filmmakers' tourism has an immense impact on local rhythms as it completely brings them to a stop. When a film crew is shooting, streets are blocked, passing through is not allowed, there is noise and sometimes smell harassment. Moreover, what may have the most powerful impact is the fact that film companies pay the city government for their right to screen in the city. Hence, there is a possibility that this leads to some sort of belief that the city belongs to the film crew, due to their payment. This can lead to conflicts with locals, who experience the Old Town as their home and not as a filmset.

With digital nomads, it is quite the opposite. Digital nomads live in a destination and as they often stay longer, they may start to adapt to local rhythms. They probably stay in flats, where they cook their own meals and therefore go shopping and follow local rhythms. If the apartments in the Old Town were more aligned towards the needs of digital nomads, life could be brought back to the historical city centre with digital nomads living there. However, the biggest problem for locals – the possibility to rent and buy flats and houses for affordable prices – would not be solved by this development. Locals are more and more pressed to the outskirts of the city, by which they become visitors to the Old Town themselves (Baumann, 2021a). Whereas 5,000 people were living in the Old Town before the Homeland War, the number decreased to about 250 today. Most of the apartments in the Old Town were bought by foreign investors and turned into tourist homes. So maybe even digital nomads would seek for more affordable flats in the outskirts of the city and therefore would not stay in the city centre. Hence, they would also have to travel from the outskirts to the city centre, just like lots of locals do.

However, the COVID-19 pandemic also changed locals' way of living. People stopped being as outgoing as in pre-pandemic times. One reason might be the loss of money during the pandemic, which leads to them being more spendable than before. Hence, local life in post-pandemic times slowed down a bit. However, slowly it comes back to normal.

7. Discussion and Outlook

Events such as the COVID-19 pandemic have positive and negative side effects. The pandemic served as a break for societies: On the one side, everyday life was shut down, and on the other side, the pandemic gave the opportunity to rethink current and future developments. In particular in regard to tourism, these two sides of the effect of the pandemic became clear: The stillstand in tourism brought economic problems, but also gave the chance to change developments which could not be changed easily in a running system.

Analysing the rhythms of cruise tourism and local life in pre-pandemic times in Dubrovnik, it becomes obvious that the rhythms of locals adapted to cruise tourism rhythms. The reasons for this are that the latter rhythms are more powerful and assertive due to the spatial and temporal concentration of cruise passengers in the city, the economic relevance of cruise tourism for the local society and the focus on cruise tourism rhythms by the city government's measures.

During the pandemic, cruise tourism in Dubrovnik came to a stillstand, which allowed locals to recapture their city and enjoy it without being affected by tourist rhythms. However, the economic loss as well as pandemic-related regulations clouded happy feelings of Dubrovnik's locals.

When the pandemic regulations slowly came to an end and cruise tourism started again, Dubrovnik's local narrative of the cruise ship as the 'symbol of hope' repeated itself as it had during the three wars that Dubrovnik had been facing in the past. However, the city government planned to focus on new tourism groups, such as digital nomads and filmmakers' tourism. Whereas filmmakers' tourism has an enormous impact on local rhythms, digital nomads could theoretically adapt to local rhythms.

These findings show that analysing local rhythms of movement can help city governments and destination management organisations to understand which kind of tourism fits their city in the best way and has the least impact on local life. This helps to generate socially sustainable tourism and to adjust tourism to local circumstances.

For the tourist world, the COVID-19 pandemic was horror and hope at the same point: horror for existing models of tourism and the economic situation; and hope to implement solutions for the future, which will lead to a better relationship between locals and tourists (Baumann, 2021b). In the future, we will have to see if city governments made use of the situation and if their developments in tourism turn out to be successful. In the best-case scenario, measures and solutions for future tourism focus on local rhythms and try to synchronise tourist rhythms with local rhythms and not vice versa.

References

Arora, S., & Sharma, A. (2021). Covid-19 Impact on overtourism: Diversion from mass tourism to alternative tourism. In A. Sharma & A. Hassan (Eds.), *Overtourism as destination risk (tourism security-safety and post conflict destinations)* (pp. 275–283). Emerald Publishing Limited. https://doi.org/10.1108/978-1-83909-706-520211018

Baumann, A. C. (2021a). *From the cruise to the city – A rhythmanalysis of cruise tourism circulation on the traffic infrastructure in Dubrovnik.* [Dissertation, TU Darmstadt, Darmstadt].

Baumann, A. C. (2021b). On the path towards understanding overtourism – Cruise tourism and the transportation infrastructure. In C. Lusby (Ed.), *Benefits and threats of travel and tourism in a globalized cultural context*, Special Issue (pp. 5–13).

Baumann, A. C. (2021c). Spaces for encounters between tourists and locals in times of cruise tourism and overtourism. In C. Lusby (Ed.), *Destination unknown* (pp. 5–18). Common Ground Publishing.

Connolly, K. (2019). A rising tide: 'Overtourism' and the curse of the cruise ships. *The Guardian.* https://www.theguardian.com/business/2019/sep/16/a-rising-tide-overtourism-and-the-curse-of-the-cruise-ships

D'Eramo, M. (2018). *Die Welt im Selfie. Eine Besichtigung des touristischen Zeitalters.* Suhrkamp.

Dodds, R., & Butler, R. W. (Eds.) (2019). *Overtourism. Issues, realities and solutions.* De Gruyter (De Gruyter Studies in Tourism, 1).

Edensor, T. (2000). Moving through the city. In D. Bell & A. Haddour (Eds.), *City visions* (pp. 121–138). Pearson Education Limited.

Edensor, T., & Holloway, J. (2008). Rhythm analysing the coach tour: The ring of kerry, Ireland. In *Transactions of the Institute of British Geographers*, *33*(4), 483–501. https://doi.org/10.1111/j.1475-5661.2008.00318.x

Flemsaeter, F., Stokowski, P., & Frisvoll, S. (2020). The rhythms of canal tourism: Synchronizing the host-visitor interface. *Journal of Rural Studies*, *78*, 199–210. https://doi.org/10.1016/j.jrurstud.2020.06.010

Freytag, T., & Kagermeier, A. (Eds.) (2019). *Touristifizierung urbaner Räume.* MetaGIS Fachbuch.

Galloway, L. (2019). What's it like to live in an over-touristed city? *BBC.* https://www.bbc.com/travel/article/20190818-whats-it-like-to-live-in-an-over-touristed-city

Gibson, P. (2012). *Cruise operation management: Hospitality perspective* (2nd ed.) Routledge.

Ito, H., Hanaoka, S., & Kawasaki, T. (2020). The cruise industry and the COVID-19 outbreak. *Transportation Research Interdisciplinary Perspectives*, *5*. https://doi.org/10.1016/j.trip.2020.100136

Koens, K., Postma, A., & Papp, B. (2018). Is overtourism overused? Understanding the impact of tourism in a city context. *Sustainability*, *10*(12). doi:10.3390/su10124384https://www.mdpi.com/2071-1050/10/12/4384

Koh, E. (2020). The end of over-tourism? Opportunities in a post-Covid-19 world. *International Journal of Tourism Cities*, *6*(4), 1015–1023.

Lefebvre, H. (2021 [1992]). *Rhythmanalysis – Space, time and everyday life*. Bloomsbury.

Lefebvre, H., & Régulier, C. (2021 [1992]). Attempt of the rhythmanalysis of Mediterranean cities. In H. Lefebvre (Ed.), Rhythmanalysis – *Space, time and everyday life* (pp. 93–106). Bloomsbury.

Milano, C. (2017). Overtourism and tourismphobia - Global trends and local contexts. *The OSTELEA School of Tourism & Hospitality*. DOI:10.13140/RG.2.2.13463.88481.

Minihane, J. (2018). 12 Destinations travelers might want to avoid in 2018. *CNN*. https://edition.cnn.com/travel/article/places-to-avoid-2018/index.html.

Raab, K. (2019). *Endlicher Spaß. Die Zeit*. https://www.zeit.de/entdecken/2019-10/tourismus-reisen-zukunft-flugscham-overtourism-branche?utm_referrer=https%3A%2F%2Fwww.google.com%2F

Rosin, U., & Gombault, A. (2021). Venice in crisis. The brutal marker of Covid-19. *International Journal of Arts Management*, *23*(2), 75–88. https://gestiondesarts.hec.ca/wp-content/uploads/2021/04/IJAM_v23_n2_6_44313.pdf

Thomas, M. (2021). First viking cruise ship arrives in dubrovnik since pandemic began. *The Dubrovnik Times*. https://www.thedubrovniktimes.com/news/dubrovnik/item/11778-first-viking-cruise-ship-arrives-in-dubrovnik-since-pandemic-began

Trkanjec, Z. (2022). Mayor: The pandemic gave birth to new ideas for Dubrovnik's future. *Euractiv*. https://www.euractiv.com/section/economy-jobs/news/mayor-the-pandemic-gave-birth-to-new-ideas-for-dubrovniks-future/

UNWTO. (2018). *'Overtourism'? – Understanding and managing urban tourism growth beyond perceptions* (Vol. 1). UNWTO.

UNWTO. (2020). *World tourism barometer N°18 January 2020*. UNWTO. https://www.unwto.org/world-tourism-barometer-n18-january-2020

Chapter 8

Tourist Xenophobia and Residents' Perspective in the VUCA Era: The Case of Japan During the COVID-19 Pandemic

Wataru Uehara and Hiromi Kamata

School of Business Administration, Hitotsubashi University, Tokyo, Japan

Abstract

This study explores how tourist xenophobia (TXO) and residents' acceptance of tourists changed during the COVID-19 pandemic. If tourists feel TXO when travelling abroad during the pandemic, then, as residents in their home country, they may not welcome other tourists. Previous research on xenophobia in tourism has focused on tourists' perspectives, but few studies have examined residents' perspectives. Therefore, this study attempts to identify the influence of TXO on residents' acceptance during COVID-19 in Japan. The national government required residents to stay at home and avoid unnecessary outings while implementing a campaign to promote the tourism industry by subsidising travel expenses. Analysis of data from residents in tourist destinations showed that TXO negatively influences residents' acceptance of tourists and their travel intentions. There was a significant covariance between travel intention and tourist acceptance. Thus, TXO affects tourist intention and residents' acceptance. Destination managers must explain to residents the importance of attracting tourists to boost the economy and mitigate xenophobia. Mitigating residents' xenophobia and welcoming tourists are crucial for becoming a sustainable tourist destination in the volatile, uncertain, complex, and ambiguous (VUCA) era of the pandemic.

Keywords: Tourist xenophobia; residents' perspective; COVID-19; tourist acceptance; travel intention

Tourism in a VUCA World: Managing the Future of Tourism, 105–118

Copyright © 2024 by Emerald Publishing Limited

All rights of reproduction in any form reserved

doi:10.1108/978-1-83753-674-020241008

1. Introduction

This chapter explores the relationship between tourist xenophobia (TXO) and residents' acceptance during COVID-19. Tourism during COVID-19 was volatile, uncertain, complex, and ambiguous (VUCA), with both tourists and residents altering their behaviours. Visiting tourists during the pandemic can include residents of other tourist destinations who may view things from the residents' perspective. Kock et al. (2019a) defined TXO as tourists' negative feelings and anxiety when encountering residents in foreign destinations; they found that TXO significantly negatively affects tourists' intentions. If tourists feel TXO when travelling abroad during the pandemic, they may not welcome other tourists as residents in their home country. In a crisis, such as the COVID-19 pandemic, many tourists may face TXO, which could affect their attitude regarding tourist acceptance as residents. For example, the reputation of Asian tourists has changed during the COVID-19 pandemic (Wassler & Talarico, 2021). Bigotry towards Asian people worldwide became widespread in 2020 (Nikkei Asia, 2020a, 2020b). In the USA, concerns about the virus were associated with anti-Asian discrimination, along with xenophobic behaviours and policy preferences (Reny & Barreto, 2022). Asians seemed to have similar experiences both as tourists and residents. Asians who live in non-Asian countries or regions in this situation seem to have the same experiences as tourists, and they might not accept tourists. Thus, anti-Asian discrimination can be linked to TXO.

This chapter investigated a sample of Japanese people for two reasons: First, residents in tourist destinations in Japan have encountered the dilemma of choosing between promoting tourism or banning it amid fears of accepting tourists who may spread the infection (Kamata, 2022). The Japanese government has occasionally declared a state of emergency for some prefectures, such as Tokyo and Osaka, since April 2020, according to the number of COVID-19 infections. The state of emergency in Japan was different from that in other countries. Specifically, lockdowns were not mandatory in these regions. The government did require residents to stay at home and avoid unnecessary outings but also implemented a campaign called 'GO TO TRAVEL' to promote the tourism industry by subsidising travel expenses. As a result of the campaign, the number of domestic tourists increased. Data revealed that the number of overnight tourists in May 2020 was approximately 9 million (82.6% less than that in May 2019); however, during the campaign, the general number of tourists increased to approximately 37 million in November 2020 (Japan Tourism Agency, 2020). One of the concerns associated with this campaign was that the number of infected people would increase as more tourists visited the area. If a COVID-19 outbreak were to occur in a tourist area, the residents would suffer the inconvenience of crowded hospitals. Furthermore, the Japanese government has aimed to increase the number of international tourists visiting Japan since 2003. From November 2022 onwards, the government reopened international travel and once again tried to attract tourists from abroad. If the residents in tourist destinations did not accept domestic tourists during the pandemic, they might also not accept international tourists. Therefore, understanding residents' attitudes during the pandemic is important for attracting international tourists without resistance from the residents after reopening the border.

2. Literature Review and Hypotheses

2.1. Literature Review

2.1.1. Tourist and Resident Aspects

Some studies have focused on both tourists' and residents' behaviour. Kock et al. (2019b) were the first to investigate tourism ethnocentrism that captured tourists' and residents' motivations to support domestic tourism. They developed a scale for tourism ethnocentrism and estimated its effects on both tourists and residents. The results showed that tourism ethnocentrism affected willingness to visit, word of mouth, and residents' support for tourism but did not affect residents' hospitality. Josiassen et al. (2022) investigated tourism affinity and animosity in the specific context of foreign visitors. The results showed that tourism affinity positively influenced residents' attitudes, whereas tourism animosity had a negative influence. One implication of this study is that both attraction and repulsion affect not only tourist but also resident behaviour.

Many studies have examined the interaction between tourists and residents in a destination and the intergroup bias in tourist behaviour (Chien & Ritchie, 2018; Griffiths & Sharpley, 2012; Ikeji & Nagai, 2021; Kock et al., 2019a). Kock et al. (2019a) pointed out that 'tourism is inextricably linked to the encounter between tourists and residents. When members of two different groups interact, intergroup biases are likely to play an important role' (Kock et al., 2019a, p. 163).

2.1.2. Residents' Attitude in the COVID-19 Pandemic

Joo et al. (2021) and Kamata (2022) conducted initial studies on residents' attitudes during and after the COVID-19 pandemic. Joo et al. (2021) estimated residents' support for tourism in Jeju, South Korea. Residents' support was found to affect perceived risk from tourists through emotional solidarity. Besides perceived risk negatively affecting every factor of emotional solidarity, emotional solidarity positively affected support for tourism. Joo et al. (2021) suggested that the negative relationship between perceived risk and support for tourism may be partially mediated by emotional solidarity. Kamata (2022) revealed a dilemma in residents' attitudes towards welcoming tourists during and after the pandemic. During the pandemic, the residents tended not to accept tourists owing to individual infection control, which was called the 'effect on personal life'. Conversely, after the pandemic (defined as the time after vaccination or the development of treatments for COVID-19), the residents intended to accept tourists, considering the boost it provided to the local economy. The residents expressed positive attitudes towards tourism despite not having accepted tourists during the pandemic. Following the initial studies, various studies on resident attitudes towards the COVID-19 pandemic have been published (e.g. Antwi et al., 2023; Erul et al., 2022; Jiang et al.,

2023; Lee et al., 2022; Li et al., 2023; Liu et al., 2022; Rey-Carmona et al., 2023; Ryu et al., 2023; Wong & Lai, 2022; Woosnam et al., 2022; Xu et al., 2022; Yin et al., 2022). However, a few studies have focused on both tourist and resident attitudes or behaviours.

In summary, regarding tourists and residents of tourist destinations, xenophobia is an important factor influencing travel intentions, travel behaviour, and resident attitudes. Therefore, this study attempts to identify the influence of TXO on residents' acceptance.

2.2. Conceptual Model and Hypotheses

The conceptual model is shown in Fig. 1. This study employed the TXO framework developed by Kock et al. (2019a, 2019b). TXO influences the willingness to accept tourists during the pandemic (Acc) and travel intention (TI). Considering the COVID-19 pandemic, the effects on personal life (EP) (Kamata, 2022) are employed as a control variable for TXO, Acc, and TI.

In this study, TXO was defined as influencing Acc and TI. If a person imagined that TXO might occur when travelling abroad during the COVID-19 pandemic, they, as residents, might not accept tourists. In the questionnaire survey, to obtain a more realistic perspective of TXO, respondents answered the items on TXO with the assumption that they had been vaccinated. This study was conducted in February 2021, at a time when the vaccine was expected to mitigate the pandemic. This study employed the vaccine as an image of safety in a questionnaire survey.

The factor 'Acc', which is a newly defined term, is the acceptance of tourists during the pandemic. Here, the important point was vaccination against COVID-19, which could be considered evidence that the person had a lower risk of infection. Residents might welcome international tourists who have been vaccinated, and residents who have been vaccinated might feel safe accepting tourists who are not vaccinated. In this study, 'International tourists' refers to vaccinated tourists.

'TI' refers to travel intention after vaccination. Respondents were asked about their domestic and international travel intentions. Their answer was expected that low intention for the travels. Thus, responses to these questions were reverse-scored

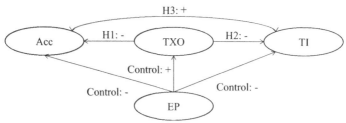

Fig. 1.   Conceptual Model. *Note*: Acc: willingness to accept tourists during the pandemic; TI: travel intention during the pandemic; EP: effect on personal life; TXO: tourist xenophobia. 'H' means hypothesis, and the sign of plus or minus means assumed in hypothesis. *Source*: The authors.

for estimation. The covariance between Acc and TI was assumed to be positive to examine the tourist and resident perspectives during the pandemic.

The hypotheses are defined below. The signs in parentheses indicate the assumed relationship (the same applies hereafter).

H1. TXO negatively influences Acc (-).

H2. TXO negatively influences TI (-).

H3. The covariance between Acc and TI is positive (+).

As shown in Fig. 1, EP was employed as a control variable. Kamata (2022) defined EP as the effect of COVID-19 on personal life. Similar to TXO, it was defined as influencing Acc and TI. To avoid infection, the residents might not want to welcome tourists even though they are vaccinated; this relationship was demonstrated by Kamata (2022). Similarly, as a tourist, EP might influence the lack of travel intention. Conversely, EP and TXO will have a positive relationship; people will control their behaviour according to EP, and might also experience increased TXO. Kock et al. (2020) also revealed that TXO is negatively influenced by perceived COVID-19 infectability.

3. Materials and Methods

3.1. Data Collection

Considering the COVID-19 situation, this study collected data between 18 and 22 February 2021 through an online questionnaire survey. The survey was conducted by a survey company in Japan (Intage, Inc.) and distributed to their panels. Respondents answered the questions using a five-point Likert scale (from 5: agree to 1: disagree). A summary of the targeted sample and the sample size goal is shown in Table 1. The sample size for each city was 400. Naha had a

Table 1. The Targeted Sample and the Total Number of Overnight Guests in 2019.

	City (Prefecture)	Sample Size Goal	Total Number of Overnight Guests	Total Number of Overnight International Guests
1	Sapporo (Hokkaido)	400	9.1 million	2.7 million
2	Naha (Okinawa)	200	3.0 million	0.9 million
3	Kyoto (Kyoto)	400	6.6 million	3.4 million
4	Kanazawa (Ishikawa)	400	3.4 million	0.6 million

Note: All targeted cities were prefectural capitals.
Source: The total number of guests and international guests for each city was sourced from the statistics data of each city.

sample size of 200, owing to its smaller population. As previous studies have mentioned, increased availability of the COVID-19 vaccination might mitigate residents' perceived risk of accepting tourists (e.g. Kamata, 2022; Woosnam et al., 2022). In other countries, such as the USA and the UK, vaccination began in December 2020. However, Japan began vaccinating only its medical frontliners in February 2021. Vaccination for the general population started in May 2021. However, at the time of data collection for this study, the citizens did not know when they would be able to get vaccinated. In summary, the Japanese people have faced an increasing number of infections as of February 2021 and were uncertain regarding the timing of their vaccination.

The respondents were residents living in the following cities: Sapporo, Naha, Kyoto, and Kanazawa. These cities were selected because they are popular destinations in Japan for domestic and international tourists (Table 1). However, the definition of 'tourist destination' is unclear because there are some industries that contribute economically to a city. Thus, some residents might perceive their region as a 'tourist destination', while others may not. Kamata (2022) defines tourist destinations based on the subjective perceptions of their residents. Specifically, the residents who responded 'agree' or 'almost agree' to the item 'I think my living area economically depends on tourism' were used in the analysis. This study employed the same definition and asked respondents similar screening questions.

The questionnaire was distributed to panels of people aged 20–70 years old and residing in the targeted cities. Regarding occupation, students were excluded, but unemployed individuals were included. Respondents agreed to answer the questionnaire through the online survey company. Both the company and researchers protected respondents' privacy, and the questionnaire data were kept anonymous.

3.2. Data Analysis

To confirm the content of each latent factor, exploratory factor analysis (EFA) and confirmatory factor analysis (CFA) were conducted. In the EFA, the items that structured each factor were assessed. This study employs the following criteria to assess the items: communality, factor loadings larger than 0.4, and correlations among items smaller than 0.6. In the CFA, latent factors derived from the EFA, reliability, and convergent and discriminant validity were evaluated. The criteria were as follows: Cronbach's alpha larger than 0.7, construct reliability (CR) larger than 0.6, and average variance extracted (AVE) larger than 0.5 (Fornell & Larcker, 1981).

4. Results

4.1. Estimation Results

Completed surveys were collected from 1,577 respondents. To avoid potential bias, employees of tourism-related companies were excluded because they might be eager to attract tourists to boost the local economy for their income stability. This reduced the sample to 1,286 (Sapporo: 385; Naha: 171; Kyoto: 360; Kanazawa: 370). Table 2 shows the demographics of these respondents. The numbers

Table 2.   Respondent Demographics.

Demographic	Number of Respondents	Ratio
Sex		
Male	683	53.1%
Female	603	46.9%
Age (years)		
20s	34	2.7%
30s	143	11.1%
40s	307	23.9%
50s	377	29.3%
60s	300	23.3%
70s	125	9.7%
Academic background		
Junior high school	32	2.5%
High school	403	31.3%
Vocational school	165	12.8%
Junior college	147	11.4%
Undergraduate	481	37.4%
Other	58	4.6%
Occupation		
Executive	38	3.0%
Company worker	422	32.8%
Government worker	101	7.9%
Temporary worker	180	14.0%
Self-employed	78	6.1%
Other	57	4.4%
Unemployed	410	31.9%
Length of residency		
Less than 10 years	279	21.7%
Over 10 years	247	19.2%
Over 20 years	760	59.1%

Source: The authors.

of men and women were almost equal. Most respondents were aged between 30 and 60 years. Regarding academic background, approximately 30% of respondents held undergraduate and high school degrees. Regarding employment, 60% of respondents were employed (including temporary workers) and 26.0% were unemployed. Approximately 60% of respondents had lived in the area for more than 20 years.

Tables 3 and 4 present the results of CFA discriminant validity, respectively. Discriminant validity tested the correlations between each pair of latent variables to see if they were less than the root of the AVE values. All factors of Cronbach's alpha, CR, and AVE satisfied the acceptance level of each criterion mentioned in Section 3.2.

As shown in Table 3, the mean of TXO was 3.38. Respondents answered the items based on the assumption that they had been vaccinated. The item with the highest mean was 'I doubt that the locals would welcome tourists like me', while the item with the second-highest mean was 'I would probably feel uneasy engaging with the locals'. This implies that respondents might be concerned about interacting with the locals even though they are vaccinated. Acc was 2.56, and TI was 2.08. Comparing the means of these factors, respondents tended to accept tourists as residents rather than travel somewhere as tourists. Among the Acc items, the item with the highest mean was 'It is not a problem if international tourists visit this area since we can confirm their vaccination status'. This implies that vaccination seems to have a certain effect on the acceptance of tourists. The means of EP were also high, suggesting that respondents felt that COVID-19 affected their lives.

The proposed model was analysed by covariance-based structural equation modelling (SEM) using AMOS 25.0, and the fit indices were as follows: chi-squared = 295.14, $p < 0.001$, GFI = 0.97, NFI = 0.95, CFI = 0.98, and RMSEA = 0.046. Some items in Acc and TXO were modified according to the modification indices. Fig. 2 and Table 5 illustrate the SEM results. All parameters were statistically significant at $p < 0.001$.

4.2. Hypotheses Tests

Table 5 presents the hypotheses test results. All hypotheses were supported. TXO negatively influenced Acc (*H1*). This indicates that the acceptance of tourists is influenced by TXO, a factor from the tourist's perspective, and suggests that when respondents feel TXO as tourists, they tend not to accept tourists. TXO negatively influences TI, supporting the findings of Kock et al. (2019a) (*H2*).

The covariance between Acc and TI was positive (*H3*), implying that people will accept tourists when they have the intention to travel as tourists. This reveals that respondents' decisions were affected by both tourists and residents.

Regarding the control variable, EP negatively influenced both TI and Acc. Kamata (2022) also showed that EP negatively affects Acc. When people attempt to control the spread of infection, they tend not to welcome tourists to their area

Table 3.   Constructs and Measurement Items.

Items	Mean	SE	FL	Alpha	CR	AVE
TXO: Tourist xenophobia (Kock et al., 2019a)	3.38			0.86	0.87	0.53
* Assumption: The respondents have been vaccinated						
1 I doubt that the locals would welcome tourists like me.	3.65	0.63	0.632			
2 I would not feel comfortable with the culture.	3.45	0.82	0.815			
3 I would probably feel uneasy engaging with the locals.	3.60	0.82	0.821			
4 There would be many misunderstandings between me and the locals.	3.34	0.85	0.846			
5 I would be suspicious towards the locals I encounter.	3.00	0.63	0.627			
6 I would be worried that the locals would meet me with reservations.	3.21	0.54	0.543			
Acc: Willingness to accept tourists during the pandemic (newly defined)	2.56			0.90		0.67
* International tourists mean vaccinated tourists						
1 As long as I am vaccinated, I have no problem interacting with tourists, foreign or Japanese.	2.52	0.91	0.752			
2 Interacting with international tourists is not a problem.	2.38	0.86	0.861			
3 It is not a problem if international tourists visit this area since we can confirm their vaccination status.	2.70	0.75	0.753			
4 As long as I am vaccinated, I do not mind foreign or Japanese tourists visiting.	2.66	0.75	0.908			

(Continued)

Table 3. (*Continued*)

Items	Mean	SE	FL	Alpha	CR	AVE
TI: Travel intention during the pandemic (reverse-scored; newly defined)	2.08			0.74	0.908	0.60
1 Even if I get the vaccine, I think I will refrain from domestic travel for the time being.	2.43	0.75	0.748			
2 Even if I get the vaccine, I think I will refrain from international travel for the time being.	1.73	0.80	0.801			
EP: Effect on personal life (**Kamata**, 2022)	3.90			0.77		0.55
1 I avoid unnecessary and non-urgent outings.	3.85	0.83	0.829			
2 I avoid crowded areas.	4.20	0.76	0.756			
3 I do not meet with family members who do not live with me.	3.64	0.63	0.628			

Note: SE = standardised estimates; FL = CFA factor loading; Alpha = Cronbach's alpha; CR = construct reliability; AVE = average variance extracted.
Source: The authors.

Table 4.   Discriminant Validity.

	TXO	Acc	EP	TI
TXO	**0.72**			
Acc	−0.21	**0.82**		
EP	0.20	−0.29	**0.74**	
TI	−0.46	0.40	−0.44	**0.78**

Note: TXO = tourist xenophobia; Acc = willingness to accept tourists during the pandemic; EP = effect on personal life; TI = travel intention.
Boldface numbers are the square root of AVE.
Source: The authors.

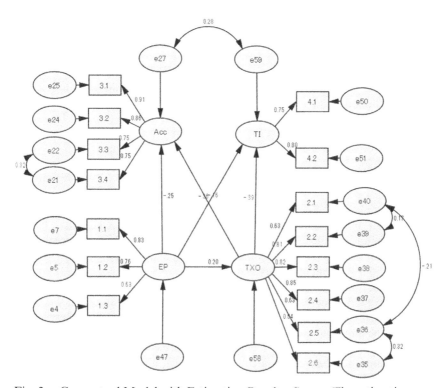

Fig. 2.   Conceptual Model with Estimation Results. *Source*: The estimation results of Amos.

of residence. EP positively influenced TXO, which supports the findings of Kock et al. (2020). However, EP and perceived COVID-19 infectability defined in this study were not the same as those defined by Kock et al. (2020).

Table 5. SEM Results.

				Assumed Sign	SE	std.	Results of the *H*-test
H1	TXO	-->	Acc	–	−0.16	0.05	Supported
H2	TXO	-->	TI	–	−0.39	0.07	Supported
H3	Acc	<-->	TI	+	0.28	0.02	Supported
Control	EP	-->	Acc	–	−0.25	0.04	Supported
Control	EP	-->	TXO	+	0.20	0.03	Supported
Control	EP	-->	TI	–	−0.36	0.05	Supported

Note: SE: Standardised estimates.
Source: The authors.

5. Discussion and Conclusions

The results of this study showed the relationship between TXO and residents' acceptance of tourists. TXO not only influences TI but also whether they will be welcomed to the travel destination. Kock et al. (2019a, 2019b) showed that tourism ethnocentrism influences both residents and tourists. Almost all previous research on xenophobia in tourism has focused only on tourists. This study found that TXO not only affects TI as a tourist but also the attitude towards tourist acceptance as a resident. As the attraction and repulsion matrix proposed by Josiassen et al. (2022) showed, tourism has positive and negative dimensions, and these effects impact not only tourists' but also residents' behaviour. The current study analysed data from the COVID-19 pandemic, which should be captured because people in tourist destinations might face a dilemma between TI and Acc. Kock et al. (2020) revealed that TXO by pathogen threat affected tourist behaviour. This study revealed that tourist destination residents' TXO as tourists arose from the fear of COVID-19 infections, and this influenced their attitudes towards accepting tourists from other destinations.

Regarding managerial implications, decision-makers at the destination (e.g. destination marketing/management organisations) should understand that TXO affects residents' acceptance of tourists. Destination managers should explain to residents the importance of attracting tourists to boost the economy and mitigate TXO. Some previous studies have also found that perceived risk might be mitigated by communication between residents and the local government (Rey-Carmona et al., 2023; Ryu et al., 2023; Woosnam et al., 2022). The Japanese government aims to increase international tourism; therefore, understanding residents' attitudes during the pandemic is important for attracting international tourists without resistance from residents after reopening the border. Furthermore, tourists visiting the destination might be satisfied by the residents' hospitality.

The future directions for this study are as follows. First, the sample should comprise respondents from more locations for a more comprehensive comparison of the results. This study only employed respondents residing in tourist destinations in Japan and excluded tourism-related workers. The sample can be expanded by surveying respondents with different characteristics, such as those from different locations or with varying employment types. Second, the COVID-19 pandemic and each country or region's strategies towards reopening their borders are still changing. People's intentions and perceptions may also change according to these strategies. Understanding people's intentions and perceptions based on a more up-to-date dataset is required.

References

Antwi, C. O., Ntim, S. Y., Boadi, E. A., Asante, E. A., Bobbey, P., & Ren, J. (2023). Sustainable cross-border tourism management: COVID-19 avoidance motive on resident hospitality. *Journal of Sustainable Tourism, 31*(8), 1831–1851. https://doi.org/10.1080/09669582.2022.2069787

Chien, P. M., & Ritchie, B. W. (2018). Understanding intergroup conflicts in tourism. *Annals of Tourism Research, 72*, 177–179. https://doi.org/10.1016/j.annals.2018.03.004

Erul, E., Uslu, A., Cinar, K., & Woosnam, K. M. (2022). Using a value-attitude-behaviour model to test residents' pro-tourism behaviour and involvement in tourism amidst the COVID-19 pandemic. *Current Issues in Tourism*, 1–14. https://doi.org/10.1080/13683500.2022.2153013

Fornell, C., & Larcker, D. (1981). Structural equation models with unobservable variables and measurement error. *Journal of Marketing Research, 31*(3), 39–50. https://doi.org/10.1177/002224378101800104

Griffiths, I., & Sharpley, R. (2012). Influences of nationalism on tourist-host relationships. *Annals of Tourism Research, 39*(4), 2051–2072. https://doi.org/10.1016/j.annals.2012.07.002

Ikeji, T., & Nagai, H. (2021). Residents' attitudes towards peer-to-peer accommodations in Japan: Exploring hidden influences from intergroup biases. *Tourism Planning and Development, 18*(5), 491–509. https://doi.org/10.1080/21568316.2020.1807400

Japan Tourism Agency. (2020). Accommodation travel statistics survey. https://www.mlit.go.jp/kankocho/siryou/toukei/shukuhakutoukei.html

Jiang, Y., Guo, Y., & Zhou, H. (2023). Residents' perception of tourism impact, participation and support in destination under the COVID-19 pandemic: The intermediary role of government trust. *Sustainability, 15*, 2513. https://doi.org/10.3390/su15032513

Joo, D., Xu, W., Lee, J., Lee, C.-K., & Woosnam, K. M. (2021). Residents' perceived risk, emotional solidarity, and support for tourism amidst the COVID-19 pandemic. *Journal of Destination Marketing and Management, 19*, 100553. https://doi.org/10.1016/j.jdmm.2021.100553

Josiassen, A., Kock, F., & Nørfelt, A. (2022). Tourism affinity and its effects on tourist and resident behavior. *Journal of Travel Research, 61*(2), 299–313. https://doi.org/10.1177/0047287520979682

Kamata, H. (2022). Tourist destination residents' attitudes towards tourism during and after the COVID-19 pandemic. *Current Issues in Tourism, 25*(1), 134–149. https://doi.org/10.1080/13683500.2021.1881452

Kock, F., Josiassen, A., & Assaf, A. G. (2019a). The xenophobic tourists. *Annals of Tourism Research, 74*, 155–166. https://doi.org/10.1016/j.annals.2018.11.005

Kock, F., Josiassen, A., Assaf, A. G., Karpen, I., & Farrelly, F. (2019b). Tourism ethnocentrism and its effects on tourist and resident behavior. *Journal of Travel Research, 58*(3), 427–439. https://doi.org/10.1177/0047287518755504

Kock, F., Nørfelt, A., Josiassen, A., Assaf, A. G., & Tsionas, M. G. (2020). Understanding the COVID-19 tourist psyche: The evolutionary tourism paradigm. *Annals of Tourism Research*, *85*, 103053. https://doi.org/10.1016/j.annals.2020.103053

Lee, N., Lee, S., & Lee, T. J. (2022). Resident reactions to a pandemic: the impact on community-based tourism from social representation perspective. *Asia Pacific Journal of Tourism Research*, *27*(9), 967–985. https://doi.org/10.1080/10941665.2022.2131441

Li, S., Fu, T., Qu, H., & Chen, M. (2023). Understanding residents' hospitality toward tourists amid the COVID-19 pandemic: A conservation of resources perspective. *Journal of Sustainable Tourism*, *31*(8), 1944–1962. https://doi.org/10.1080/0966958 2.2022.2131798

Liu, Y., Cao, X-Y., Font, X., & Gao, X-P. (2022). Standing with our hometowns? The relationship between residents' perceived threat from COVID-19 and intention to support tourism recovery in their hometown. *Journal of Destination Marketing & Management*, *25*, 100726. https://doi.org/10.1016/j.jdmm.2022.100726

Nikkei Asia. (2020a). *Anti-Asian Hate, the New Outbreak Threatening the World*. https://asia.nikkei.com/Spotlight/Coronavirus/Anti-Asian-hate-the-new-outbreak-threatening-the-world

Nikkei Asia. (2020b). *We are not COVID-19: Asian Americans speak out on racism*. https://asia.nikkei.com/Spotlight/Coronavirus/We-are-not-COVID-19-Asian-Americans-speak-out-on-racism

Reny, T. T., & Barreto, M. A. (2022). Xenophobia in the time of pandemic: Othering, anti-Asian attitudes, and COVID-19. *Politics, Groups, and Identities*, *10*(2), 209–232. https://doi.org/10.1080/21565503.2020.1769693

Rey-Carmona, F. J., Núñez-Tabales, J. M., Durán-Román, J. L., & Pulido-Fernández, J. I. (2023). Open the doors to tourism or remain cautious: Residents' dilemma amidst a pandemic. *Current Issues in Tourism*, *26*(5), 835–850. https://doi.org/10.1080/136 83500.2022.2047162

Ryu, K., Promsivapallop, P., Kannaovakun, P., Kim, M., & Insuwanno, P. (2023). Residents' risk perceptions, willingness to accept international tourists, and self-protective behaviour during destination re-opening amidst the COVID-19 pandemic. *Current Issues in Tourism*, *26*(8), 1367–1383. https://doi.org/10.1080/13683500.2022.2054782

Wassler, P., & Talarico, C. (2021). Sociocultural impacts of COVID-19: A social representations perspective. *Tourism Management Perspectives*, *38*, 100813. https://doi.org/10.1016/j.tmp.2021.100813

Wong, J. W. C., & Lai, I. K. W. (2022). The mechanism influencing the residents' support of the government policy for accelerating tourism recovery under COVID-19. *Journal of Hospitality and Tourism Management*, *52*(9), 219–227. https://doi.org/10.1016/j.jhtm.2022.06.018

Woosnam, K. M., Russell, Z., Ribeiro, M. A., Denley, T. J., Rojas, C., Hadjidakis, E., Barr, J., & Mower, J. (2022). Residents' pro-tourism behaviour in a time of COVID-19. *Journal of Sustainable Tourism*, *30*(8), 1858–1877. https://doi.org/10.1080/0966958 2.2021.1985128

Xu, J. (B.), Choi, H. S. C., Lee, S. W., & Law, R. (2022). Residents' attitudes toward and intentions to participate in local tourism during and after the COVID-19 pandemic. *Asia Pacific Journal of Tourism Research*, *27*(5), 473–488. https://doi.org/10.1080/10941665.2022.2091945

Yin, J., Kim, E. J., & Hwang, Y.-H. (2022). Changes in residents' attitudes toward tourism and perceptions of tourism contribution pre- and peri-Covid-19 pandemic: Role of perceived gratitude and damage. *Asia Pacific Journal of Tourism Research*, *27*(6), 637–651.

Chapter 9

Psychological and Socio-Demographic Drivers of Pro-environmental Behaviour in Generation Z

Dora Ivković[a] and Ante Mandić[a,b]

[a]*Faculty of Economics, Business and Tourism, University of Split, Split, Croatia*
[b]*Faculty of Economics, Business and Tourism, University of Split, Croatia*
Warner College of Natural Resources, Colorado State University, USA

Abstract

This study explores the socio-demographic and psychological factors influencing pro-environmental behavior among Generation Z individuals. Aimed at deciphering the impact of socio-demographic characteristics on psychological drivers and identifying significant psychological factors affecting pro-environmental behavior, the research utilizes an inductive approach with a sample of 225 Generation Z members from Splitsko-Dalmatia County, Croatia. Data were collected via an online questionnaire focusing on attitudes, beliefs, and behaviors related to the environment. Findings reveal that gender, education level, and residential area significantly influence psychological drivers such as guilt, moral obligations, and self-identity, with women, individuals with higher education levels, and those residing in suburban areas exhibiting higher levels of these drivers. This study contributes to the understanding of pro-environmental behavior in Generation Z by highlighting the importance of socio-demographic variables and psychological factors, thus offering insights for promoting sustainable behaviors among this demographic.

Keywords: Generation Z; pro-environmental behaviour; psychological drivers; socio-demographic drivers; Western society perspective

Tourism in a VUCA World: Managing the Future of Tourism, 119–141
Copyright © 2024 by Emerald Publishing Limited
All rights of reproduction in any form reserved
doi:10.1108/978-1-83753-674-020241009

1. Introduction

Human attitudes and behaviour determine the state of the environment (Palupi & Sawitri, 2018). The way people relate to the environment affects the quality of human life. Neglecting the environment causes global harm, which prompts people today to change their behaviour to reduce negative environmental impacts (Gifford & Nilsson, 2014). Tourism, as one of the largest global industries significantly impacts the environment. Its strong expansion and inappropriate tourist behaviour frequently result in the degradation of various ecosystem components, especially during the tourism season (Juvan & Dolnicar, 2017). Protecting and restoring the environment are the main challenges faced by today's society, so it is essential to understand and comprehend the environmental behaviour in society and the factors that influence it.

A new generation is entering adulthood amidst a changing global reality and concerns such as climate change and technological advancement (Robinson & Schänzel, 2019). Generation Z, as the youngest generation, consists of individuals born in 1995 and later, with the oldest members being 27 years old. Generation Z is mainly the offspring of Generation X and has been raised during the changes brought about by the internet, smartphones, laptops, freely accessible networks, and digital media (Robinson & Schänzel, 2019). The knowledge, attitudes, skills, values, and behaviours of Generation Z members, a significant majority of whom are students, are of particular interest since university education aims to prepare students for critical social roles as researchers, experts, and future decision-makers (Hansmann et al., 2020). The results of previous research show that Generation Z is the most concerned about global warming (Morrin & Gillespie, 2021). According to the survey data from Deloitte in 2021, Generation Z adopts more sustainable behaviours than any other group: 50% have reduced their consumption, and 45% have stopped buying certain brands due to sustainability or ethical concerns (Deloitte, 2021). Moreover, the data show that younger generations feel more motivated to reduce the impacts of climate change and pollution (Deloitte, 2021). The attitudes, knowledge, behaviours, and concerns about the environment that members of this generation have directly or indirectly influence future decisions regarding natural resources and how their usage can be sustainable (Mandić et al., 2023a, 2023b; Palupi & Sawitri, 2018). Therefore, it is necessary to motivate each individual to become a pioneer of pro-environmental behaviour.

Tourism must become more environmentally sustainable to ensure long-term growth and prosperity of the global community and the tourism industry. This is particularly important for countries like Croatia, where interventions to promote pro-environmental behaviour are just starting to enter political agendas and where there has been little research on factors related to pro-environmental behaviour (Balunde et al., 2019). Individuals can play a key role in reducing pressure on ecosystems. However, they are often unaware of their environmental footprints because they behave in ways that support their own interests (Mandić & Vuković, 2021). Tourists have several behavioural options that can help reduce the negative impacts of tourism on the environment. They can take fewer vacations, spend their holidays closer to home, offset their carbon footprint, avoid unsustainable modes of transportation, use certified providers of environmentally sustainable tourism, avoid engaging in harmful destination activities, and refuse to use services provided by unsustainable tourism providers (Juvan & Dolnicar, 2017).

Anthropogenic climate change currently threatens existing human societal systems, and psychology plays a significant role in researching and identifying predictors of sustainable behaviour and environmental concern (Smith & Kingston, 2021). In other words, as environmental concerns grow, so does the interest in understanding the psychological determinants of pro-environmental behaviour. Environmental psychologists and researchers in related disciplines have sought to identify the most influential predictors of pro-environmental behaviour and develop models that represent the role of intrapersonal factors (e.g. attitudes, beliefs, and values), interpersonal factors (e.g. social norms), and external factors (e.g. rewards and punishments) (Kormos & Gifford, 2014). Behaviour focused on environmental protection is crucial for ensuring environmental sustainability. Similarly, it can be said that the pro-environmental behaviour of tourists plays an essential role in mitigating the negative impacts of tourism on the natural environment. However, adopting pro-environmental behaviour is complicated, with various factors influencing its formation. Focusing on the mechanism of promotion alone is far from sufficient. To better understand the formation of pro-environmental behaviour, it is necessary to delve into why people do not engage in it (Wu et al., 2020).

Questions regarding the key factors that motivate people to adopt pro-environmental behaviour are increasingly capturing the interests of researchers (Li et al., 2019). This chapter aims to explore the psychological and socio-demographic factors related to specific sustainable tourist behaviours. Based on the above, it is possible to pose two research questions addressed in this chapter:

- Which socio-demographic characteristics significantly influence the psychological drivers of pro-environmental behaviour among Generation Z?
- Which psychological factors are most significant in pro-environmental behaviour among Generation Z individuals?

2. Literature Review

2.1. Impacts of Tourism and Tourist Behaviour on the Environment

Research on the environmental impacts of tourism dates back to the 1960s and 1970s, with early concerns emerging in the mid-1970s by scholars like Budowski, Krippendorf, and Cohen (Fennell, 1999). These early researchers identified three key relationships between tourism and environmental conservation: conflict, coexistence, and symbiosis (Biddle et al. 1987; Budowski, 1976; Cohen, 1978; Krippendorf, 1977). In the 1980s, the focus shifted towards assessing tourism's environmental impacts, with Pearce providing a framework for studying tourism and environmental stress (Pearce, 1985). These impacts encompass trampling, access roads, built facilities, and water edges, which have enduring consequences (Zahedi, 2008).

Despite relying on the natural environment, tourism can have detrimental effects due to abuse, overuse, and neglect (Anderson & Westcott, 2021). Global tourist arrivals saw significant growth in 2022, raising concerns about transportation emissions (OECD, 2016; UNWTO, 2022). Climate change affects tourism demand and resilience, necessitating climate action (Colombàs, 2020; Hall, 2010). Although mitigation policies and awareness efforts exist, public perception suggests that governments must do more (Gössling et al., 2012; Lorenzoni et al., 2007).

Tourists often contribute to environmental degradation, yet their responsibility is not always emphasised, leading to careless behaviour (Krippendorf, 1987). To instil ecological values in destinations, consumer orientation is crucial alongside the destination's commitment to environmental preservation. Responsible tourist behaviour is essential for destinations to remain competitive. Irresponsible behaviour, such as littering and vegetation destruction, can harm the environment (He et al., 2018). Thus, a key challenge for destinations is the sustainable management of tourism activities, requiring comprehensive research to promote ecologically responsible tourist behaviour. Such research is the foundation for preserving the environment's quality, authenticity, and competitiveness (Marques et al., 2021).

Ecologically responsible behaviour indicates an individual's ecological commitment, care, and knowledge, manifesting through environmentally friendly and pro-environmental actions (Marques et al., 2021). Ecologically responsible tourist behaviour involves activities by tourists to promote sustainable resource use and minimise environmental impacts at destinations (Liu et al., 2022). It is influenced by internal psychological factors like subjective norms, perceived value, and satisfaction, as well as external factors such as environmental quality, policies, and destination characteristics (Liu et al., 2022).

Managing pro-environmental tourist behaviour is vital to mitigate tourism's negative environmental impacts (Becken, 2007). Destinations employ various approaches to encourage pro-environmental behaviour, including motivation, education, infrastructure, and policies. However, tourists are less likely to engage in such behaviour while on vacation, facing barriers like unfamiliarity with the destination and a reluctance to exert additional effort (Dolnicar & Leisch, 2008a, 2008b). Few studies explore destination's external influences on tourist behaviour (Leung & Rosenthal, 2019), including the relatively unexamined factor of destination ecological image. This image encompasses tourists' perceptions of environmental preservation, sustainable practices, destination commitment, and environmental quality (Bilynets & Cvelbar, 2022). Research indicates that pro-environmental actions at a destination enhance its image as environmentally friendly, with tourists perceiving the destination as sustainable when exposed to 'green' activities (Bilynets & Cvelbar, 2022). Furthermore, the daily behaviour of the local population has a spillover effect on tourist behaviour, highlighting the transformative power of tourism on the environment (micro to macro scales) globally.

2.2. Defining the Concept of Pro-Environmental Behaviour

Human activities have emerged as a leading driver of environmental change and degradation, impacting ecological processes, environmental quality, and human health globally (Alzubaidi, 2018). These activities encompass unsustainable resource consumption, increased hazardous waste production, air and water pollution, and biodiversity loss. Consequently, research has highlighted environmentally harmful human behaviour as a fundamental contributor to these issues, emphasising the need for increased pro-environmental behaviour to mitigate destruction and achieve sustainable development (Rampedi & Ifegbesan, 2022).

Pro-environmental behaviour, as defined by Lange and Dewitte (2019), involves actions that benefit the environment and refrain from those that harm it. In essence, it encompasses various choices made by individuals or groups aimed at preserving the environment and reducing natural resource consumption and destruction (Rodríguez-Barreiro et al., 2013). This behaviour manifests at the individual level through practices like household waste recycling and reduction, decreased car usage, avoidance of air travel and plastic bags, and the conservation of resources like water and energy (Patel et al., 2017). Given these activities, the question arises about the factors that either promote or discourage pro-environmental behaviour among individuals in different countries.

2.3. Psychological Drivers of Pro-Environmental Behaviour

Psychological drivers of pro-environmental behaviour encompass various factors. Self-efficacy, a key determinant, influences intention and, subsequently, behaviour (Bandura, 1997). In the context of pro-environmental actions, self-efficacy reflects individuals' belief in their ability to perform environmental measures, such as waste sorting (Huang, 2016). It not only directly impacts environmental behaviour but also drives interest in obtaining information about global warming solutions (Huang, 2016).

Perceived behavioural control is another critical factor, encompassing beliefs related to controlling elements that can facilitate or hinder behaviour (Ajzen, 2020). If individuals feel in control of their actions, they are more likely to act in line with their intentions. This control relates to an individual's perception of their ability to align their behaviour with environmental goals (Karimi & Mohammadimehr, 2022). It positively affects various pro-environmental behaviours, such as reducing food waste and adopting green purchasing or recycling practices (Mohiuddin et al., 2018; Soorani & Ahmadvand, 2019; Wu et al., 2022).

Morality plays a significant role in motivating altruistic pro-environmental behaviour (Han & Hyun, 2017). Higher moral reasoning aligns with a greater likelihood of altruistic behaviour (Wu et al., 2020). Tourists' moral obligations correlate positively with pro-environmental actions, including low-effort actions like recycling and using environmentally friendly shopping bags, as well as high-effort behaviours like volunteering for conservation projects (Harland et al., 2007; Lam & Chen, 2006; Saphores et al., 2012).

Self-identity, defined as internal self-definitions within social contexts, influences behaviour (Turner, 2013). Identity is linked to actions and consumer behaviours, with those perceiving themselves as typical recyclers more likely to engage in recycling (Mannetti et al., 2004). Identity can override attitudes, especially when it aligns with societal roles (Whitmarsh & O'Neill, 2010). Environmental self-identity, as well as place identity, can mediate positive spill-over effects, influencing behaviours such as choosing environmentally friendly products and protecting local areas from development threats (Cornelissen et al., 2008; Lacasse, 2016; Stets & Biga 2003; Truelove et al., 2021; Van der Werff et al., 2014b).

Social norms are unwritten rules that define acceptable actions within a group, guiding behaviour (Farrow et al., 2017). They have evolved, influencing actions like recycling and reducing single-use plastics (Perry et al., 2021). These norms are contextual and require repeated interactions within a group for establishment (Perry et al., 2021). They are challenging to foster among strangers and in unfamiliar situations (Duffy et al., 2013).

Environmental knowledge is a fundamental driver of pro-environmental behaviour, encompassing awareness of environmental issues and actions to address them (Laroche et al., 2001). Factual knowledge, which pertains to environmental issues and potential solutions, differs from action-specific knowledge, which focuses on actions for environmental protection. Action-specific knowledge, translating into concrete and informed decisions, has a more significant impact on pro-environmental behaviour compared to factual knowledge (Liobikienė et al., 2016; Liobikienė & Poškus, 2019). It simplifies decision-making and directly influences behaviour, especially when addressing practical choices like transportation or energy consumption (Liobikienė & Poškus, 2019; Zhao et al., 2014).

2.4. Socio-Demographic Drivers of Pro-Environmental Behaviour

Socio-demographic drivers significantly influence pro-environmental behaviour. Education level, for instance, shows a positive correlation with environmentally oriented actions, with higher education often associated with greater environmental consciousness (Rowlands et al., 2003; Sánchez et al., 2015; Tilikidou, 2007). Educated individuals tend to acquire environmental knowledge through their education, which positively affects their behaviour (Chen et al., 2011).

Age is another socio-demographic factor related to pro-environmental behaviour, with numerous studies revealing a positive relationship between age and environmentally friendly actions (Chen et al., 2011; Oerke & Bogner, 2010; Pavalache-Ilie & Unianu, 2012; Rowlands et al., 2003; Samarasinghe, 2012). Younger individuals are often more environmentally conscious compared to older generations (Getzner & Grabner-Kraüter, 2004; Roberts & Bacon, 1997), and an increase in age is linked to greater environmentally friendly behaviour and awareness (Abeliotis et al., 2010; Tilikidou, 2007).

Residential area, particularly urbanisation, influences pro-environmental behaviour. Urbanised areas can result in a detachment from nature, reducing environmental concerns (Weinstein et al., 2015). Less contact with nature during childhood can lead to fewer pro-ecological behaviours in adulthood (Evans et al., 2018; Wells & Lekies, 2006). Exposure to urban environments compared to natural settings can decrease the sense of connectedness to nature and willingness to engage in sustainable behaviour (Mayer et al., 2009; Zelenski et al., 2015).

Income level also plays a role, with higher income positively associated with pro-environmental behaviour. Income satisfaction strengthens this relationship, indicating a stronger connection when individuals are content with their income.

Engagement in organised environmental protection, such as volunteering or donating, represents another demographic factor. While it's commonly assumed that environmental activism correlates with pro-environmental behaviour, empirical evidence supporting this link requires further exploration (Dono et al., 2010). Some studies have found a limited correlation between environmental activism and different types of pro-environmental behaviour (Stern et al., 1999). Hence, there is a need for more investigation into the relationship between pro-environmental behaviour and environmental activism (Dono et al., 2010).

Household type also influences pro-environmental behaviour. Individuals living alone or in childless couples tend to exhibit higher levels of pro-ecological behaviour, regardless of their environmental attitudes and values (Longhi, 2013). The behaviours and attitudes of both partners play a role in household decisions related to pro-environmental choices, with variations based on the specific context (Longhi, 2013).

2.5. Characteristics of Pro-Environmental Behaviour in Generation Z

Generation Z exhibits distinct environmentally focused behaviours characterised by awareness, action, advocacy, and innovation (Parzonko et al., 2021). They are highly aware of environmental issues due to growing up in an era where such concerns are prevalent in the media and widely recognised as global problems (Francis & Hoefel, 2018). This awareness extends to actively seeking to influence policy and business actions on various issues, including the environment (Francis & Hoefel, 2018). Deloitte's 2021 survey indicates that Generation Z takes actions to reduce environmental impacts, such as increased recycling, greater use of public transportation, dietary changes, and even considering the environment when making decisions about family size (Deloitte, 2021).

Generation Z translates their awareness into action by engaging in pro-environmental behaviours like reducing, reusing, and recycling, conserving energy and water, and supporting eco-friendly products and companies. Their easy access to information through technology and the internet allows them to educate themselves about environmental issues and understand the consequences of their actions. Additionally, their strong emphasis on social connections makes them highly influenced by the environmentally conscious behaviours of their peers.

Advocacy is another hallmark of Generation Z's environmental engagement. They are more likely to actively advocate for environmental causes and participate in campaigns and movements focused on the environment (Tyson et al., 2021). Compared to older generations, they are more vocal about climate change, engage with online content about the issue, and participate in activities like volunteering and protests (Tyson et al., 2021).

Generation Z's innovative spirit extends to their approach to environmental issues, as they are more inclined to devise creative and novel solutions to environmental challenges. Their passion for problem-solving, combined with idealism, drives them to actively seek ways to influence and improve the world. Despite their own perspectives and upbringing, they have access to diverse global perspectives and information, which further fuels their innovative thinking.

3. Empirical Research

3.1. Methodology and Sample

An inductive research approach was used in this study. The sample consisted of 225 members of Generation Z (aged 15 to 28 years) from the Splitsko-Dalmatia County area (Croatia). Data were collected using an online questionnaire. Each variable had a certain number of statements for which respondents determined their level of agreement on a Likert scale ranging from 1 to 5 (1 – strongly disagree, 5 – strongly agree). Accordingly, the study was conducted on a convenience sample, meaning that the subjects selected for the sample were available and willing to participate (Golem, 2018). The questionnaire consisted of two main sets of questions. The first set of questions included socio-demographic characteristics (age, gender, education, and income level). The second set of questions focused on psychological aspects and included questions about attitudes, beliefs, and behaviour related to the environment. Respondents used a five-point Likert scale to rate various aspects of pro-environmental behaviour, including environmental awareness, knowledge of environmental issues, sense of responsibility towards the environment, intention to engage in pro-environmental behaviour and actual engagement in pro-environmental behaviour. The data were collected through an online questionnaire and presented using tabular representation, and they were analysed using the statistical program SPSS Statistics 26 (Statistical Package for Social Sciences). Kruskal–Wallis H test will be used to test and determine the relationship between socio-demographic and psychological variables and specific behaviour.

3.2. Results of the Analysis

3.2.1. Sample Description

There is no significant difference in the gender structure of Generation Z members in the sample. 54.2% of the respondents are female, while 45.8% are male. Regarding age structure, the age group of 19 to 24 is the most represented, accounting for 44% of the respondents. This is followed by the age group of 25 to 28 years, which means 31.6% of the respondents, and the age group of 15 to 18 years, with 24.4% of the respondents. The ranks of age groups are determined by educational status. Therefore, the age group of 15 to 18 consists of high school students. The age group of 19 to 24 consists of university students, while the age group of 25 to 28 consists of postgraduate students or young employees.

Regarding the level of education, the most common is a graduated level (37.3% of the respondents), followed by a secondary professional degree (30.2% of the respondents), and an undergraduate level degree (21.8% of the respondents).

On the other hand, the smallest percentage consists of respondents with completed postgraduate studies (2.7% of the respondents) and highly qualified workers (1.8% of the respondents). Considering income, the most represented group is those with an income less than 560 euros, accounting for 43.1% of the sample. This is followed by respondents with a gain of 801–1,200 euros, representing 21.8% of the sample.

3.2.2. Hypothesis Testing

Table 1 presents the corresponding ranks of the given sample according to socio-demographic characteristics, specifically gender, education level, and residential area. It can be stated that a lower rank indicates a lower level of agreement with statements that explore psychological factors as drivers of pro-environmental behaviour. Observing the average rank by gender, it can be said that women generally have a higher degree of agreement, indicating a stronger sense of Perception of behavioural control, moral obligation, and self-identity compared to men. Regarding education level and psychological factors, it can be noted that individuals with a high school education (THREE-YEAR HIGH SCHOOL EDUCATION) have the highest sense of Perception of behavioural control and moral obligation, while individuals with a secondary professional degree (FOUR-YEAR HIGH SCHOOL EDUCATION) have the highest level of action-specific

Table 1. The Average Ranks of Selected Socio-Demographic Characteristics for the Given Sample Are Analysed in Relation to Various Psychological Factors.

	Variable	Sample	Average Rank
	Gender		
Self-efficiency	Female	122	119,14
	Male	103	105,72
	Total	225	
Perception of behavioural control	Female	122	119,44
	Male	103	105,37
	Total	225	
Perception of behavioural control	Female	122	129,96
	Male	103	92,91
	Total	225	
Perception of behavioural control	Female	122	121,53
	Male	103	102,90
	Total	225	

(*Continued*)

Table 1.   (*Continued*)

	Variable	Sample	Average Rank
Self-identity	Female	122	122,16
	Male	103	102,16
	Total	225	
Social norms	Female	122	117,25
	Male	103	107,97
	Total	225	
Factual knowledge	Female	122	116,93
	Male	103	108,34
	Total	225	
Action-specific knowledge	Female	122	120,12
	Male	103	104,56
	Total	225	
	Education level		
Self-efficiency	Lower vocational education	14	85,61
	Three-year high school education	4	142,13
	Four-year high school education	68	118,37
	Undergraduate studies	49	122,42
	Graduate studies	84	108,89
	Postgraduate studies	6	77,33
	Total	232	
Perception of behavioural control	Lower vocational education	14	85,79
	Three-year high school education	4	121,00
	Four-year high school education	68	120,46
	Undergraduate studies	49	121,61
	Graduate studies	84	107,23
	Postgraduate studies	6	97,00
	Total	225	
Perception of behavioural control	Lower vocational education	14	86,96
	Three-year high school education	4	174,50
	Four-year high school education	68	116,72
	Undergraduate studies	49	132,08

Table 1. (*Continued*)

	Variable	Sample	Average Rank
	Graduate studies	84	99,59
	Postgraduate studies	6	122,50
	Total	225	
Perception of behavioural control	Lower vocational education	14	59,11
	Three-year high school education	4	135,13
	Four-year high school education	68	129,47
	Undergraduate studies	49	120,54
	Graduate studies	84	106,11
	Postgraduate studies	6	72,25
	Total	225	
Self-identity	Lower vocational education	14	97,32
	Three-year high school education	4	122,50
	Four-year high school education	68	125,45
	Undergraduate studies	49	103,99
	Graduate studies	84	108,27
	Postgraduate studies	6	141,92
	Total	225	
Social norms	Lower vocational education	14	103,00
	Three-year high school education	4	101,38
	Four-year high school education	68	130,10
	Undergraduate studies	49	107,70
	Graduate studies	84	104,89
	Postgraduate studies	6	107,08
	Total	225	
Factual knowledge	Lower vocational education	14	86,32
	Three-year high school education	4	122,63
	Four-year high school education	68	121,17
	Undergraduate studies	49	120,69
	Graduate studies	84	106,69
	Postgraduate studies	6	101,75
	Total	225	

(*Continued*)

Table 1. (*Continued*)

	Variable	Sample	Average Rank
Action-specific knowledge	Lower vocational education	14	92,39
	Three-year high school education	4	129,13
	Four-year high school education	68	135,82
	Undergraduate studies	49	118,54
	Graduate studies	84	96,43
	Postgraduate studies	6	78,42
	Total	225	
	Residential area		
Self-efficiency	Rural	39	100,09
	Semi-urban	41	134,30
	Urban	145	110,45
	Total	225	
Perception of behavioural control	Rural	39	92,28
	Semi-urban	41	125,50
	Urban	145	115,04
	Total	225	
Perception of behavioural control	Rural	39	94,13
	Semi-urban	41	138,63
	Urban	145	110,83
	Total	225	
Perception of behavioural control	Rural	39	117,04
	Semi-urban	41	135,72
	Urban	145	105,49
	Total	225	
Self-identity	Rural	39	112,59
	Semi-urban	41	118,59
	Urban	145	111,53
	Total	225	
Social norms	Rural	39	120,90
	Semi-urban	41	127,41
	Urban	145	106,80
	Total	225	

Table 1. (*Continued*)

	Variable	Sample	Average Rank
Factual knowledge	Rural	39	95,67
	Semi-urban	41	124,38
	Urban	145	114,44
	Total	225	
Action-specific knowledge	Rural	39	118,47
	Semi-urban	41	114,10
	Urban	145	111,22
	Total	225	

knowledge. On the other hand, individuals with a non-secondary education (NSS) have the lowest sense of Perception of behavioural control and moral obligation, while those with postgraduate studies have the lowest level of action-specific knowledge. Furthermore, the average rank by residential area indicates that individuals living in rural areas have the lowest level of self-efficacy, while those living in suburban areas have the highest level of self-efficacy. Additionally, individuals living in rural areas have the most inferior sense of Perception of behavioural control, while those living in suburban areas experience the highest sense of Perception of behavioural control. Finally, individuals living in urban areas have the lowest sense of moral obligation, while those living in suburban areas exhibit the highest sense of moral obligation.

Table 2 presents the results of the Kruskal–Wallis *H* test for the given sample of participants, along with their associated socio-demographic characteristics such as gender, education level, and residential area.

The results of the Kruskal–Wallis *H* test for the sample of participants based on *gender* indicate that the empirical significance for self-efficacy is $\alpha^* \approx 0.120 = 12\%$, which means that $\alpha^* > 5\%$. Therefore, we conclude that gender does not significantly influence self-efficacy as a psychological driver of pro-environmental behaviour. The empirical significance for perceived behavioural control is $\alpha^* = 0.103 = 10.3\%$, indicating that $\alpha^* > 5\%$. Hence, we conclude that gender does not statistically significantly affect perceived behavioural control, with a test significance level of 5%. Furthermore, the empirical significance for the perception of behavioural control is $\alpha^* \approx 0.00 = 0\%$, implying that $\alpha^* < 5\%$. Therefore, we conclude that gender significantly influences the perception of behavioural control, while the empirical significance for a moral obligation is $\alpha^* \approx 0.032 = 3.2\%$, indicating that $\alpha^* < 5\%$. In other words, gender significantly affects the sense of moral obligation as a psychological driver of pro-environmental behaviour. Similarly, the empirical significance for self-identity is $\alpha^* \approx 0.021 = 2.1\%$, suggesting that $\alpha^* < 5\%$, and thus we conclude that gender significantly influences self-identity. Specifically, females have a higher average rank for the perception of behavioural

Table 2.   Results of the Kruskal–Wallis *H* Test for the Given Sample of
Respondents Based on Socio-Demographic Characteristics.

	Kruskal–Wallis *H*	df	Asymp. sig
Gender			
Self-efficiency	2,411	1	0,120
Perception of behavioural control	2,652	1	0,103
Guilt	18,335	1	0,000
Moral commitment	4,620	1	0,032
Self-identity	5,328	1	0,021
Social norms	1,148	1	0,284
Factual knowledge	0,982	1	0,322
Action-specific knowledge	3,224	1	0,073
Education			
Self-efficiency	7,014	5	0,220
Perception of behavioural control	5,372	5	0,372
Guilt	14,118	5	0,015
Moral commitment	18,544	5	0,002
Self-identity	6,013	5	0,305
Social norms	6,904	5	0,228
Factual knowledge	5,206	5	0,391
Action-specific knowledge	17,672	5	0,003
Residential area			
Self-efficiency	6,246	2	0,044
Perception of behavioural control	5,701	2	0,058
Guilt	9,926	2	0,007
Moral commitment	7,145	2	0,028
Self-identity	0,381	2	0,826
Social norms	3,942	2	0,139
Factual knowledge	4,124	2	0,127
Action-specific knowledge	0,400	2	0,819

control, with a value of 129.96, compared to males, with an average rank of 92.91. For moral obligation, females have an average rank of 121.53, while males have an average rank of 102.90. In terms of self-identity, females have an average rank of 122.16, whereas males have an average rank of 102.16. Finally, the empirical significance for social norms is $\alpha^* \approx 0.284 = 28.4\%$, indicating that $\alpha^* > 5\%$. Therefore, we conclude that gender does not significantly influence social norms as a driver of pro-environmental behaviour. The empirical significance for factual knowledge is $\alpha^* \approx 0.322 = 32.2\%$, implying that $\alpha^* > 5\%$, and thus we conclude that gender does not significantly affect factual knowledge. Additionally, the empirical significance for action-specific knowledge is $\alpha^* \approx 0.073 = 7.3\%$, indicating that $\alpha^* > 5\%$, and therefore we conclude that gender does not significantly influence action-specific knowledge.

The results of the Kruskal–Wallis test for the sample of participants based on *education level* indicate that the empirical significance for self-efficacy is $\alpha^* = 0.220 = 22\%$, which means that $\alpha^* > 5\%$. Hence, we conclude that education level does not affect self-efficacy among Generation Z individuals. The empirical significance for perceived behavioural control is $\alpha^* = 0.372 = 37.2\%$, indicating that $\alpha^* > 5\%$. Therefore, we conclude that education level does not statistically significantly influence perceived behavioural control. The empirical significance for the perception of behavioural control is $\alpha^* = 0.015 = 1.5\%$, suggesting that $\alpha^* < 5\%$. Thus, we conclude that education level significantly affects the perception of behavioural control among Generation Z individuals, with a significance level of 5%. Specifically, individuals with lower vocational education have the highest average rank for the perception of behavioural control, with a value of 174.50, while those with non-secondary education have the lowest presence of the perception of behavioural control, with an average rank of 86.96. The empirical significance for a moral obligation as a psychological driver of pro-environmental behaviour is $\alpha^* = 0.002 = 0.2\%$, indicating that $\alpha^* < 5\%$. Therefore, we conclude that education level significantly influences the sense of moral obligation among Generation Z individuals, with a significance level of 5%. More specifically, individuals with lower vocational education have the most pronounced sense of moral obligation, with an average rank of 135.13, while those with non-secondary education have the least pronounced sense of moral obligation, with an average rank of 59.11. The empirical significance for self-identity is $\alpha^* = 0.305 = 30.5\%$, suggesting that $\alpha^* > 5\%$, and thus we conclude that education level does not significantly influence self-identity. The empirical significance for social norms is $\alpha^* = 0.228 = 22.8\%$, indicating that $\alpha^* > 5\%$, and therefore we conclude that education level does not statistically significantly affect social norms as a driver of pro-environmental behaviour. The empirical significance for factual knowledge is $\alpha^* = 0.391 = 39.1\%$, implying that $\alpha^* > 5\%$, and thus we conclude that education level does not significantly influence factual knowledge. Lastly, the empirical significance for action-specific knowledge as a psychological driver of pro-environmental behaviour is $\alpha^* = 0.003 = 0.3\%$, indicating that $\alpha^* < 5\%$, and therefore we conclude that education level significantly affects action-specific knowledge among Generation Z individuals, with a significance level of 5%. Specifically, individuals with completed secondary education have the highest level of action-specific knowledge, with an average rank of 135.82, while those with completed postgraduate studies have the lowest level of action-specific knowledge, with an average rank of 78.42.

The results of the Kruskal–Wallis H test for the given sample of participants based on residential area indicate that the empirical significance for self-efficacy is $\alpha^* \approx 0.044 = 4.4\%$, which means that $\alpha^* < 5\%$. Therefore, we conclude that residential area significantly influences self-efficacy as a psychological driver of pro-environmental behaviour. Specifically, individuals living in suburban areas have the highest self-efficacy, with an average rank of 134.30, while those living in rural areas have the lowest self-efficacy, with an average rank of 100.09. The empirical significance for perceived behavioural control is $\alpha^* = 0.058 = 5.8\%$, indicating that $\alpha^* > 5\%$. Hence, we conclude that residential areas do not statistically significantly affect perceived behavioural control, with a test significance level of 5%. The empirical significance for the perception of behavioural control as a psychological driver of pro-environmental behaviour is $\alpha^* = 0.007 = 0.7\%$, suggesting that $\alpha^* < 5\%$. Therefore, we conclude that residential area significantly influences the perception of behavioural control among Generation Z individuals, with a significance level of 5%. Specifically, individuals living in suburban areas have the highest perception of behavioural control, with an average rank of 138.63, while those living in rural areas have the least perception of behavioural control, with an average rank of 94.13. Similarly, the empirical significance for a moral obligation is $\alpha^* \approx 0.028 = 2.8\%$, indicating that $\alpha^* < 5\%$. Thus, we conclude that residential area significantly affects the sense of moral obligation, with individuals living in suburban areas having the highest average rank of 135.72, while those living in urban areas have the lowest average rank of 105.49. The empirical significance for self-identity is $\alpha^* = 0.826 = 82.6\%$, suggesting that $\alpha^* > 5\%$, and thus we conclude that residential area does not significantly influence self-identity. Likewise, the empirical significance for social norms is $\alpha^* = 0.139 = 13.9\%$, indicating that $\alpha^* > 5\%$, and therefore we conclude that residential area does not statistically significantly affect social norms. The empirical significance for factual knowledge is $\alpha^* = 0.127 = 12.7\%$, implying that $\alpha^* > 5\%$, and thus we conclude that residential areas do not significantly influence factual knowledge. Finally, the empirical significance for action-specific knowledge is $\alpha^* = 0.819 = 81.9\%$, indicating that $\alpha^* > 5\%$, and therefore we conclude that residential area does not statistically significantly affect action-specific knowledge, with a test significance level of 5%.

4. Discussion and Conclusion

Through the conducted research, an attempt was made to provide answers to two research questions. The first question was, 'Which socio-demographic characteristics significantly influence the psychological drivers of pro-environmental behaviour among Generation Z individuals?' After statistical analysis of the collected data, we conclude that gender, education level, and residential area influence psychological drivers of pro-environmental behaviour. Other socio-demographic variables from the questionnaire did not show statistical significance concerning any psychological factor. The second question was, 'Which psychological factors play the most significant role in pro-environmental behaviour among Generation Z individuals?' Overall, it can be concluded that all the mentioned socio-demographic variables (gender, education level, and residential area) significantly influence the psychological drivers of pro-environmental behaviour, such as guilt feelings and moral obligations. Regarding gender as a socio-demographic factor, guilt feelings, moral obligations, and self-identity are more prevalent among females compared to males, where they are less prominent.

Approaching this topic with caution is crucial, recognising that psychological traits and behaviours are influenced by complex interactions of social, cultural, and individual factors (Cislaghi & Heise, 2020). On one hand, socialisation can play a significant role. Traditional gender roles and societal expectations in research often emphasise women's care, responsibility, and social obligations (Cislaghi & Heise, 2020). As a result, women may internalise these expectations more deeply, leading to increased guilt when they perceive themselves as not meeting societal or personal ideals, including environmental responsibilities (Miceli & Castelfranchi, 2018). According to Julián and Guevara de Molina, women are more prone to adopting a holistic perspective, recognising the interdependencies between human well-being, social justice, and environmental sustainability (Julián & Guevara de Molina, 2013). This broader moral framework can enhance their sense of responsibility and moral obligation towards the environment.

Furthermore, personal values, beliefs, and experiences vary significantly among individuals, regardless of gender. Moreover, social attitudes and gender norms evolve, which can shape and redefine perceptions of moral obligation over time (Julián & Guevara de Molina, 2013). One explanation could be self-identify's historical association with concepts such as nurturing, harmony, and connection with nature (Qasim et al., 2019). This connection may lead women to develop a stronger self-identity that includes a sense of responsibility and care for the environment. The desire to create a better future for their children and future generations can contribute to a stronger sense of responsibility and motivation to engage in pro-environmental behaviours (Qasim et al., 2019). However, it is crucial to avoid generalisations and acknowledge that individual differences and evolving social dynamics play a significant role in shaping one's identity and pro-environmental behaviour (Wallis & Loy, 2021).

Regarding education level, previous research cited in the theoretical part of the study shows a positive correlation between individuals with higher education and pro-environmental behaviour. They suggest that individuals with higher education acquire knowledge and awareness of the environment through their learning and education, leading them to act proactively towards the environment. On the other hand, individuals with lower education levels do not show the same level of pro-environmental behaviour. In this study, it can be concluded that the psychological factor of guilt plays a greater role in individuals with higher education, while other psychological factors, such as moral obligation and action-specific knowledge, play a greater role in individuals with lower education. This can be explained by the fact that the research was conducted on a sample of Generation Z individuals aged 15–28, where individuals with lower education are currently in the process of schooling, attending primary or secondary schools, and thus learning about the environment and possible negative/positive impacts on the environment and ways in which they can proactively act.

Examining the residential area, many studies have emphasised that individuals living in urban areas have less contact with nature, leading to a diminished sense of connection to the environment and, ultimately, a lower need for pro-environmental behaviour. On the other hand, individuals living outside major cities still possess that sense of connection, and their proactive environmental actions are more pronounced. In this study, psychological factors such as self-efficacy, guilt feelings, and moral obligations play the most significant role among individuals living in suburban areas. Since the research was conducted in the Split-Dalmatia County area, it can be said that suburban areas such as Solin, Podstrana, Stobreč, Žrnovnica, and others often provide better access to resources that support environmentally friendly behaviours. These resources can include recycling facilities, community gardens, farmers' markets, public transportation options, and green spaces (Alcock et al., 2020). The availability of such resources can increase individuals' belief in their ability to engage in environmentally friendly practices, thereby strengthening their self-efficacy. Suburbs often prioritise environmental sustainability and may have infrastructure designed to facilitate recycling, energy efficiency, and sustainable living practices (Alcock et al., 2020). Proximity to nature and the potential visibility of environmental degradation, such as pollution or deforestation, can increase individuals' awareness of their impact on the environment. This heightened awareness can lead to a stronger sense of guilt when people in suburban areas see their actions as contributing to the degradation of their immediate surroundings (Nash et al., 2019). Similarly, shared values and expectations within these communities can create a more substantial moral obligation to act environmentally responsibly (Nash et al., 2019).

References

Abeliotis, K., Koniari, C., & Sardianou, E. (2010). The profile of the green consumer in Greece. *International Journal of Consumer Studies, 34*, 153–160.

Ajzen, I. (2020). The theory of planned behaviour: Frequently asked questions. *Human Behavior and Emerging Technologies, 2*, 314–324. https://doi.org/10.1002/hbe2.195

Alcock, I., White, M. P., Pahl, S., Duarte-Davidson, R., & Fleming, L. E. (2020). Associations between pro-environmental behaviour and neighbourhood nature, nature visit frequency and nature appreciation: Evidence from a nationally representative survey in England. *Environment International, 136*, 105441. https://doi.org/10.1016/j.envint.2019.105441

Alzubaidi, H. (2018). Factors affecting consumers' pro-environmental behaviours in Saudi Arabia. In *Emerging markets from a multidisciplinary perspective* (pp. 303–331). Springer.

Anderson, W., & Westcott, M. (Eds.). (2021). *Introduction to tourism and hospitality in B.C* (2nd ed.). BCcampus. https://opentextbc.ca/introtourism2e/

Balunde, A., Perlaviciute, G., & Steg, L. (2019). The relationship between people's environmental considerations and pro-environmental behaviour in Lithuania. *Frontiers in Psychology 10*, 2319. https://doi.org/10.3389/fpsyg.2019.02319

Bandura, A. (1997). Self-efficacy: The exercise of control. New York, NY: W. H. Freeman and Company.

Becken, S. (2007). Tourists' perception of international air travel's impact on the global climate and potential climate change policies. *Journal of Sustainable Tourism, 15*(4), 351–368. https://doi.org/10.2167/jost710.0

Biddle, B. J., Bank, B. J., & Slavings, R. R. L. (1987). Norms, preferences, identities and retention decisions. *Social Psychology Quarterly*, *50*(4), 322–337.

Bilynets, I., & Cvelbar, K. L. J. (2022). Tourist pro-environmental behaviour: The role of environmental image of destination and daily behaviour. *Annals of Tourism Research Empirical Insights*, *3*(2). https://doi.org/10.1016/j.annale.2022.100070

Budowski, G. (1976). Tourism and environmental conservation: Conflict, coexistence, or symbioses. *Environmental Conservation*, *3*(1), 27–310.

Chen, X., Peterson, M. N., Hull, V., Lu, C., Lee, G. D., Hong, D., & Liu, J. (2011). Effects of attitudinal and socio-demographic factors on pro-environmental behaviour in urban China. *Environmental Conservation*, *38*, 45–52.

Cislaghi, B., & Heise, L. (2020). Gender norms and social norms: Differences, similarities and why they matter in prevention science. *Sociology of Health & Illness*, *42*(2), 407–422. https://doi.org/10.1111/1467-9566.13008

Cohen, E. (1978). The impact of tourism on the physical environment. *Annals of Tourism Research*, *5*(2), 215–237.

Colombàs, L. N. (2020). *Tourist behaviour and environmental protection*. Universitat de les Illes Balears.

Cornelissen, G., Pandelaere, M., Warlop, L., & Dewitte, S. (2008). Positive cueing: Promoting sustainable consumer behaviour by cueing common environmental behaviours as environmental. *International Journal of Research in Marketing*, *25*, 46–55. https://doi.org/10.1016/j.ijresmar.2007.06.002

Deloitte. (2021). *A call for accountability and action*. Retrieved February 6, 2023, from https://www2.deloitte.com/content/dam/Deloitte/mk/Documents/about-deloitte/2021-deloitte-global-millennial-survey-report.pdf

Dolnicar, S., & Leisch, F. (2008a). An investigation of tourists' patterns of obligation to protect the environment. *Journal of Travel Research*, *46*(4), 381–391.

Dolnicar, S., & Leisch, F. (2008b). Selective marketing for environmentally sustainable tourism. *Tourism Management*, *29*(4), 672–680. https://doi.org/10.1016/j.tourman.2007.07.010

Dono, J., Webb, J., & Richardson, B. (2010). The relationship between environmental activism, pro-environmental behaviour and social identity. *Journal of Environmental Psychology*, *30*(2), 178–186. https://doi.org/10.1016/j.jenvp.2009.11.006

Duffy, J., Xie, H., & Lee, Y.-J. (2013). Social norms, information, and trust among strangers: Theory and evidence. *Economic Theory*, *52*, 669–708. https://doi.org/10.1007/s00199-011-0659-x

Evans, G. W., Otto, S., & Kaiser, F. G. (2018). Childhood origins of young adult environmental behaviour. *Psychological Science*, *29*(5), 679–687. https://doi.org/10.1177/0956797617741894

Farrow, K., Grolleau, G., & Ibanez, L. (2017). Social norms and pro-environmental behaviour: A review of the evidence. *Ecological Economics*, *140*, 1–13. https://doi.org/10.1016/j.ecolecon.2017.04.017

Fennel, David, A. (1999) Ecotourism, an introduction, second eddition, Routledge, London and New York.

Francis, T., & Hoefel, F. (2018). *True Gen: Generation Z and its implications for companies*. McKinsey & Company.

Getzner, M., & Grabner-Kraüter, S. (2004). Consumer preferences and marketing strategies for 'green shares'. *The International Journal of Bank Marketing*, *22*, 260–278.

Gifford, R., & Nilsson, A. (2014). *Pro-environmental concern and behaviour: A review* (pp. 1–17).

Gössling, S., Scott, D., Hall, C. M., Ceron, J. P., & Dubois, G. (2012). Consumer behaviour and demand response of tourists to climate change. *Annals of Tourism Research*, *39*(1), 36–58.

Hall, M. C. (2010). Crisis events in tourism: Subjects of crisis in tourism. *Current Issues in Tourism, 13*(5), 401–417.

Hansmann, R., Laurenti, R., Mehdi, T., & Binder, C. (2020). Determinants of pro-environmental behaviour: A comparison of university students and staff from diverse faculties at a Swiss University (Vol. 268), 121864. https://doi.org/https://doi.org/10.1016/j.jclepro.2020.12186

Harland, P., Staats, H., & Wilke, H. A. (2007). Situational and personality factors as direct or personal norm mediated predictors of pro-environmental behaviour: Questions derived from norm-activation theory. *Basic and Applied Social Psychology, 29*(4), 323–334.

Huang, H. (2016). Media use, environmental beliefs, self-efficacy, and pro-environmental behaviour. *Journal of Business Research, 69*(6), 2206–2212. https://doi.org/10.1016/j.jbusres.2015.12.031

Julián, I. P., & Guevara de Molina, S. (2013). Towards an integrative approach to sustainability: Exploring potential synergies between gender and environment. *Cepal Review, 110.*

Juvan, E., & Dolnicar, S. (2017). Drivers of pro-environmental tourist behaviours are not universal. *Journal of Cleaner Production.* https://doi.org/10.1016/j.jclepro.2017.08.087

Karimi, S., & Mohammadimehr, S. (2022). Socio-psychological antecedents of pro-environmental intentions and behaviours among Iranian rural women: An integrative framework. *Frontiers in Environmental Science,* 979728. https://doi.org/10.3389/fenvs.2022.979728

Kormos, C., & Gifford, R. (2014). The validity of self-report measures of proenvironmental behaviour: A meta-analytic review. *Journal of Environmental Psychology, 40*(2014), 359–3371. http://dx.doi.org/10.1016/j.jenvp.2014.09.003

Krippendorf, J. (1977). Les devoreurs des paysages, Lausanne: 24 Heures, In Fennel, Opcit.

Krippendorf, J. (1987). *The holiday makers: Understanding the impact of leisure 26 and travel.* Butterworth-Heinemann.

Lacasse, K. (2016). Don't be satisfied, identify! Strengthening positive spillover by connecting pro-environmental behaviours to an "environmentalist" label. *Journal of Environmental Psychology, 48,* 149–158. https://doi.org/10.1016/j.jenvp.2016.09.006

Lam, S. P., & Chen, J. K. (2006). What makes customers bring their bags or buy bags from the shop? A survey of customers at a Taiwan hypermarket. *Environment and Behaviour, 38*(3), 318–332.

Lange, F., & Dewitte, S. (2019). Cognitive flexibility and pro-environmental behaviour: A multimethod approach. *European Journal of Personality, 33,* 488–505.

Laroche, M., Bergeron, J., & Barbaro-Forleo, G. (2001). Targeting consumers who are willing to pay more for environmentally friendly products. *Journal of Consumer Marketing, 18,* 503–520.

Leung, Y. W., & Rosenthal, S. (2019). Explicating perceived sustainability-related climate: A situational motivator of pro-environmental behaviour. *Sustainability (Switzerland), 11*(1). https://doi.org/10.3390/su11010231

Li, Q. C., & Wu, M. Y. (2019). Rationality or morality? a comparative study of pro-environmental intentions of local and nonlocal visitors in nature-based destinations. *Journal of Destination Marketing & Management, 11,* 130–139.

Li, D., Zhaoc, L., Ma, S., Shao, S., & Zhang, L. (2019). What influences an individual's pro-environmental behaviour? A literature review. *Resources, Conservation & Recycling, 146*(2019), 28–34. https://doi.org/10.1016/j.resconrec.2019.03.024

Liobikienė, G., Niaura, A., Mandravickaitė, J., & Vabuolas, Ž. (2016). Does religiosity influence environmental attitude and behaviour? The case of young Lithuanians. *European Journal of Science and Theology, 12,* 77–86.

Liobikienė, G., & Poškus, M. S. (2019). The importance of environmental knowledge for private and public sphere pro-environmental behaviour: Modifying the value-belief-norm theory. *Sustainability*, *11*, 3324. https://doi.org/10.3390/su11123324

Liu, J., Li, J., Jang, S. C.(S), & Zhao, Y. (2022). Understanding tourists' environmentally responsible behaviour at coastal tourism destinations. https://doi.org/10.1016/j.marpol.2022.105178

Longhi, S. (2013). *Individual pro-environmental behaviour in the household context.* [ISER Working Paper Series, No. 2013-21, University of Essex, Institute for Social and Economic Research (ISER), Colchester].

Lorenzoni, I., Nicholson-Cole, S., & Whitmarsh, L. (2007). Barriers perceived to engaging with climate change among the UK public and their policy implications. *Global Environmental Change*, *17*(3–4), 445–459.

Mandić, A., & Vuković, M. (2021). Millennials attitudes, choices and behaviour – Integrative analysis. *Journal of Ecotourism*. https://doi.org/10.1080/14724049.2021.1932925

Mandić, A., Walia, S., & Kautish, P. (2023a). The antecedents of pro-environmental tourist behaviour of Gen Z: An eastern society perspective. *Anatolia*, *00*(00), 1–10. https://doi.org/10.1080/13032917.2023.2224368

Mandić, A., Walia, S. K., & Rasoolimanesh, S. M. (2023b). Gen Z and the flight shame movement: Examining the intersection of emotions, biospheric values, and environmental travel behaviour in an Eastern society. *Journal of Sustainable Tourism*. https://doi.org/10.1080/09669582.2023.2254950

Mannetti, L., Pierro, A., & Livi, S. (2004). Recycling: Planned and self-expressive behaviour. *Journal of Environmental Psychology*, *24*, 227–236.

Marques, C., Vinhas da Silva, R., & Antova, S. (2021). Image, satisfaction, destination and product post-visit behaviours: How do they relate in emerging destinations? *Tourism Management*, *85*. raspoloživo na: https://doi.org/10.1016/j.tourman.2021.104293

Mayer, F. S., Frantz, C. M., Bruehlman-Senecal, E., & Dolliver, K. (2009). Why is nature beneficial?: The role of connectedness to nature. *Environment and Behaviour*, *41*(5), 607–643. https://doi.org/10.1177/0013916508319745

Miceli, M., & Castelfranchi, C. (2018). Reconsidering the differences between shame and guilt. *Europe's Journal of Psychology*, *14*(3), 710–733. https://doi.org/10.5964/ejop.v14i3.1564

Mohiuddin, M., al Mamun, A., Syed, F., Mehedi Masud, M., & Su, Z. (2018). Environmental knowledge, awareness, and business school students' intentions to purchase green vehicles in emerging countries. *Sustainability*, *10*, 1534. https://doi.org/10.3390/su10051534

Morrin, E., & Gillespie, C. (2021). *What Americans are worrying about right now, from the silent generation to gen Z.* Verywellmind. Retrieved August 29, 2022, from https://www.verywellmind.com/what-americans-of-all-ages-are-worrying-about-right-now-5202028

Nash, N., Capstick, S., Whitmarsh, L., Chaudhary, I., & Manandhar, R. (2019). Perceptions of local environmental issues and the relevance of climate change in Nepal's Terai: Perspectives from two communities. *Frontiers in Sociology*, *4*. https://doi.org/10.3389/fsoc.2019.00060

OECD. (2016). *OECD tourism trends and policies 2016 policy highlights.*

Oerke, B., & Bogner, F. X. (2010). Gender, age and subject matter: Impact on teachers' ecological values. *Environmentalist*, *30*, 111–122.

Palupi, T., & Sawitri, D. R. (2018). The importance of pro-environmental behaviour in adolescent. *E3S Web of Conferences*, *31*, 09031. ICENIS 2017. https://doi.org/10.1051/e3sconf/20183109031

Parzonko, A. J., Balińska, A., & Sieczko, A. (2021). Pro-environmental behaviours of Generation Z in the context of the concept of homo socio-oeconomicus. *Energies*, *14*(6), 1597. MDPI AG. http://dx.doi.org/10.3390/en14061597

Patel, J., Modi, A., & Paul, J. (2017). Pro-environmental behaviour and socio-demographic factors in an emerging market. *Asian Journal of Business Ethics, 6,* 189–214.

Pavalache-Ilie, M., & Unianu, E. M. (2012). Locus of control and the pro-environmental attitudes. *Procedia - Social and Behavioural Sciences, 33,* 198–202.

Pearce, D. G. (1985). 'Tourism and environmental research: A review'. *International Studies, 25,* 247–255.

Perry, G. L., Richardson, S. J., Harré, N., Hodges, D., Lyver, P. O., Maseyk, F. J., Taylor, R., Todd, J. H., Tylianakis, J. M., Yletyinen, J., & Brower, A. (2021). Evaluating the role of social norms in fostering pro-environmental behaviours. *Frontiers in Environmental Science, 9,* 620125. https://doi.org/10.3389/fenvs.2021.620125

Qasim, H., Yan, L., Guo, R., Saeed, A., & Ashraf, B. (2019). The defining role of environmental self-identity among consumption values and behavioural intention to consume organic food. *International Journal of Environmental Research and Public Health, 16*(7), 1106. https://doi.org/10.3390/ijerph16071106

Rampedi, I. T., & Ifegbesan, A. P. (2022). Understanding the determinants of pro-environmental behaviour among South Africans: evidence from a structural equation model. *Sustainability, 14*(6), 3218. MDPI AG. http://dx.doi.org/10.3390/su14063218

Roberts, J. A., & Bacon, D. R. (1997). Exploring the subtle relationships between environmental concern and ecologically conscious consumer behaviour. *Journal of Business Research, 40,* 79–89.

Robinson, M. V., & Schänzel, A. H. (2019). *A tourism inflex: Generation Z travel experiences* (Vol. 5, no. 2, pp. 127–141). Emerald Publishing Limited, ISSN 2055-5911. https://doi.org/10.1108/JTF-01-2019-0014

Rodríguez-Barreiro, L. M., Fernández-Manzanal, R., Serra, L. M., Carrasquer, J., Murillo, M. B., & Morales, M. J. (2013). Approach to a causal model between attitudes and environmental behaviour. A graduate case study. *Journal of Cleaner Production, 48,* 116–125.

Rowlands, I. H., Scott, D., & Parker, P. (2003). Consumers and green electricity: Profiling potential purchasers. *Business Strategy and the Environment, 1*(2), 36–48.

Samarasinghe, D. S. R. (2012). A green segmentation: Identifying the green consumer demographic profiles in Sri Lanka. *International Journal of Marketing and Technology, 2,* 318–331.

Sánchez, M., Natalia, L.-M., & Lera-López, F. (2015). Improving pro-environmental behaviours in Spain: The role of attitudes and socio-demographic and political factors. *Journal of Environmental Policy & Planning, 18*(1), 47–66.

Saphores, J. D. M., Ogunseitan, O. A., & Shapiro, A. A. (2012). Willingness to engage in a pro-environmental behaviour: An analysis of e-waste recycling based on a national survey of US households. *Resources, Conservation and Recycling, 60,* 49–63.

Smith, M. A., & Kingston, S. (2021, February). Demographic, attitudinal, and social factors that predict pro-environmental behaviour. *Sustainability and Climate Change,* 47–54. http://doi.org/10.1089/scc.2020.0063

Soorani, F., & Ahmadvand, M. (2019). Determinants of consumers' food management behaviour: Applying and extending the theory of planned behaviour. *Waste Management, 98,* 151–159. https://doi.org/10.1016/j.wasman.2019.08.025

Stern, P. C., Dietz, T., Abel, T., Guagnano, G. A., & Kalof, L. (1999). A value-belief-norm theory of support for social movements: The case of environmentalism. *Human Ecology Review, 6,* 81–97.

Stets, J. E., & Biga, C. F. (2003). Bringing identity theory into environmental sociology. *Sociological Theory, 21*(4), 398–423.

Tilikidou, I. (2007). The effects of knowledge and attitudes upon Greeks' pro-environmental purchasing behaviour. *Corporate Social Responsibility and Environmental Management, 14,* 121–134.

Truelove, H. B., Carrico, A. R., Yeung, K. L., & Wolff, J. M. (2021): Identity and guilt as mediators of pro-environmental spillover. *Frontiers in Psychology, 12*, 1664–1078. https://doi.org/10.3389/fpsyg.2021.659483

Turner, J. H. (2013). *Contemporary sociological theory*. Sage Publications.

Tyson, A., Kennedy, B., & Funk, C. (2021). *Gen Z, millennials stand out for climate change activism, social media engagement with issue*. Pew Research Center.

UNWTO. (2022). *Tourism enjoys strong start to 2022 while facing new uncertainties*. World Tourism Organization (UNWTO).

Van der Werff, E., Steg, L., & Keizer, K. (2014b). I am what I am, by looking past the present: The influence of biospheric values and past behaviour on environmental self-identity. *Environment & Behavior, 46*, 626–657. https://doi.org/10.1177/0013916512475209

Wallis, H., & Loy, L. S. (2021). *What drives pro-environmental activism of young people? A survey study on the Fridays For Future movement*. https://doi.org/10.1016/j.jenvp.2021.101581

Weinstein, N., Balmford, A., DeHaan, C. R., Gladwell, V., Bradbury, R. B., & Amano, T. (2015). Seeing community for the trees: The links among contact with natural environments, community cohesion, and crime. *BioScience, 65*(12). https://doi.org/10.1093/biosci/biv151

Wells, N. M., & Lekies, K. S. (2006). Nature and the life course: Pathways from childhood nature experiences to adult environmentalism. *Children Youth and Environments, 16*(1), 1–24.

Whitmarsh, L., & O'Neill, S. (2010). Green identity, green living? The role of pro-environmental self-identity in determining consistency across diverse pro-environmental behaviours. *Journal of Environmental Psychology, 30*(3), 305–314. https://doi.org/10.1016/j.jenvp.2010.01.003

Wu (Snow), J., Font, X., & Liu, J. (2020). Tourists' pro-environmental behaviours: Moral obligation or disengagement? *Journal of Travel Research*, 1–14. https://doi.org/10.1177/0047287520910

Wu, L., Zhu, Y., and Zhai, J. (2022). Understanding waste management behavior among university students in China: environmental knowledge, personal norms, and the theory of planned behavior. Front. Psychol. 12:771723. doi: 10.3389/ fpsyg.2021.771723

Zahedi, S. (2008). Tourism impact on coastal environment. *Environmental Problems in Coastal Regions* (Vol. 99). https://doi.org/10.2495/CENV080051

Zelenski, J. M., Dopko, R. L., & Capaldi, C. A. (2015). Cooperation is in our nature: Nature exposure may promote cooperative and environmentally sustainable behaviour. *Journal of Environmental Psychology, 42*, 24–31. https://doi.org/10.1016/j.jenvp.2015.01.005

Zhao, H.-H., Gao, Q., Wu, Y.-P., Wang, Y., & Zhu, X. D. (2014). What affects green consumer behaviour in China? A case study from Qingdao. *Journal of Cleaner Production, 63*, 343–351.

Part III

Organisational and Strategy Transformations Under VUCA

Chapter 10

Tourism's Vitality After COVID-19 Pandemic: Embracing Healing as a Significant Concept

Ricardi S. Adnan

Universitas Indonesia, Depok, Indonesia

Abstract

During the pandemic, people have been experiencing the effects of the VUCA era, which has led to changes in lifestyle, including the way we approach tourism. In the past, tourism focused on enjoying nature and cultural heritage, but now there are many different forms, such as sports adventure, edu-tourism, and Sustainable Tourism. Recently, there has been a new trend in tourism called 'healing', which emphasises activities that promote relaxation and wellness, such as meditation, yoga, herbal therapy, and forest healing. In Indonesia, there have been over 100 promotional activities for healing tourist attractions, and the term has become increasingly popular in tweets and online searches. This trend reflects the growing need for people to restore their fitness and energy, not just seek pleasure. Studies have shown that travel can help reduce stress and improve mental health, making healing tourism an attractive option for many. By analysing digital data, this article seeks to explain this phenomenon and how it relates to the demands and stresses of modern life. The COVID-19 pandemic has only heightened the need for healing tourism as people seek to fulfil their basic human needs for relaxation and rejuvenation.

Keywords: COVID-19; healing tourism; Indonesia; stress; VUCA

Tourism in a VUCA World: Managing the Future of Tourism, 145–156
Copyright © 2024 by Emerald Publishing Limited
All rights of reproduction in any form reserved
doi:10.1108/978-1-83753-674-020241010

Introduction

Various rapid and drastic changes that are often unanticipated in the last two decades have caused various shocks that drain a lot of energy and resources owned by individuals. Namely, the ever-increasing demands of daily life, developments, and challenges from workplaces/companies/agencies that are constantly changing, especially in the use of information technology, as well as demands for a professional and family environment which are increasing from time to time. This condition is quite a heavy burden for many people, considering their ability to adapt is often not as fast as the development of an increasingly complex environment. Facts that are full of various pressures encourage people to take the time to calm their thoughts and feelings by indulging in tourism activities that aim to restore and improve their mental and psychological conditions.

The most real moment of this can be felt in the COVID-19 pandemic situation which reflects the VUCA condition (Adnan et al., 2022) which has caused a lot of stress in society (Droit-Volet et al., 2020; Muslim, 2020; Yasmin et al., 2020) – so people need medical and psychological therapy in the form of relaxation. The concept of healing is an alternative or even considered a solution. After the pandemic was declared over, tourist attractions developed in Indonesia that facilitate individual healing needs. Healing tourism has become a valuable concept in the recovery of tourism that has been hit hard by the pandemic (Ma et al., 2021).

This chapter was written based on desk research from various scientific publications and mass media coverage from 2020 to February 2023 and reinforced with digital data via Google trend searches from 2018 to 2022 as an effort to explain the phenomenon of the increasing health tourism trend in Indonesia.

Indonesian Tourism After the COVID-19 Pandemic

The COVID-19 pandemic has had a significant impact on the people of Indonesia (Adnan et al., 2021; Yasmin et al., 2020), with many social activities being restricted due to fear of spreading the deadly disease. This has created a VUCA (volatile, uncertain, complex, and ambiguous) condition, with tight rules and surveillance by authorities and the community. Daily activities such as work, study, and leisure have been affected, leading to increased stress levels within society (Adnan et al., 2022). As seen in other parts of the world, individuals in Indonesia are experiencing immense pressure due to disrupted activities and restrictions on previously considered human rights.

The COVID-19 pandemic has had a significant impact not only on individuals but also on various organisations and institutions in Indonesia. In 2019, the country had 12,376 tourism workers, which was the fourth largest number in the world. However, due to the pandemic, the number of workers in the Indonesian tourism sector has decreased to 10,947 in 2021. Despite this, the impact of the pandemic on Indonesia is relatively less severe than that on the United States, as indicated by the absorption indicator for the number of workers in the tourism sector. Previously ranked fourth in the world, Indonesia has now risen to the third spot. This is likely due to the country's labour system, which allows workers to be temporarily laid off rather than permanently dismissed, giving them a chance to rest until economic conditions improve. See Table 1.

According to the World Travel and Tourism Council, the tourism industry is expected to see a positive growth trend after the COVID-19 pandemic ends. In 2024, the industry is projected to grow by approximately 3%, with a Travel and Tourism (T&T) employment value of 340 million people. This growth is expected to continue in the following years, with an annual industry growth rate of 22%, and an estimated workforce of 425 million.

Indonesia is expected to see significant growth in its tourism industry, following China, India, and the United States. This is reflected in the rise of new job opportunities in the sector. The British media company, The Telegraph, has also acknowledged Indonesia's achievement by including it in its list of 'The Top 20 Fastest Growing Travel Destinations' (Fitriana, 2020).

Indonesia has made significant progress in its tourism competitiveness, as indicated by the World Economic Forum's tourism competitiveness index. From 2015 to 2017, the country's ranking improved from 50th to 42nd. In 2017, the tourism industry experienced a growth of 22%, which was the second highest in the region after Vietnam (29%). The average growth rate for tourism in Indonesia was 6.4%, while the ASEAN region experienced a growth rate of 7%. The 'Wonderful Indonesia' branding has been successful, earning 150 awards between 2016 and March 2019. Prior to the pandemic, Indonesia's tourism sector had been thriving, resulting in a steady increase in income.

According to EIR data for 2022, it is predicted that around 126 million new job opportunities will be created worldwide from 2022 to 2032. The Asia Pacific region is expected to have the highest number of job openings, accounting for 64.8% of the total. Indonesia, among other countries in the region, is ranked fourth with a 4.2% share (Travel & Tourism Economic Impact Global Trends, 2022).

Table 1.   Travel and Tourism Employment.

No	2019 Rank	Millions	No	2021 Rank	Millions
1	China	82.2	1	China	73.3
2	India	40.3	2	India	32.1
3	United States	16.8	3	Indonesia	10.9
4	Indonesia	12.4	4	United States	10.5
5	Philippines	9.5	5	Philippines	7.8
6	Thailand	8.2	6	Thailand	6.9
7	Brazil	7.6	7	Brazil	6.4
8	Mexico	7.0	8	Mexico	6.0
9	Germany	5.9	9	Japan	5.5
10	Japan	5.8	10	Germany	5.1

Source: World Travel & Tourism Council (2022). Retrieved from https://wttc.org/Portals/0/Documents/Reports/2022/EIR2022-Global%20Trends.pdf

This suggests that tourism growth in Indonesia plays a crucial role in the development of tourism in the Asia Pacific region.

Healing Tourism

The term 'healing' is often associated with the soul, feelings, and thoughts in psychology (Baldwin et al., 2016; Luong et al., 2016). Recently, the term 'self-healing' has emerged, referring to the process of treating emotional wounds that disturb a person's emotional condition. This process is generally influenced by several factors, such as anxiety about being unable to carry out tasks well. Signs that someone is harbouring emotional wounds include being more emotional than usual, experiencing frequent anxiety or negative feelings, engaging in repeated negative actions, having difficulty forgiving or trusting others, and being ignorant or apathetic. In today's digital era, public awareness of these symptoms seems to be increasing, and people are increasingly interested in 'me time' activities such as mindfulness, meditation, and forming a peaceful relationship with oneself and the environment. These activities are welcomed by tourism activities that aim to reduce stress levels and encourage individuals or families to refresh, making healing tourism a relevant activity.

The term 'healing tourism' refers to trips that centre around medical treatment and the use of health services. This can include tourist trips that incorporate medical services (Yang et al., 2015). The synergy of medical services in health tourism encompasses a wide range of services, from preventive and therapeutic health services to rehabilitation and curative travel. Healing tourism, also known as medical tourism, has a rich history spanning thousands of years. Many cultures and religions have practiced the tradition of travelling for medicinal purposes, often referred to as 'journeying to holy places'.

Throughout various cultures around the world, the concept of healing has been recognised for thousands of years. One example can be seen in ancient Greece, where individuals would visit the temple of Asklepion in Epidaurus to receive both spiritual and physical healing. Modern healing tourism, however, began to develop in the early 20th century when Americans and Europeans started to visit hot resorts in Europe and North America to alleviate medical conditions and ailments like rheumatism, asthma, and skin problems.

During the 18th and 19th centuries, Europe was a popular destination for people seeking health services from all over the world. Wealthy individuals from Asia, Africa, and Latin America would travel to Europe to receive medical care from renowned doctors while enjoying the healthier surroundings of Switzerland and France. As the 20th century began, the United States also became a destination for people seeking more advanced medical care. The Mayo Clinic and Cleveland Clinic gained international recognition in the 1910s for their high-quality medical care. Towards the end of the 20th century, countries like India, Thailand, and Singapore emerged as popular healing tourism destinations. These countries offer lower healthcare costs and more advanced medical facilities than Western countries, while also providing attractive environments for visitors to enjoy after their medical treatment.

Over the past few years, countries like South Korea, Malaysia, and Mexico have emerged as popular destinations for those seeking top-notch medical care at a reasonable cost. Healing tourism has become a massive global industry, with the medical tourism market projected to reach USD 54.0 billion by 2027 according to a Transparency Market Research report. But there are risks involved in travelling overseas for medical reasons, as we previously mentioned. Visitors must be prepared to bear the high expenses incurred and the lack of a guarantee of complete recovery. It's essential to consider these risks seriously.

As time passes, healing tourism is becoming more organised and popular in various countries like Japan, Thailand, and India. This type of tour offers different healing packages, including alternative medicine, spas, yoga, meditation, and other health practices as part of the tourism activity. The response from the public towards the healing tour concept is different from general tourism promotions. Although casual tourism remains a massive and popular industry, many people are seeking more holistic experiences. Public's response to healing tourism is greatly influenced by their culture and background. Some individuals prefer traditional tour packages such as sunbathing on the beach, visiting historical sites, or trying local cuisine. Others are more interested in holistic health and spiritual experiences.

In numerous publications, the reasons for why individuals engage in healing practices have been discussed (Bhalla et al., 2021; Han & An, 2022; Kim et al., 2020; Ma et al., 2021; Speier, 2011):

1. Alleviating mental strain. Maintaining individual quality and productivity can be a challenge when faced with a large workload. Practicing self-care and relaxation is key to overcoming the mental burdens of various limitations. Many professionals, including doctors, medical personnel, electronic and digital media experts, and even tourism practitioners, often talk about the therapeutic benefits of relaxation and healing.
2. Maintaining good mental health should be a top priority. In our fast-paced world, both work and school demands are on the rise, causing heightened stress levels and psychological pressure on individuals. This is reflected in the growing number of reported cases of psychological and psychiatric conditions. To counteract this trend, healthcare professionals and psychologists have placed greater emphasis on the benefits of mindfulness and mental relaxation for stress reduction. By improving mental well-being, individuals can reinvigorate their energy levels and overcome stagnation.
3. Take a moment to relax and clear your thoughts. Healing activities are a form of relaxation that reduces tension and pressure on a person's mind. Moreover, if healing is combined with fun activities in the form of enjoying the beauty of nature, it will calm a confused mind.
4. More able to love yourself. Healing has the ability to revive both the body and mind, providing much-needed peace and relaxation from various issues. This allows a person to gain self-awareness and understand their own importance, ultimately leading to greater self-love.

5. Restore spirit. Engaging in healing activities can be a great way to relax and relieve stress on the mind. Combining healing with enjoyable activities, such as immersing oneself in nature's beauty, can help to soothe a troubled mind. Restoring the body's health can have a positive impact on the spirit, which is why healing has become increasingly popular amongst many individuals.

Healing tourism has rapidly developed in recent decades and is now a significant market segment in the global tourism industry. According to a report by Allied Market Research, the medical tourism market is expected to reach USD 143.8 billion by 2027, growing annually at 12.9% from 2020 to 2027. In 2019, global health travel, which includes healing tourism, reached USD 639.4 billion, an increase of approximately 6.5% from the previous year, according to a report by the Global Wellness Institute. The same report also indicates that wellness travel is among the top 5 categories of global tourism spending, along with business travel, overseas travel to visit friends or family, lifestyle travel, and adventure travel.

In a broader sense, health tourism is commonly referred to as healing tourism or medical tourism (Yang et al., 2015). People are more health-conscious and seek travel experiences that promote wellness (Shiaty et al., 2016). Here are some current trends in healing tourism across the globe. Firstly, medical spas and wellness centres are on the rise, offering a variety of services such as acupuncture, massage, yoga, meditation, and special diet programs. Secondly, more individuals are seeking travel experiences that provide spiritual benefits, such as meditation retreats, trips to holy places, and other spiritually based health activities. Thirdly, an increasing number of destinations offer comprehensive wellness experiences, including hot spring accommodations, spas and wellness centres, traditional healing, and other wellness programs. Fourthly, health technologies are becoming more readily available to help visitors care for and monitor their health while travelling, such as activity trackers, health sensors, and health apps. Lastly, group health trips are gaining popularity as more people travel with friends or family to receive social support and motivation to achieve their health goals.

Healing tourism involves travelling while engaging in activities that improve physical, emotional, and spiritual health, and is influenced by various factors that contribute to the growing trend of tourism.

1. More and more communities are recognising the significance of health and wellness and seeking innovative ways to enhance their overall quality of life. Healing tourism presents a compelling opportunity for individuals who wish to integrate travel with activities that promote their physical and mental well-being.
2. Developing medical technology and affordable care in developing countries are driving medical tourism to various destinations worldwide.
3. With modern life being fast-paced and stressful, many individuals are searching for ways to manage stress and boost their health. Healing tourism presents an escape from everyday routine and a chance to unwind the mind and body.

4. Due to high market demand, the healing tourism industry rapidly expands and offers customisable tour packages.
5. The rise of social media has led to a trend of travellers seeking out unique and shareable health and fitness experiences.

Healing tourism is becoming a popular alternative to traditional tourism and has created its own market segment. However, more research and promotion are necessary to increase awareness and demand for this concept within the wider community.

An industry that is currently experiencing significant growth is Japanese healing tourism. It offers a wide range of distinct health and wellness experiences for visitors seeking travel opportunities that promote overall well-being. This form of tourism in Japan presents numerous options for anyone looking to improve their health and wellness:

1. Onsen (hot springs). In Japan, there are several tour packages that include onsen experiences, such as in Hakone, Beppu, or Noboribetsu. These tours are known as 'onsen ryokan' or hot spring inns, which are popular for healing tourism. Typically, hot spring inns are situated in serene rural areas, allowing visitors to appreciate the stunning natural views and relax in a peaceful atmosphere. Japanese onsen are believed to provide health benefits as they are rich in minerals and can help alleviate stress, enhance blood circulation, alleviate headaches, and reduce symptoms of skin diseases.
2. Yoga and meditation. Yoga and meditation classes are now widely available in numerous locations, including Kyoto and Okinawa. Moreover, several cities offer government-sponsored health programs under the name 'Kenko-tourism' or 'health tourism'.
3. There are some traditional therapies that have been around for centuries, including shiatsu, acupuncture, and moxibustion. There are several locations in Japan that provide tour packages that consist of this customary therapy.
4. Indulge in a nutritious culinary journey. Japan is renowned for its nutritious and flavourful cuisine, including sushi, ramen, and soba. Numerous locations throughout Japan provide tour packages that offer culinary experiences or the chance to savour healthy Japanese dishes.
5. Outdoors and hiking. Japan boasts numerous stunning natural attractions, including Mount Fuji, Nikko National Park, and Hokkaido's natural area. Many tour packages offer hiking and trekking options to these locations.

Post COVID-19 Concept for Indonesian Tourism

In the wake of COVID-19, the tourism industry has undergone strategic management changes, particularly in marketing, to adapt to the changing environment. Despite the abundance of beautiful natural attractions in Indonesia (Krisnawati et al., 2021), there has been a recent trend towards well-being tourism (Ma et al., 2021). To increase tourism, the government is focusing on promoting popular destinations abroad with a new tagline: 'Bali, the Soul of Indonesia' in 2021. This promotes Bali as a main attraction while also seeking to advertise other Indonesian destinations.

Building on the previous marketing concept of 'Wonderful Indonesia', we have developed a new approach called 'Sustainable Tourism'. This travel concept aims to have a lasting impact that benefits the environment, society, culture, and economy for both locals and tourists. Sustainable tourism involves managing environmental, economic, and human resources to minimise negative impacts and maximise positive benefits. This ensures that destinations are eco-friendly and can be enjoyed by all, while also promoting human health and welfare. Ultimately, the key to achieving sustainable tourism lies in balancing the interests of tourism with ecological and social sustainability.

Tourism that is sustainable can also promote healing tourism by offering experiences that have positive effects on both human health and the environment. This can be achieved by providing healthy activities, like yoga, meditation, hiking, and other natural activities that offer mental and physical health benefits to visitors. Additionally, destinations that prioritise local culture and preserve the environment can provide social and spiritual benefits to visitors. On the flip side, healing tourism can help to achieve sustainable tourism goals by encouraging responsible environmental and social practices.

Indonesia Requires Healing Tourism

Tourism in Indonesia has experienced substantial transformations from the New Order period (1966–1998) to the reform era (1998–2019) and the current millennial phase (2019–present). During the New Order period, tourism campaigns were geared towards foreign visitors, emphasising the allure of Bali Island's scenic wonders like the beaches, mountains, and lakes. Meanwhile, other tourist destinations were promoted by regional authorities or local media outlets.

During the reform era, the promotion of Indonesian tourism shifted towards highlighting cultural diversity and natural beauty beyond Bali. Popular destinations now include Yogyakarta, Lombok, Raja Ampat, and Labuan Bajo, each showcasing local culture through dance, music, handicrafts, and culinary arts. Sustainable development has become a key focus, with campaigns promoting eco-friendly and responsible tourism. In 2019 and prior, the term 'healing' was typically used in reference to psychiatric treatment for individuals.

During the Millennial phase, tourism promotion aims to offer tourists distinctive experiences, such as culinary delicacies, cultural attractions, and adventurous activities. With the current socio-economic advancements, the government is targeting Millennials and Generation Z tourists with modern tourism promotions that use social media platforms. The latest trends in this phase include the emergence of halal tourism and health tourism, which have become crucial factors in promotional strategies.

According to the Indonesia National Adolescent Mental Health Survey (I-NAMHS), which is the first national mental health survey that measures the incidence of mental disorders in Indonesian adolescents aged 10 to 17 years, it has been found that 15.5 million teenagers, which is one in three Indonesian adolescents, are facing mental health issues. Additionally, 2.45 million Indonesian teenagers, which is one in 20 teenagers, have been diagnosed with mental disorders as per the Diagnostic and Statistical Manual of Mental Disorders Fifth Edition (DSM-5) guidelines. Adolescents suffering from mental disorders find it challenging to perform their daily activities. The pandemic (2020–2021) has worsened the situation, resulting in a threefold increase in the level of depression among Indonesian teenagers.

It is interesting to note that the growth of healing tourism in Indonesia seems to coincide with the rise in stress levels among people. However, further research is required to establish a clear correlation between the two variables. The health and beauty tourism sector has experienced a 28 per cent increase in 2019, compared to the previous two years. This number is expected to rise again to 32 per cent in 2021. The Central Statistics Agency (BPS) reported that foreign tourists spent 21.1 trillion rupiah in Indonesia during the first quarter of 2020, including expenses related to health and beauty tourism.

The Indonesian government is focusing on improving healthcare services in tourist destinations, with a special emphasis on developing health facilities such as hospitals and services that cater to health tourism. For instance, Gadjah Mada University Hospital (UGM) in Yogyakarta has developed such services. The city is highly cognizant of the significance of meeting the needs of health tourism, and as a result, it is collaborating with Gadjah Mada Wisata to offer Medical Tourism and Wellness Tourism Facilities. These facilities incorporate tourism activities that are recommended and monitored by medical professionals, with the aim of providing a pleasurable experience for UGM Academic Hospital patients undergoing medical procedures.

Bali Island is a popular tourist destination for foreigners and has been known to offer healing tourism for many years. This beautiful island is home to many traditional healing places that provide various alternative therapies that are believed to help heal various diseases and health conditions. Ubud, famous for its art, yoga, and spa centres, and Lovina, known for diving tourism and dolphin therapy, are some of the popular healing destinations in Bali. Moreover, Bali has many modern healing centres that offer various medical facilities and services, such as Bali Royal Hospital, BIMC Hospital, and several beauty clinics and modern spas. Recently, the regional government of Bali and the central government of Indonesia have focused on developing healing tourism as part of their tourism development strategy. With the advancement in technology and growing tourist demand, innovative healing services are being developed with modern packaging to attract more tourists.

Stress and Healing

According to the Indonesian Basic Health Research conducted in 2018, more than 19 million individuals above the age of 15 have suffered from emotional and mental disorders, while over 12 million have experienced depression. In 2016, the Research and Development Agency of the Ministry of Health reported that 1,800 people died by suicide annually, which translates to an average of five deaths per day. Shockingly, 47.7% of these victims belonged to the age group of 10–39 years, comprising teenagers and individuals in their productive years. Currently, mental disorders affect nearly 20% of Indonesia's population, which means that one in five individuals are susceptible to experiencing such conditions.

According to I-NAMHS, it is predicted that there will be a rise in stress levels among teenagers in 2022. Doctors and psychiatrists have suggested various solutions to tackle this issue, including methods related to healing. While there is no concrete evidence linking stress problems with an increase in healing tourism, the term 'healing' became more prevalent during the COVID-19 pandemic, which led to a rise in stressful conditions.

According to Google Trends (see Fig. 1), there has been an increase in searches for the term 'healing' compared to 'tourism' following the impact of the COVID-19 pandemic on different aspects of human life. Interestingly, since August 2021, the term 'healing' has been searched for more frequently than 'stress'.

The word 'healing' was only mentioned once in tourism news in 2020, but increased to seven mentions in 2021. As of 2022, there are now 93 portals that offer healing tours. In the first two months of 2023, there were already 32 sources of information promoting healing tours. This trend is indicative of the challenges that society is facing amidst the pandemic, including economic and social issues, as well as barriers to various activities. These challenges have a psychological impact on individuals, which is why the tourism industry has started using the term 'healing tourism'.

Sum Up and Discussion

Currently, healing tourism is a significant aspect of the tourism industry in Indonesia, with positive prospects for the future. This is particularly true following the pandemic, which has caused an increase in stress levels. Healing tours offer a

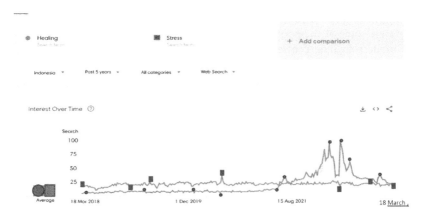

Fig. 1.   The Emergence of the Words Stress and Healing March 2018–March 18, 2023, from Google Trend.

promising solution for those seeking affordable and high-quality treatment while maintaining their health. The Indonesian community is becoming more aware of the benefits of incorporating health into their travel activities.

There are several factors that contribute to the growth of health tourism. Firstly, the demand for health services abroad is increasing as more and more people seek medical treatment for various reasons. Secondly, medical treatment in developed countries such as the United States and Europe tends to be very expensive, which has led many people to explore more affordable alternatives in Asian countries. Thirdly, people who seek medical treatment often take the opportunity to visit local tourist destinations before or after their treatment, creating a potential partnership between the health tourism and conventional tourism industries. Fourthly, advancements in medical technology have led to more sophisticated treatments that include not only clinical but also aesthetic and preventive procedures, which increases people's interest in seeking treatment while also enjoying relaxation and tourism activities. Lastly, health tourism can offer a more economical option for those seeking affordable healthcare services, attracting more patients in need of cost-effective solutions.

External environmental conditions can have an impact on people's daily routines, which can, in turn, affect tourism activities, including health tourism in Indonesia and worldwide. Hence, it is crucial to conduct in-depth research on the current positive trends in health tourism. To achieve this, a comprehensive analysis that encompasses various significant variables is necessary.

References

Adnan, R. S., Anam, F. K., & Radhiatmoko. (2021). The VUCA era creates Covid-19 pandemic in Indonesia being complicated. *Sosiohumaniora*, *3*(23). https://doi.org/ 10.24198/sosiohumaniora.v23i3.29744

Adnan, R. S., Harmadi, S. H. B., Hardjosoekarto, S., & Muhammaditya, N. (2022). Institutional reconstruction of promoting and maintaining the level of compliance with health protocols in Indonesia during the pandemic. *Systemic Practice and Action Research*, 1–30. https://doi.org/10.1007/s11213-022-09611-1

Baldwin, P. R., Velasquez, K., Koenig, H. G., Salas, R., & Boelens, P. A. (2016). Neural correlates of healing prayers, depression and traumatic memories: A preliminary study. *Complementary Therapies in Medicine*, *27*, 123–129. https://doi.org/10.1016/ j.ctim.2016.07.002

Bhalla, R., Chowdhary, N., & Ranjan, A. (2021). Spiritual tourism for psychotherapeutic healing post COVID-19. *Journal of Travel & Tourism Marketing*, *38*(8), 769–781. https://doi.org/10.1080/10548408.2021.1930630

Droit-Volet, S., Gil, S., Martinelli, N., Andant, N., Clinchamps, M., Parreira, L., Rouffiac, K., Dambrun, M., Huguet, P., Dubuis, B., Pereira, B., Bouillon, J., Dutheil, F., & COVISTRESS Network. (2020). Time and covid-19 stress in the lockdown situation: Time free, "Dying" of boredom and sadness. *PloS One*, *15*(8), e0236465. https:// doi.org/10.1371/journal.pone.0236465

Fitriana, I. N. (2020). *Mengulik potensi wisata indonesia pasca pandemi*. https://www. researchgate.net/publication/346463247_Mengulik_Potensi_Wisata_Indonesia_ Pasca_Pandemi

Han, J. H., & An, K. S. (2022). Comparison of perceptions of wellness tourism in Korea before and after COVID-19: Results of social big data analysis. *Global Business and Finance Review*, 27(2), 1–13. https://doi.org/10.17549/gbfr.2022.27.2.1

Kim, S., Um, S., & Lee, T. J. (2020). Healing effects from the on-site experiences of tourists. *The International Journal of Tourism Research*, 22(2), 192–201. https://doi.org/10.1002/jtr.2328

Krisnawati, E., Darsono, H., Amalia, R. M., Sujatna, E. T. S., & Pamungkas, K. (2021). Metaphors in Indonesian Nature Tourism Discourse: Disclosing cognition about nature. *Pertanika Journal of Social Sciences & Humanities*, 29(4), 2469–2482. https://doi.org/10.47836/pjssh.29.4.21

Luong, G., Wrzus, C., Wagner, G. G., & Riediger, M. (2016). When bad moods may not be so bad: Valuing negative affect is associated with weakened affect-health links. *Emotion (Washington, D.C.)*, 16(3), 387–401. https://doi.org/10.1037/emo0000132

Ma, S., Zhao, X., Gong, Y., & Wengel, Y. (2021). Proposing "healing tourism" as a post-COVID-19 tourism product. *Anatolia: An International Journal of Tourism and Hospitality Research*, 32(1), 136–139. https://doi.org/10.1080/13032917.2020.1808490

Muslim, M. (2020). Manajement stress pada masa pandemi Covid-19 ESENSI. *Jurnal Manajemen Bisnis*, 23(2). https://doi.org/10.55886/esensi.v23i2

Shiaty, R. E., Taalab, M., & Osama, I. (2016). Evaluating the performance of the outdoor spaces in healing eco-tourism. *Procedia Environmental Sciences*, 34, 461–473. https://doi.org/10.1016/j.proenv.2016.04.041

Speier, A. R. (2011). Health tourism in a Czech health spa. *Anthropology & Medicine*, 18(1), 55–66. https://doi.org/10.1080/13648470.2010.525879

Travel & Tourism Economic Impact Global Trends. (2022, August). World Travel & Tourism Council.

Yang, J. Y., Paek, S., Kim, T., & Lee, T. H. (2015). Health tourism: Needs for healing experience and intentions for transformation in wellness resorts in Korea. *International Journal of Contemporary Hospitality Management*, 27(8), 1881–1904. https://doi.org/10.1108/IJCHM-11-2013-0505

Yasmin, H., Khalil, S., & Mazhar, R. (2020, December). Covid 19: Stress management among students and its impact on their effective learning. *International Technology and Education Journal*, 4(2). https://doi.org/10.29062/edu.v4i2

Chapter 11

Resilience of Tourism Enterprises Facing VUCA Environment

Krzysztof Borodako, Jadwiga Berbeka and Michał Rudnicki

Krakow University of Economics, Krakow, Poland

Abstract

The aim of the study is to assess the resilience of tourism enterprises in the face of the pandemic crisis and the war in Ukraine. It was achieved on the base of the results of surveys conducted among Małopolska (Poland) tourism enterprises in the years 2021–2022. The research was conducted using the CAWI technique, it has been collected 517 completed questionnaires. Regression analysis was used to check the relationships between the studied variables. The findings confirm that the surveyed companies react agilely to changing, volatile, uncertain, and complex business conditions. These companies undertook numerous innovative (most often in the scale of the company) solutions in the organisational area. Changes noticed in the behaviour of contractors were also confirmed by constant monitoring of the environment forced by dynamic changes in conditions. Among the factors determining the activities of tourist companies in the context of international factors, one can undoubtedly mention the uncertainty caused by the war in Ukraine (and thus the energy crisis). The research focuses on the important subject of resilience, organisational changes, and agility in adapting to conditions in the face of volatility and uncertainty in the environment.

Keywords: Resilience; agile management; innovations; volatility; uncertainty; tourism

Tourism in a VUCA World: Managing the Future of Tourism, 157–170

Copyright © 2024 by Emerald Publishing Limited
doi:10.1108/978-1-83753-674-020241011

1. Introduction

The outbreak of the COVID-19 pandemic and the imposed administrative restrictions have had a huge impact on the tourism sector around the world (Duro et al., 2021). After some months, countries managed to control the spread of the pandemic, some tools and methods to deal with the situation were rapidly developed, restrictions were loosened and there were signs of improvement in the tourism industry (Yeh, 2021). Unfortunately, in 2022, the war broke out in Ukraine and the tourist demand there and in neighbouring countries, in particular international demand, was again limited by the uncertainty about safety (Plzáková & Smeral, 2022). The energy crisis as an indirect result of the war has had a strong impact on all industries, including tourism (Karabag & Imre, 2022).

The issue of operating under conditions of uncertainty, defined by four factors and called VUCA as their acronym, has become the subject of scientific studies (Stein, 2021). Some of them were purely theoretical (Stein, 2021). Empirical studies focus on analysing the impact of the pandemic on the global tourism sector (Duro et al., 2021), on a particular continent: for example, the European market (Plzáková & Smeral, 2022) or on a country: in the UK (Ntounis et al., 2022), Indonesia (Pramana et al., 2022) or Iran (impact of government policies on tourism SMEs (Estiri et al., 2022). The regional aspect was less frequently addressed. This chapter fills this gap.

In the chapter, the focus is on the organisational resilience (Duchek et al., 2020) of tourism enterprises. The attitudes of entrepreneurs from the Małopolska region (a very popular touristic region in Poland) and the actions taken by them to adapt to the new conditions were empirically examined. These attitudes concerned the area of organisational solutions introduced in the light of perceived changes in the tourism market and identified positive and negative factors in the international environment.

2. Literature Review

2.1. VUCA Environment

A review of both scientific and business literature confirms the opinion that today's enterprises are forced to operate in very hard conditions (Minciu et al., 2020; Sthapit, 2020). Some of them are unable to adapt to these changes and use the new environment as a stimulant to increase their competitiveness. The authors of publications after 2020 very often emphasise that the global situation is VUCA, that is, volatile, unpredictable, complex, and ambiguity (Stein, 2021). Some authors use the terms 'unknown' (Wakelin-Theron et al., 2019) or 'uncertain' (Lubowiecki-Vikuk et al., 2023; Weerapattanawong et al., 2022) interchangeably for 'unpredictable'.

The dynamic environmental factors that affect the world economy and societies force us to act non-routinely and lead to unpredictable consequences. One of the significant factors in the last decade was the outbreak of the COVID-19 pandemic, which disrupted many spheres of life of the population and the functioning of enterprises. According to WTO (2023) data, within 3 years of the declaration of a pandemic, according to official data, over 750 million people in the world were infected, and over 6.8 million people died from this disease. The pandemic also caused a sharp decline in sales and profits of enterprises – however, varying these values depending on individual industries (Al-Awadhi et al., 2020). An extensive discussion on each part of the VUCA environment was presented by Bennett and Lemoine (2014) in their chapter.

The consequences caused by the pandemic were also very visible in the area of employment. Striving to save money and cut costs, many companies have decided to reduce employment primarily of low-paid and temporary workers (Hurley et al., 2021). Another event of an unprecedented nature after the pandemic is Russia's attack on Ukraine in the spring of 2022, which has had multiple consequences. On the one hand, over 12 million people fled the war from Ukraine, mainly to EU countries (the vast majority of them staying in Poland) (UNHCR, 2023); on the other hand, the hybrid war caused a global energy and humanitarian crisis (International Energy Agency, 2023).

These four conditions of volatility, unpredictability, complexity, and ambiguity require some kind of awareness of external risks from the managers. External factors most often force certain actions in the organisation, which cause a chain reaction in many other firm's processes (Bukłaha & Cabała, 2023). Managers introduce changes in marketing activities, work organisation, and technological changes (which may also apply to the two previously mentioned areas). Introducing such changes is based on information from the environment that the company needs to pick up, analyse, and evaluate (Buckley & Carter, 2004). In the light of sudden, unpredictable, as well as complex, and ambiguous changes, this task is even more difficult and time-consuming. In such environmental changes with a powerful impact on the operational activities of companies, adjustments of work organisation become necessary (Bennett & Lemoine, 2014; Janssen & van der Voort, 2020), but also changes in employment policy seem to play a key role (Sobotka, 2021). Companies, operating in such a complex and dynamic environment, undertake changes in the organisational structure (Kaya, 2022), changes in the employees' duties (Kolga, 2021), changes in the remuneration regulations (Kinowska, 2021), and the introduction of remote or rotational work (Jacks, 2021).

2.2. Resilience in Tourism

Due to the described above uncertainty, a resilience has become an important feature of enterprises, that is why many researchers have taken up the topic (Denyer, 2017; Duchek et al., 2020; Pettit et al., 2010). Resilience – considered from the point of view of the organisation – is the ability to plan for, react to and recover from disaster events (like pandemics or wars) or financial risks and uncertainties (Hollnagel, 2014; Sinha & Ola, 2021). Crucial factors: the ability to anticipate, monitor, respond, recover, and learn from disadvantageous events, contribute to an organisation's performance during these events (Hollnagel, 2014) and afterwards.

Bouaziz and Smaoui Hachicha (2018) stress that resilience is more than resistance or adaptation to change. They draw attention to the fact that it involves adopting a proactive attitude, anticipating and leveraging change. What's more, as Duchek et al. (2020) highlight, resilience allows for effectively crisis handling and can even be a source of competitive advantage (Hamel & Välikangas, 2003) and long-term success (Coutu, 2002). Therefore, it is stressed that organisations must develop resilience by being agile and adapting positively to the economic activities affected by disasters (like pandemic), war, and financial fluctuations to improve performance. This is especially important in the case of tourism industry companies, which are affected by crisis situations in the first place.

Williams et al. (2017) stress that organisational resilience evolves, resulting in organisational reactions and responses to unexpected changes in the business environment and alternative plans to recover from these situations. However, the organisation requires information and knowledge to transform from reactive organisational resilience to dynamic or proactive organisational resilience (Giroux & Prior, 2012; Williams et al., 2017).

Resilience can be analysed from many perspectives. One involves distinguishing three levels of resilience: individual, group, and organisational (Ma et al., 2018). From the point of view of our research, the second and third levels are particularly important. Employees in a company, creating a team focused on acquiring new skills, mastering new situations, and improving competencies are more likely to positively adapt to difficult conditions and achieve better results in the long run. Positive adaptation is more likely because groups that have refined their competencies are more likely to register and deal with the complexities of dynamic decision-making environments and may be more motivated to endure obstacles and adversities (Sutcliffe & Vogus, 2003). One of the mechanisms of positive adaptation is accumulated knowledge (Cohen & Levinthal, 1990). The second mechanism concerns the diversity of group (team) composition. In addition to broadening the group's collective knowledge base (i.e. competencies, response repertoire, and ability to understand new situations), the diversity of group members can build resilience, influencing the group's ability to sense, register, and regulate complexity (Weick & Sutcliffe, 2011). A third (closely related mechanism) is the diversity of experiences brought by individual group members.

At the level of organisational resilience, organisational learning and adaptation, dynamic capabilities, and high-reliability impact the business performance (Sutcliffe & Vogus, 2003). Organisational resilience is anchored in organisational processes aimed at the empowerment of general competencies and development of the organisation (especially the ability to learn and learn from mistakes) and restoring efficiency by increasing the ability to quickly process feedback and flexibly rearrange or transfer knowledge and resources to deal with emerging situations (Sutcliffe & Vogus, 2003).

Due to the nature of the industry, it is particularly difficult to achieve resilience in tourism.

2.3. Tourism Development in Małopolska Region (2019–2022)

Małopolska is one of the 16 regions in Poland, whose capital is Krakow. The whole region of Krakow is very rich in terms of tourism, which is very famous for domestic and foreign tourists.

According to the study of tourist traffic carried out since 2003, the region recorded an increase in the number of tourists, approaching 14 million tourists in the pre-pandemic period. Looking at the number of tourists, there was a strong decrease in the total number of tourists in 2020 (from 13.80 to 7.66 million). The latest available data confirm that tourism is recovering (despite the war in Ukraine, the energy crisis, and the difficult economic situation caused by, among others, rising inflation) – Fig. 1.

The growing number of tourists was also related to the growing offer of the region—from tourist attractions to accommodation. Małopolska operates 13.4% of all hotel facilities in Poland and 15% of all hotels in this country. In 2021, there are 378 hotels, 69 boarding houses, and 77 other hotel facilities in Małopolska. In 2020, there were 101 museums (including branches) operating in this region, which had 3.12 million pieces of exhibits. The international tourist importance of this region is evidenced by the fact that as many as six historic complexes from Małopolska were included on the UNESCO World Heritage List (Statistical Office in Krakow, 2022). The three main aims of travel to the Małopolska region are presented in Fig. 2.

3. Methodology

This chapter aims to assess the resilience of tourism enterprises in the face of the pandemic crisis and the war in Ukraine. The survey method was applied. The data collection tool was a questionnaire that was conducted by the Małopolska Tourist Organization among the companies of the tourism industry in Małopolska.

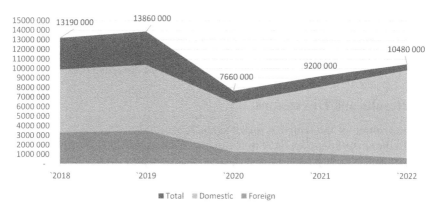

Fig. 1.   Number of Tourists in Małopolska Region in 2018–2022. *Source*: Own elaboration on the data of Borkowski et al. (2023).

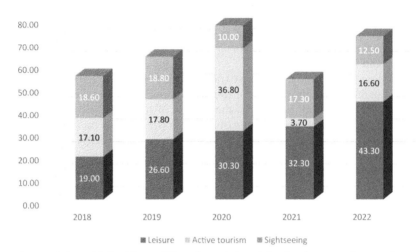

Fig. 2.   Three Main Aims of Travel to Małopolska Region [%]. *Source*: Own elaboration on the data of Borkowski et al. (2023).

The research was conducted using the CAWI technique via the ProfiTest.pl platform in two rounds, September–November 2021 and September–November 2022. Due to the difficult situation caused by the post-pandemic reality and the war in Ukraine, the vast majority of Małopolska tourist companies were reluctant to participate in the research. After numerous requests and reminders, we managed to obtain 517 completed questionnaires.

The following tourism companies' characteristics were used in the study: size (in the number of employees), time of presence on the market (in years), and tourism industry (hospitality, gastronomy, and others). The starting point for the conducted analyses was the changes observed in employment, which influenced organisational changes within the resilience of tourism enterprises facing the VUCA environment.

The analysis method employed was the regression analysis to evaluate whether variables were related. The results show only relationships for which the level of test probability p, based on the Chi-square statistics, is less than 0.05.

4. Results and Discussions

A description of the sample is presented in Table 1.

In the surveyed group, there were most companies classified as 'other', including transport companies, travel agencies (tour operators and tourism brokers), service companies in MICE tourism (meetings, incentive, conferences/congress, exhibition/events) tourism guides/pilots, tourism attractions, tourism information with souvenirs. The hotel industry accounted for over 35%, and every fifth surveyed company represented gastronomy. Taking into account the time of presence on the market, a more or less equal division between the defined groups

Table 1.   Sample Description.

Tourism Industry	Hospitality	Gastronomy	Others		
Share in %	35.40%	20.31%	44.29%		
Time of presence on the market (in years)	**Up to 5 years**	**6–10 years**	**11–15 years**	**16-20 years**	**More than 20 years**
Share in %	17.21%	22.63%	18.38%	18.18%	21.66%
Number of employees	**1 - person activity**	**Up to 9 employees**	**10–49 employees**	**50–249 employees**	**More than 250 employees**
Share in %	21.66%	51.26%	21.28%	4.64%	0.58%

Source: Own elaboration on the data of Seweryn et al. (2021, 2022).

was observed, amounting to about 20% (+/− 3%). In accordance with the trends observed in the tourism industry, nearly 3/4 were MSMEs. A decreasing share of companies was observed along with an increase in their size. Every fifth surveyed company was a one-person company run by self-employed persons.

The main objective was to assess the resilience of tourism enterprises in the face of the pandemic crisis and the war in Ukraine. Taking into account, that organisational resilience evolves, resulting in organisational reactions and responses to unexpected changes (Williams et al., 2017) we analysed changes in the number of employees and their impact on the implementation of organisational changes as alternative plans to recover from these situations (Table 2). In the face of the VUCA environment changes in employment in the tourism industry (which is also characterised by high seasonality of employment) are one of the first reactions of entrepreneurs (Hurley et al., 2021; Janssen & van der Voort, 2020). Reducing the size of employment or increasing it is also a premise for further organisational changes introduced in companies (Sobotka, 2021). As a result of the chi-square test analysis, we identified a significant relationship between changes in employment and the introduction of organisational changes ($p = 0.00003$).

The percentage of companies introducing organisational changes was the highest among companies that were forced to reduce employment in the face of VUCA, which is consistent with the results of research conducted by Hurley et al. (2021). Among the companies that increased employment, more than 40% of companies decided to introduce organisational changes. The lowest percentage was observed among companies that did not change their employment. However, it amounted to nearly 40%, which shows that organisational changes are necessary for the face of VUCA, but they do not always have to be immediately conditioned by changes in employment. Duchek et al. (2020) highlight that resilience should allow for managing crisis effectively – a proactive attitude and maintaining the current size of human resources as part of organisational resilience can be a

Table 2. Dependencies of Introducing Organisational Changes.

Variables	Organisational Changes Introduced	Organisational Changes Not Introduced	*p*-value
Changes in employment			**0.00003**
Increased	42.37%	57.63%	
Stayed at the same level	37.60%	62.40%	
Decreased	49.37%	50.63%	
Not applicable	19.61%	80.39%	
Number of employees			**0.00000**
1 - person activity	18.92%	81.08%	
Up to 9 employees	38.87%	61.13%	
10–49 employees	53.64%	46.36%	
50–249 employees	54.17%	45.83%	
More than 250 employees	0.00%	100.00%	
Time of presence on the market (in years)			**0.12632**
Up to 5 years	46.07%	53.93%	
6–10 years	43.59%	56.41%	
11–15 years	37.89%	62.11%	
16–20 years	30.85%	69.15%	
More than 20 years	33.04%	66.96%	
Tourism industry			**0.00334**
Hospitality	36.61%	63.39%	
Gastronomy	52.38%	47.62%	
Others	33.33%	66.67%	

Source: Own elaboration on the data of Seweryn et al. (2021, 2022).

good example of this, especially in the case of the need to quickly return to full organisational efficiency and service capabilities.

The introduction of organisational changes was also checked due to the variables characterising the surveyed companies. *p*-Value<0.05 was obtained when examining the relationship between the fact of introducing organisational changes and the size of the company ($p = 0.00000$) and the industry ($p = 0.00334$) represented by the surveyed companies.

The largest number of organisational changes were introduced by SMEs (more than half of the surveyed companies). Also, nearly 40% of micro-enterprises introduced organisational changes in the face of VUCA, but this percentage is lower. This depends on the small human resources of these companies, which means that these changes will be directed mainly towards changes in the scope of responsibilities and competencies of leadership.

Organisational changes were mainly introduced by companies operating in gastronomy (more than half of the surveyed sample). Among the companies representing the hotel industry and the so-called 'other' every third company took action in the field of resilience in the face of VUCA.

Among the companies that introduced organisational changes, it was checked which solutions were most often implemented (Table 3).

The most frequently introduced organisational change was a change in employees' duties and/or scope of activities at individual positions, which is also confirmed by other research results (Kolga, 2021). These changes were identified as the most popular both in terms of industries and the size of the surveyed companies. Among hotel companies, apart from changes in the scope of competencies, changes in occupational health and safety conditions forced by the pandemic and sanitary requirements were also particularly important. On the other hand, for companies operating in gastronomy, important organisational changes were also changes in the remuneration regulations and changes in the scope of working time. Among the 'other' companies, due to the very large diversification of the nature of the tourism activity, it is difficult to identify leading organisational changes apart from the identified changes in the scope of competencies.

Changes in employees' duties and/or scope of activities at individual positions were also the most common organisational changes observed among all defined age groups of the surveyed companies. Our results are in line with the conclusions of Sharma and Sharma (2019). Relatively often (nearly every third surveyed company) introduced changes in the rules of remuneration and bonuses for employees, which is also confirmed by the results obtained by Kinowska (2021).

The results presented in this chapter show that a significant part of tourism companies from the Małopolska region, in the face of VUCA caused first by the pandemic and then by the war in Ukraine, took positive adaptation as part of organisational resilience. These changes were predominant in employees' duties and/or scope of activities at individual positions. Organisational changes are often observed in the literature, especially in the context of changes in competencies and leadership (Bywater & Lewis, 2019; Rath et al., 2021). What is more, companies in the tourism industry are particularly susceptible to changes that create the VUCA environment, which requires from them not only organisational resilience but also resilience in marketing and management (Lubowiecki-Vikuk & Sousa, 2021; Weerapattanawong et al., 2022).

Moreover, it should be borne in mind that many of the actions taken by Małopolska enterprises resulted from the need to quickly adapt to unpredictable and dynamically changing circumstances, thus not being long-term resilience strategies. Some of the changes introduced in companies were undoubtedly of a long-term nature, while others initiated change processes aimed at greater efficiency of their operations. The mechanisms developed in this way become unique, which according to classic studies on business strategies is often identified as a survival strategy in the long run (Collins, 2001; Collins & Porras, 2005). These

166   Krzysztof Borodako et al.

Table 3. Organisational Changes of Tourist Companies as Their Resilience in the Face of VUCA.

Variables	Changes in Organisational Structure	Changes in Employees' Duties and/or Scope of Activities at Individual Positions	Changes in the Remuneration Regulations	Changes in the Working Time of Employees	Introduction of Remote or Rotational Work	Changes in the Conditions of Occupational Health and Safety	Other Organisational Changes
Hospitality	20.90%	55.22%	23.88%	22.39%	16.42%	41.79%	0.00%
Gastronomy	27.27%	61.82%	40.00%	40.00%	9.09%	25.45%	7.27%
Others	22.37%	36.84%	30.26%	22.37%	25.00%	21.05%	10.53%
1-person activity	23.81%	33.33%	28.57%	23.81%	28.57%	23.81%	9.52%
Up to 9 employees	24.27%	46.60%	31.07%	31.07%	18.45%	29.13%	5.83%
10–49 employees	16.95%	61.02%	32.20%	23.73%	10.17%	28.81%	6.78%
50–249 employees	46.15%	46.15%	30.77%	23.08%	30.77%	46.15%	0.00%

Source: Own elaboration on the data of Seweryn et al. (2021, 2022).

unique resilience strategies of outliers enabled Małopolska tourism companies to survive in the VUCA environment and fast recovery in the tourism market.

5. Managerial Contribution

The activity of companies in the tourism industry is characterised by high sensitivity to external factors. Changeable weather conditions, epidemics, cataclysms, and wars, causing fears about the safety of tourists in neighbouring countries, force managers of the tourism industry to be very resilient. Due to the fact that tourism is dominated by SMEs, the flexibility of action, and resistance to emerging problems should be relatively easy to implement quickly and effectively.

The conducted research allows for the formulation of certain recommendations for managers of tourism companies regarding the introduction of changes in response to significant changes in the environment. The research context was based on the very strong impact of the pandemic period, and thus large personnel changes (dismissals of some employees). Therefore, based on research, it is possible to recommend the management build a competitive advantage based on the diversification of organisational changes. Changes in the scope of duties of employees and (short-term) savings through changes in salaries were the most frequently practiced actions, which exceptional circumstances seemed to explain the difficulty to carry out measures to save companies.

6. Limitations and Future Research

Each study must be based on certain assumptions and performed within certain limitations. In this study, analyses of organisational changes in travel companies operating in the VUCA conditions were carried out. This study analysed various types of changes in the work organisation, but the previously defined research objective did not allow for estimating the effects of the actions introduced by the companies. Therefore, the limitation of this study could be the difficulty in identifying the long-term effects of the changes introduced during the crisis. Another aspect is the short-term nature of analysed data, the short perspective of effects of organisational changes, and the unique character of resilience strategies, so there are also some difficulties in imitating these strategies by others in the market. In this case, a solution to these limitations could be to conduct long-term studies. In this context, it becomes important to observe the unique resilience strategies of outliers from a wider perspective and their impact on companies' performance operating in the VUCA environment.

The research provided important information for the tourism industry about the processes taking place in companies during a major triple crisis (pandemic, war across the eastern border of the country, energy crisis), but interpreting the results does not allow for isolating the individual effects of each of these sources. It is impossible to determine to what extent individual crises 'overlapped' and to what extent one or two of them occurred.

In light of the results, it is still worth seeking answers to two key questions in future research. The first is to check to what extent the organisational resilience of tourism companies varies depending on the duration of a given hindering factor. To what extent very difficult operating conditions (of a seasonal nature) are more easily absorbed by the immune mechanisms of companies, and to what extent do strong global factors contribute to the bankruptcy of maladjusted companies? The second question that arose based on this research is certainly the need to define the strategic role of crisis management in tourism companies while making aware of the dominant role of MSMEs in the tourism industry.

References

Al-Awadhi, A. M., Alsaifi, K., Al-Awadhi, A., & Alhammadi, S. (2020). Death and contagious infectious diseases: Impact of the COVID-19 virus on stock market returns. *Journal of Behavioral and Experimental Finance*, *27*, 100326.

Bennett, N., & Lemoine, G. J. (2014). What VUCA really means for you. *Harvard Business Review*, Jan–Feb, 1–4.

Borkowski, K., Seweryn, R., Mazanek, L., & Alejziak, B. (2023). *Research on tourist traffic in Krakow and Lesser Poland in 2022* (Vol. 1/2023). Małopolska Tourist Organization.

Buckley, P. J., & Carter, M. J. (2004). A formal analysis of knowledge combination in multinational enterprises. *Journal of International Business Studies*, *35*(5), 371–384.

Bukłaha, E., & Cabała, P. (2023). Przydatność wybranych koncepcji zarządzania zmianą w świecie VUCA. *Studia i Prace Kolegium Zarządzania i Finansów*, (186), 19–131.

Bouaziz, F., & Smaoui Hachicha, Z. (2018). Strategic human resource management practices and organizational resilience. *Journal of Management Development*, 37(7), 537–551. https://doi.org/10.1108/JMD-11-2017-0358

Bywater, J., & Lewis, J. (2019). Leadership: What competencies does it take to remain engaged as a leader in a VUCA world. *Assessment & Development Matters*, *11*(3), 2–9.

Cohen, W. M., & Levinthal, D. A. (1990). Absorptive capacity: A new perspective on learning and innovation. *Administrative Science Quarterly*, *35*, 128–152.

Collins, J. C., & Porras, J. (2005). *Built to last: Successful habits of visionary companies*. Random House.

Collins, J. (2001). *Good to great: Why some companies make the leap and others don't*. HarperCollins.

Coutu, D. L. (2002). How resilience works. *Harvard Business Review*, *80*(5), 46–56.

Denyer, D. (2017). Organizational resilience. In *Organizational resilience. A summary of academic evidence, business insights and new thinking*. https://doi.org/10.1093/acprof :oso/9780199791057.001.0001

Duchek, S., Raetze, S., & Scheuch, I. (2020). The role of diversity in organizational resilience: A theoretical framework. *Business Research*, *13*(2), 387–423. https:// doi.org/10.1007/s40685-019-0084-8

Duro, J. A., Perez-Laborda, A., Turrion-Prats, J., & Fernández-Fernández, M. (2021). Covid-19 and tourism vulnerability. *Tourism Management Perspectives*, *38*. https:// doi.org/10.1016/j.tmp.2021.100819

Estiri, M., Heidary Dahooie, J., & Skare, M. (2022). COVID-19 crisis and resilience of tourism SME's: A focus on policy responses. *Economic Research-Ekonomska Istraživanja*, *35*(1), 5556–5580. https://doi.org/10.1080/1331677X.2022.2032245

Giroux, J., & Prior, T. (2012). *Factsheet expressions of resilience: From bounce back to adaptation.* Risk and Resilience Research Group, Center for Security Studies, ETH Zürich.

Hamel, G., & Välikangas, L. (2003). The quest for resilience. *Harvard Business Review*, *81*(9), 52–63. http://proquest.umi.com/pqdweb?did=395498971&Fmt=7&clientId=4574&RQT=309&VName=PQD%5Cnpapers3://publication/uuid/5041D63D-7A0F-47F7-B447-EF0EE63A7D9D

Hollnagel, E. (2014). Resilience engineering and the built environment. *Building Research and Information*, *42*(2), 221–228.

Hurley, J., Fana, M., Adăscăliței, D., Ortolani, G. M., Mandl, I., Peruffo, E., & Vacas-Soriano, C. (2021). *What just happened? COVID-19 lockdowns and change in the labour market.* Joint Research Centre (Seville site).

International Energy Agency. (2023). *Russia's War on Ukraine.* Retrieved April 10, 2023, from https://www.iea.org/topics/russias-war-on-ukraine

Jacks, T. (2021). Research on remote work in the era of COVID-19. *Journal of Global Information Technology Management*, *24*(2), 93–97.

Janssen, M., & van der Voort, H. (2020). Agile and adaptive governance in crisis response: Lessons from the COVID-19 pandemic. *International Journal of Information Management*, *55*(June), 102180.

Karabag, S. F., & Imre, Ö. (2022). The global, regional, national, sectoral, economic, and commercial impact of the Russo-Ukrainian war and the emerging second cold war. *Journal of Applied Economics and Business Research*, *12*(2), 58–70.

Kaya, Y. (2022). The importance of the organizational structure to be competitive in VUCA World. In *Agile Management and VUCA-RR: Opportunities and threats in Industry 4.0 towards Society 5.0* (pp. 207–214). Emerald Publishing Limited.

Kinowska, H. (2021). Core features for the design of remuneration systems for sustainable human resource management during the Covid-19 pandemic: Polish companies' experiences. *Entrepreneurship and Sustainability Issues, VsI Entrepreneurship and Sustainability Center*, *8*(4), 389–402.

Kolga, M. (2021). Initiating leadership development in a VUCA environment. In *The organizational improvement plan at Western University.* https://ir.lib.uwo.ca/oip/197/

Lubowiecki-Vikuk, A., Budzanowska-Drzewiecka, M., Borzyszkowski, J., & Taheri, B. (2023). Critical reflection on VUCA in tourism and hospitality marketing activities. *International Journal of Contemporary Hospitality Management.* https://doi.org/10.1108/IJCHM-04-2022-0479

Lubowiecki-Vikuk, A., & Sousa, B. (2021). Tourism business in a vuca world: Marketing and management implications. *Journal of Environmental Management and Tourism*, *12*(4), 867–876.

Ma, Z., Xiao, L., & Yin, J. (2018). Toward a dynamic model of organizational resilience. *Nankai Business Review International*, *9*(3), 246–263. https://doi.org/10.1108/NBRI-07-2017-0041

Minciu, M., Berar, F. A., Dobrea, R. C., & Dima, C. (2020). New approaches of managers in the context of the VUCA world. In *Public recreation and landscape protection - with sense hand in hand? Conference Proceedings.*

Ntounis, N., Parker, C., Skinner, H., Steadman, Ch., & Warnaby, G. (2022). Tourism and Hospitality industry resilience during the Covid-19 pandemic: Evidence from England. *Current Issues in Tourism*, *25*(1), 46–59. https://doi.org/10.1080/13683500.2021.1883556

Pettit, T. J., Fiksel, J., & Croxton, K. L. (2010). Ensuring supply chain resilience: Development of a conceptual framework. *Journal of Business Logistics*, *31*(1), 1–21.

Plzáková, L., & Smeral, E. (2022). COVID-19 pandemic, the war in Ukraine and looming risks for tourism's recovery. *Tourism Economics*. https://doi.org/10.1177/13548166221131722

Pramana, S., Paramartha, D. Y., Ermawan, G. Y., Deli, N. F., & Srimulyani, W. (2022). Impact of COVID-19 pandemic on tourism in Indonesia. *Current Issues in Tourism*, 25(15), 2422–2442. https://doi.org/10.1080/13683500.2021.1968803

Rath, C. R., Grosskopf, S., & Barmeyer, Ch. (2021). Leadership in the VUCA world – A systematic literature review and its link to intercultural competencies. *European Journal of Cross-Cultural Competence and Management*, 5(3), 195–219.

Seweryn, R., Niemczyk, A., Borodako, K., & Rudnicki, M. (2021). *Małopolska Tourist Industry in 2021*. Małopolska Tourist Organization.

Seweryn, R., Niemczyk, A., Borodako, K., & Rudnicki, M. (2022). *Małopolska Tourist Industry in 2022*. Małopolska Tourist Organization.

Sharma, A., & Sharma, L. (2019). VUCA world: The road ahead for HR. *NHRD Network Journal*, 12(2), 151–158.

Sinha, R., & Ola, A. (2021). Enhancing business community disaster resilience. A structured literature review of the role of dynamic capabilities. *Continuity and Resilience Review*, 3(2), 132–148. https://doi.org/10.1108/crr-03-2021-0009

Sobotka, B. (2021). Labour market changes and challenges for education in the VUCA era. *Journal of Modern Science*, 46(1), 191–208.

Statistical Office in Krakow. (2022). *Tourism in Małopolskie Voivodship in 2020 and 2021*.

Stein, S. (2021). Reimagining global citizenship education for a volatile, uncertain, complex, and ambiguous (VUCA) world. *Globalisation, Societies and Education*, 19(4), 482–495.

Sthapit, A. (2020). The VUCA world: What management is for? *Journal of Business and Social Sciences Research*, 5(1). https://doi.org/10.3126/jbssr.v5i1.30194

Sutcliffe, K. M., & Vogus, T. J. (2003). Organizing for resilience. In K. S. Cameron, J. E. Dutton, & R. E. Quinn (Eds.), *Positive organizational scholarship: Foundations of a new discipline* (pp. 94–110). Berrett-Koehler. https://doi.org/10.4324/9780429298974

UNHCR. (2023). Ukraine refugee situation. *United Nations High Commissioner for Refugees*. https://data.unhcr.org/en/situations/ukraine

Wakelin-Theron, N., Ukpere, W. I., & Spowart, J. (2019). Determining tourism graduate employability, knowledge, skills, and competencies in a VUCA world: Constructing a tourism employability model. *African Journal of Hospitality, Tourism and Leisure*, 8(3), 1–18.

Weerapattanawong, N., Hoonsopon, D., Chandrachai, A., & Triukose, S. (2022). The resilient marketing strategy framework in VUCA world. *Res Militaris*, 12(2), 7569–7582.

Weick, K. E., & Sutcliffe, K. M. (2011). *Managing the unexpected: Resilient performance in an age of uncertainty* (2nd ed.). Jossey-Bass.

Williams, T. A., Gruber, D. A., Sutcliffe, K. M., Shepherd, D. A., & Zhao, E. Y. (2017). Organisational response to adversity: Fusing crisis management and resilience research streams. *Academy of Management Annals*, 11(2), 733–769.

WHO. (2023). WHO Coronavirus (COVID-19) Dashboard – Overview. *World Health Organization*. https://covid19.who.int

Yeh, S. S. (2021). Tourism recovery strategy against COVID-19 pandemic. *Tourism Recreation Research*, 46(2), 188–194. https://doi.org/10.1080/02508281.2020.1805933

Chapter 12

Risk Preparation in Touristic Coastal Areas in Spain: COVID-19 Versus Tsunamis

Sandra Sánchez-Arcediano and Frank Babinger

Department of Geography, Faculty of Commerce and Tourism, Complutense University of Madrid, Spain

Abstract

After COVID-19, the current situation is more VUCA than ever. Tourism has shown great resilience but has been recently truncated. The question is how tourism destinations have coped with the pandemic and how are they preparing for other impacts in the future? This chapter analyses how Spanish tourism stakeholders have coped with the pandemic and whether tourism destinations are prepared for other hazards. It proposes a comparison of the preparations that have been made to deal with the crisis in the sector with those that are being made to deal with tsunamis. Even if this comparison may seem surprising, in both cases, we are dealing with the preparation for a hazard that affects a tourist destination. In view of this unprecedented situation, it has become clear that tourist destinations are vulnerable to different events that may occur, and risk management is necessary to be able to deal with all situations. This has shown that other hazards less frequent in Spain, such as tsunamis, have been relegated. Knowing how both hazards have been dealt with in the Spanish tourism sector will help to highlight weaknesses in planning. This will involve some anticipation and will avoid planning and management on the fly.

Keywords: Spain; COVID-19; tsunamis; hazards; tourism planning; VUCA; coastal areas

Tourism in a VUCA World: Managing the Future of Tourism, 171–186
Copyright © 2024 by Emerald Publishing Limited
All rights of reproduction in any form reserved
doi:10.1108/978-1-83753-674-020241012

1. Introduction

In recent years, the idea that we are in a VUCA environment has been reinforced. This term, although not new (Covarrubias Moreno, 2020), has recently gained weight.

This idea has been reinforced by the emergence of COVID-19, an unprecedented virus (Mantecón, 2020) that broke out without warning, creating a climate of instability and uncertainty. Given the lack of knowledge of this virus and its uncontrolled spread, the competent administrations were obliged to take the most forceful and rapid measures possible. These measures have been a turning point, as it is the first time that such restrictive measures have been taken in an epidemic (Huertas et al., 2020).

In this framework of uncertainty and instability, and despite the fact that all sectors were affected (Castello, 2020), the tourism sector was one of the most impacted because, due to its characteristics, it is more susceptible than the rest to any change.

Although the worst moments of the pandemic are behind us, the virus is far from over and we are still living with many consequences that followed in its wake. In addition to the management conducted by the competent administrations (Romero-Saritama et al., 2021), it is important to address how this management has been conducted in tourist destinations and whether they are prepared or are already anticipating another hazard that may occur in the future.

Therefore, the main objective of this chapter is to analyse how Spanish tourism stakeholders in coastal areas have coped with the pandemic and whether they are prepared for tsunami hazards. In this sense, it will be necessary to make a comparison between the two hazards, considering that they do not require the same measures and that not all of them have the same level of risk. However, this comparison is justified since both have a direct impact on the tourism sector. It is important to highlight that this work has been based on a literature review following the proposal established by Guirao-Goris et al. (2008).

It is necessary to address how tourist destinations in coastal areas have prepared for the risk of COVID-19 since, as stated by Duro et al. (2021), tourism in seaside destinations of the Islands and the Mediterranean have shown higher vulnerability to COVID-19. In times of crisis, companies in the tourism and hospitality sector are forced to change their operational strategies (Rodríguez-Antón & Alonso-Almeida, 2020). Although attempts are being made to resume the activity with the same characteristics as before the appearance of the virus, the fact is that it has marked a before and after in societies. Therefore, this negative situation should serve to rethink the tourism model that was being developed (Arold Lario, 2021) and to learn from the experience provided by the management of COVID-19.

This learning should help tourism destinations to take the initiative and lead a change, allowing them to establish a security structure for multiple hazards that may affect the activity in their destination. In Spain, the tourism sector is an engine of the national economy, and it is its responsibility to guarantee safety and quality standards to maintain one of the fundamental pillars.

2. Theoretical Background

2.1. The Case of COVID-19

The concept of VUCA, understood as volatility, uncertainty, complexity, and ambiguity, has been widely used and analysed. Although recently the idea that we are in a global VUCA environment has been reinforced, this term has been used since the 20th century. The emergence of this concept dates back to the US military, which used this acronym to describe the future after the Cold War (Covarrubias Moreno, 2020).

The fact that we find ourselves in a social environment in which volatility, uncertainty, complexity, and ambiguity predominate, makes it difficult to predict (Covarrubias Moreno, 2020). This impedes management and decision-making prior to the event taking place and should enhance the precautionary principle. It is vital to have advance planning to guide you to avoid making decisions quickly and in an uncontrolled manner.

After many processes of change at the international level (Covarrubias Moreno, 2020), the emergence of the SARS-CoV-2 coronavirus has reinforced the VUCA environment.

Throughout history, there have been multiple epidemics that have affected humans (Moreno-Sánchez et al., 2018) and their control was not possible until the 19th century thanks to advances in medicine (Galeana, 2020). Although other contagious diseases have occurred in recent years such as Ebola (Huertas et al., 2020), COVID-19 has surprised a society that was not prepared for an epidemic of such magnitude, as there were no previous protocols for action (Mantecón, 2020).

COVID-19 was detected in 2019 with Wuhan as the infection core (Huertas et al., 2020), but cases were detected in more than 24 countries (Trilla, 2020). Given the uncontrolled spread of the virus, the World Health Organization (WHO) was forced to declare a global pandemic (Vega Falcón et al., 2020). Moreover, the WHO declared this epidemic as a Public Health Emergency of International Concern (Trilla, 2020). In the case of Spain, the state of alarm was declared on 14 March 2020 (Fernández Alles, 2020).

Globally, the impact of the pandemic has been remarkable. As indicated by data provided by Statista (2023), by the end of February 2023, the number of infectious cases was close to 700 million. However, the recovery figure is quite positive, with more than 650 million people having recovered from the virus. In terms of human losses, nearly 7 million have been counted (Statista, 2023).

Furthermore, it is a virus that has affected the world, regardless of the region; however, there are differences. In this respect, Europe has been the region most affected by the virus in terms of infections, followed by the Western Pacific region. In terms of human losses, the Americas region is the worst hit followed by the European region (Statista, 2023).

The gravity of the situation is also visible in terms of the global economic impact. This can be seen in the loss of GDP in all economies worldwide, with Latin America, emerging markets, and advanced economies losing the most, by 8.5%, 7%, and 6.5%, respectively (Statista, 2023).

As already mentioned, COVID-19 plunged the entire world into an unprecedented health crisis, affecting in particular the tourism sector (Duro et al., 2021), which by its very nature is more vulnerable to any type of change that may occur (Sánchez-Arcediano & Babinger, 2022). The tourism sector bases its activity on the movement and mobility of people and, therefore, it is in this exchange of people where there is a considerable risk of the spread of the virus and its contagion. This is why an epidemic will have direct consequences on tourism flows (Vega Falcón et al., 2020).

Using statistics provided by Statista (2022b), it can be seen that during the years of the pandemic, there has been a large decline in global GDP from tourism. The share of global GDP in 2020 – less than 6% – is the lowest in the last 23 years. In 2021, a slight recovery is beginning to emerge.

Other striking data can be found in the number of international tourist arrivals worldwide, which in 2020 experienced its lowest number since the late 1980s and early 1990s. Again, from 2021 onwards, the data started to improve, but by 2022 the figures were far from those recorded in 2019 (Statista, 2022b).

The lack of knowledge and experience in epidemiological control meant that decisions had to be taken quickly and forcefully; despite the great difficulty, a balance had to be found that would protect the health of the population without neglecting the country's economy (Velasco González, 2020). For the tourism sector, the measures were particularly harsh, as for other epidemics mobility had never been restricted to curb contagion (Huertas et al., 2020).

2.2. The Case of Tsunamis

The sudden appearance of COVID-19 on the international scene has highlighted the lack of preparedness for an unknown hazard. Given this situation, the authors question whether we are currently facing the same situation as with COVID-19, but with tsunamis. The focus here is on tsunamis, so it is vital to contextualise what a tsunami is and what the tsunami risk is within Spanish territory.

Gómez Pina (2016, p. 38) states that tsunamis are

> a set of waves generated by a very abrupt vertical displacement of a large volume of water. [...] whose origin can be diverse: an earthquake on the seabed, an underwater landslide, a meteorite, a volcanic eruption, a coastal landslide, or the collapse of a large glacier.

With this definition in mind, there are certain regions in the world that are known or associated with tsunami risk (Rodríguez Vidal, 2016) due to their short return periods. Tsunamis such as the 2004 Indian Ocean tsunami (Gómez Pina, 2016), among others, are well known.

In this particular case, the study focuses on the tsunami hazard in Spain, but is there really a risk in Spain?

To talk about tsunamis in Spain, we must go back to 1 November 1755, when the Lisbon earthquake took place (Birkmann et al., 2010). According to data, the earthquake is estimated to have had a magnitude of approximately 8.5–9.0, and it was felt throughout the Iberian Peninsula and in some areas of Europe (Birkmann et al., 2010; Cantavella Nadal, 2015).

This event was particularly destructive due to the fire and tsunami that followed (Martínez Solares, 2016), and it is estimated that the death toll from the tsunami was higher than from the earthquake itself (Cantavella Nadal, 2015).

The exact number of people who died as a result of this catastrophe is unknown, but it is estimated to be between 5,000 and 12,000 in Portugal and more than 1,200 people in Spain as a result of the tsunami (Martínez Solares, 2016).

However, this is not a unique and isolated phenomenon. As Rodríguez Vidal (2016) points out, there is evidence of nine tsunamis prior to the 1,755 tsunamis and another 4 after it, up to the 19th century.

Numerous authors have studied these phenomena; however, it is not known when they will occur again. Gracia Prieto (2016) brings together and compares some findings obtained by several authors who believe they have found a pattern in the large tsunamis that have occurred on the coasts of Cadiz. Some authors point out that the return period at around 700–1,500 years (Gracia Prieto, 2016).

In addition to the Azores-Gibraltar fault, another area at risk of tsunamis is situated in northern Morocco and Algeria, as well as in the Alboran Sea (Cantavella Nadal, 2015). There are records of this with affected areas in the Balearic Islands in 2003 (González Rodríguez, 2016).

From all of the above, it is known that the Iberian Peninsula is susceptible to a tsunami, despite the fact that the return periods are exceptionally low. However, evidence shows that a tsunami can happen at any time and Spain must act through planning and risk management. Due to the cross-cutting nature of the tourism sector, it is vital that the sector is part of this management and acts accordingly, as it is a phenomenon that will greatly affect the coastal areas that experience it.

3. Results

3.1. Measures to Curb COVID-19 Infection in Spain

In Spain, the first case of COVID-19 was detected in 2020 in La Gomera by a German tourist (RTVE, 2022). This fact, added to the situation that was being experienced at the international level, triggered social alarm.

At the national level, the establishment of the state of alarm stands out. This measure, noted for being one of the most restrictive and harshest, was extended several times (Pérez Guerra, 2020). The implications of this state of alarm meant that all non-essential businesses were obliged to remain closed, and people who did not belong to the group of essential workers had to stay at home (Pérez Guerra, 2020).

Since the first cases, schools were closed, sports competitions were cancelled, IMSERSO (Institute for the Elderly and Social Services) trips were cancelled and all events with more than 1,000 attendees were banned (Abascal, 2020; Pérez Guerra, 2020). During the first 2 years of the pandemic, provincial closures and closures by health areas were implemented, preventing population movements on different scales (Sánchez-Arcediano & Babinger, 2022).

Furthermore, the Ministry of Health (2021) established a series of general measures to be taken by each and every individual in Spain. The following measures stand out (Table 1).

All these measures were disseminated through illustrated posters, the media, social networks, etc. Moreover, documents were also created with information on the virus, how to detect close contact, how to act in case of symptoms, vaccination, etc. (Ministry of Health, 2021).

In addition, the Ministry of Health (2020a) conducted the campaign '*We can all stop this virus*', financed by the European Regional Development Fund—Spain's Multi-regional Operational Program. This campaign was created with the aim of raising awareness among the Spanish population and preventing the spread of the virus. For its dissemination, videos, banners, etc., were created.

3.2. Specific Measures for the Tourism Sector to Curb the Spread of COVID-19

Despite these measures, there is a turning point for the tourism sector brought about by two events. Firstly, tourism was seen as one of the main sources of contagion, as it was pointed out that the first contagions in Spain were at the hands of tourists who had come to the country on holiday (RTVE, 2022).

The second fact was the data collected. As is evident, confinements made travel impossible, so tourism activity came to a complete halt.

Given this situation, governments, all the relevant public administrations, tourist destinations, and companies in the sector, were forced to intervene by establishing a series of measures to help the economic recovery of tourism activity. In developing these measures, the involvement of tourism stakeholders was essential.

From here onwards we will cite Sánchez-Arcediano and Babinger (2022), who have already carried out an analysis of the measures that have been implemented in previous research.

Table 1.   Measures to Prevent COVID-19 Infection in Spain.

Use of face mask to cover nose and mouth	Maintenance of interpersonal distance of at least 1.5 m	Frequent hand washing
Use of disinfectant products such as hydroalcoholic gel	Reduction of social contact	Social relationship with a closed, small, and stable circle
Ventilation of spaces	Development of outdoor activities	Isolation at home (persons with symptoms, COVID-19 positive, in close contact and awaiting diagnosis)

Source: Prepared by the authors on the basis of the Spanish Ministry of Health (2021).

Among the tourism measures, it is important to highlight the elaboration of guides, promoted by the Secretary of State for Tourism and the Ministry of Health and drawn up by the Institute for Spanish Tourism Quality (ICTE). This resulted in a twenty-two *Guidelines for SARS-CoV-2 Coronavirus Infection Reduction in the Tourism Sector* for nearly all tourist activities (Ministry of Industry, Trade and Crafts, 2020).

These guides contain specific measures in order to guarantee safety and quality standards. This would protect tourists, local population, and workers of the establishments concerned. This measure is a milestone, as it standardises processes for services.

The implementation of the measures included in the guidelines was not compulsory but subject to the voluntary nature of each establishment.

For Spain and tourism sector in particular, the creation of these guidelines is a remarkable achievement as they resulted in the International Organization for Standardization (ISO) Specification ISO/PAS 5643 *Requirements and recommendations for the reduction of COVID-19 infection in the tourism industry.*

It also highlights the work of the Institute for Spanish Tourism Quality and the Spanish Tourist Offices Abroad (OTS), which continued during the pandemic to promote the Q mark for Tourism Quality and to promote Spain internationally as a safe destination.

In addition, Turespaña launched the *Travel Safe* campaign with the aim of promoting Spain as a safe destination internationally. This campaign led to the creation of a website with recommendations and information of interest to all tourists wishing to visit Spain.

3.3. Measures to Reduce the Risk of COVID-19 Infection in Spanish Coastal Areas

Spanish tourism has always stood out for its sun and beach destinations (Vizcaíno Ponferrada, 2015). With COVID-19 and the consequent measures to reduce contagion, these tourist areas have also been affected.

In 2020, all municipalities in coastal areas were forced to close access to beaches to prevent travel to these areas in order to curb contagion (EFE, 2020). An example is Cullera, the first town council to close beaches and tourist services and to place the red flag to ban bathing; these measures were agreed with representatives of Cullera's tourist sector (EFE, 2020).

These measures were also taken strategically as a large number of the population decided to move to their second homes in coastal areas for confinement; the municipalities wanted to avoid such movements. However, other municipalities considered that it was not necessary to close the beaches (EFE, 2020).

In Costa del Sol the measures went further, and bars, restaurants and terraces were closed because customers and tourists did not follow the recommendations to stay indoors (EFE, 2020).

In May 2020, the Ministry of Science, and Innovation with the Spanish National Research Council (CSIC, 2020) issued a *Report on SARS-CoV-2 Transmission in Beaches and Swimming Pools*, an issue of direct relevance to tourism in coastal areas. This report clarifies doubts about the transmission and survival of the virus in certain waters and their treatment. In addition, it assists and facilitates management and decision-making on the reopening of these sites and how to maintain them in the safest way.

This document mentions that it is necessary to adopt measures in these spaces that are included in other reports, such as the *Protocol and Guide to Good Practices for Commercial Activity in Physical and Non-Sedentary Establishments* of the Ministry of Industry, Trade and Tourism (MICT, 2020).

Subsequently, the Ministry of Health (2020b) promoted a report on *Recommendations for the opening of beaches and bathing areas after the COVID-19 crisis*, with the participation of other organisms. This report includes an assessment of the transmission of the virus in water, defines the actions to be conducted prior to the opening of these areas and includes preventive measures in order to guarantee safety once these areas are reopened.

3.4. Measures for the Reduction of Tsunami Hazard: The Case of Spain

In Spain, Civil Protection is the public service responsible for protecting people and property during emergencies and disasters (Law 17/2015, of 9 July, on the National Civil Protection System, 2015, Article 1). Among its functions is the creation of the National Civil Protection System Strategy, which must analyse the hazards that may affect people and property in Spanish territory (Article 4).

In 2013, Spain became a member of the Intergovernmental Coordination Group for the North-eastern Atlantic, the Mediterranean and Connected Seas Tsunami Early Warning and Mitigation System (NEAMTWS) and the National Tsunami Warning Network is created through the Spanish National Geographic Institute, the Directorate General of Civil Protection and Emergencies, State Ports and other organisations (Directorate General of the National Geographic Institute and Directorate General of Civil Protection and Emergencies, 2021).

In 2015, the Basic Civil Protection Planning Guideline for the Hazard of Tsunamis was approved. Although the tsunami hazard is not explicitly mentioned, the previous regulation does provide the possibility of considering all hazards that could affect it.

There is evidence of tsunamis and tsunamigenic zones close to the Spanish coasts, which highlight the need for a special plan at the national and regional levels (Basic Guideline for Civil Protection Planning in the Event of Tsunami Hazard, 2015, Article 1).

This Basic Guideline establishes four priority axes: risk assessment, establishment of the National Tsunami Warning System, organisation of the operability of the plans, and education and information (Article 3).

The first Tsunami hazard maps of the Spanish coasts were created in 2017 (Proes & Principia, 2017).

Despite the regulation, there was a hiatus for years, where no further progress was made.

Nevertheless, the National Civil Protection Strategy (Directorate General of Civil Protection, 2019), approved by the National Security Council, emerged, which identifies the following hazards: floods, forest fires, earthquakes and tsunamis, volcanoes, adverse weather events, accidents in installations or processes where hazardous substances are used or stored, transport of dangerous goods by road and rail and nuclear and radiological.

For all of them, a description of the hazard, risk drivers, regulatory and management instruments and priority actions are provided. Tsunamis are mentioned, and it is said that there is an extremely low perception by the population (Directorate General for Civil Protection, 2019).

In 2020, the Regional Government of Andalusia and the city council of Cádiz reported that tsunami plans are being drawn up (Hernández Mateo, 2020); practical drills were conducted in 2021 (El Confidencial, 2021). In 2021, the State Plan for Civil Protection against the Hazard of Tsunamis was also approved (Spanish National Geographic Institute, 2021).

In 2022, as part of the UNESCO Tsunami Ready Programme, the municipality of Chipiona is working towards safety certification (Bernal, 2022).

No progress has been made in this area by the tourism sector, nor is it being contemplated for the time being.

4. Discussion and Conclusions

After analysing the measures implemented for each hazard, it is necessary to put them together.

It is notable that the number of measures developed and implemented for the COVID-19 is higher than those defined for tsunamis.

There are eighteen measures to curb the COVID-19 contagion (not counting the specific measures of municipalities and autonomous communities), compared to eight for tsunamis (Table 2).

It is important to note that measures for tsunami hazards are of a normative nature. The bases are established for the creation of specific plans and the requirements that must appear in them, but at regional and local level the current regulations have not yet been complied with.

This fact poses a significant risk since the exact date of occurrence of a tsunami is unknown and there is currently no protocol for action after a tsunami warning.

It is vital to detect and convey the warning message, but this is not useful without specific measures to assist evacuation in the event of a disaster.

COVID-19 has been an unprecedented catastrophe and the numbers of infections and deaths justify all efforts to overcome this situation. This is evident from the considerable number of measures and proposals that have been put forward in recent years, the speed with which decisions have been taken and the great collaboration and cooperation in their creation.

In the specific case of Spain, tourism is a driving force of the economy, and it was necessary to take decisions as quickly as possible to control the dramatic situation.

Decision-making has not been an easy task and particularly complicated because of the need to strike a balance between protecting the population and the

Table 2.   Actions Conducted for COVID-19 and Tsunamis in Spain.

General Measures	
COVID-19	**Tsunamis**
1. Establishment of the state of alarm.	1. Member of the North-eastern Atlantic, the Mediterranean, and Connected Seas Tsunami Early Warning and Mitigation System (NEAMTWS).
2. Non-essential businesses closed.	2. National Tsunami Warning Network.
3. Non-essential workers had to stay at home.	3. Royal Decree 1053/2015 of 20 November 2015, approving the Basic Guideline for Civil Protection Planning in the Event of Tsunami Hazard.
4. Schools were closed.	4. Tsunami hazard maps of the Spanish coasts.
5. Sports competitions were cancelled.	5. National Civil Protection Strategy.
6. Events with more than 1,000 attendees were banned in communities with high incidence.	6. Some simulation exercises.
7. Provincial closures and health areas were implemented.	7. The Andalusian Territorial Emergency Plan for Andalusia and the Emergency Plan for the hazard of tsunamis.
8. Use of face mask.	8. The city council of Chipiona is working to achieve the UNESCO Tsunami Ready certification.
9. Frequent hand washing.	
10. Use of disinfectant products.	
11. Ventilation of spaces.	
12. Interpersonal distance of 1.5 m.	
13. Reduction of social contact.	
14. Development of outdoor activities.	
15. Isolation at home.	
16. Relationship with closed circles.	
17. Dissemination of information on the virus, vaccines, etc.	
18. Awareness campaigns.	

Table 2. (*Continued*).

Measures for the Tourism Sector	
COVID-19	**Tsunamis**
1. IMSERSO trips were cancelled.	No measures to cope with tsunamis have been implemented in the tourism sector.
2. Perimeter and border closures.	
3. Access to beaches closed.	
4. Red flags to ban bathing.	
5. Bars, restaurants, and terraces were closed.	
6. Guidelines for SARS-CoV-2 Coronavirus Infection Reduction in the Tourism Sector.	
7. Specification ISO/PAS 5643 Requirements and recommendations for the reduction of COVID-19 infection in the tourism industry.	
8. Protocol and Guide of Good Practices for Commercial Activity in Physical and Non-Sedentary Establishments of the Ministry of Industry, Trade and Tourism.	
9. Report on SARS-CoV-2 Transmission in Beaches and Swimming Pools.	
10. Promotion of the Q mark for Tourism Quality.	
11. Promotion of Spain internationally as a safe destination.	
12. Travel Safe campaign.	
13. Recommendations for the opening of beaches and bathing areas after the COVID-19 crisis.	

Source: Prepared by the authors.

economy (Velasco González, 2020). This factor is compounded by widespread ignorance and lack of previous experience, which has led to a number of highly controversial and often unsupported measures.

Despite all of the above, it is important to focus again on the comparison made in relation to the measures for each of the hazards.

In Spain, we have not experienced a tsunami of catastrophic proportions since 1755, so there is a general lack of knowledge about this hazard. It is impossible to determine the exact date of occurrence, so a tsunami can occur at any time. If priority is given to other types of hazards with a shorter return period and planning and management of this risk is postponed, what is being done is to generate more insecurity and vulnerability, which will become more pronounced over time.

The lack of decision-making in the present will condition the future, and they will be forced to improvise on the spot, as has already happened in the case of COVID-19.

However, there is hope as planning is being conducted at the regional and municipal levels. This work has been resumed as of 2019, four years after the regulatory framework, so it is only complying with the law. In addition, not all communities are working on tsunamis, as is the case in many provinces and municipalities.

It is known that Andalusia is working on it, as is the city of Cádiz or the municipality of Chipiona, but there is still a lot of work to be done before it can be said that these places are prepared for tsunamis and even more to say that Spain is prepared for the hazard of tsunamis.

The experience with COVID-19 has served to set a precedent for the management of a pandemic. Protocols are now in place to control a situation such as the one experienced worldwide in the future. We have a certain '*head start*' in the event of an analogous situation occurring again. However, it is negative that all the knowledge acquired, preparedness and awareness-raising has been achieved once a major disaster has occurred. Do we as a society really need to find ourselves in a critical situation to make decisions? Should we wait for something bad to happen before we plan and manage?

We are in a VUCA environment where it is increasingly difficult to predict events that are going to take place, and even more so if we are talking about hazards. This uncertainty of not knowing when a phenomenon is going to occur should make us alert and start preparing for this event to avoid making decisions quickly, hastily, poorly, or even without being based on proven evidence. Of course, it is difficult to anticipate and plan for an unknown event for which you have no data or do not know what its proportions may be.

It is precisely anticipation and precaution that would help reduce volatility, uncertainty, complexity, and ambiguity. It is the lessons learned during COVID-19 that will enable us to be prepared for a similar event, since we already know how to identify the indicators detected and will allow us to manage the crisis more quickly. It will also allow us to respond better in this VUCA world.

If we continue not to plan for other hazards, we will remain in a VUCA environment where we will not know when the next catastrophe will occur and, by the time action is taken, it may be too late. Instead, if we continue to work on risk planning, we will be striving to mitigate the negative impacts of something that is unstoppable and uncontrollable.

As can be seen in Table 2, there is still a lot of work to be done in terms of tsunami risk. Even more so considering that it is a hazard that is not known by society, which has not caused a profound impact like COVID-19, that the indicators of its presence are unknown, let alone what to do in the event of a tsunami.

If Spain is to be recognised as a safe tourist destination, we must work together and address all hazards to achieve safety standards. Of course, having this preparedness in place does not eradicate the risk, but it does ensure that on the day it occurs there will be a protocol in place to help minimise the impact.

Acknowledgements

This research is part of the funding programme of the Universidad Complutense de Madrid – Banco Santander for contracts for the training of doctors who conduct a doctoral thesis and the Training of Research Staff (Predoctoral UCM).

References

Abascal, L. (25 de marzo de 2020). El Gobierno confirma el primer caso de coronavirus en España. El Plural. https://cutt.ly/4W91rRj

Arold Lario, P. (2021). Apuntes para la gestión del turismo en España tras la crisis sanitaria de la Covid-19. *Pasos. Revista de Turismo y Patrimonio Cultural*, *19*(1), 189–194. https://doi.org/10.25145/j.pasos.2021.19.012

Bernal, L. (2022, 25 de junio de). España estrena para cuando llegue el tsunami: un plan y 2 tipos de evacuaciones en una hora. *20 minutos*. https://www.20minutos. es/noticia/5019601/0/asi-se-prepara-espana-frente-a-los-tsunamis-solo-tenemos-una-hora-para-actuar-hasta-que-llegue-una-ola-de-5-metros/

Birkmann, J., Teichman, K. V., Welle, T., González, M., & Olabarrieta, M. (2010). The unperceived risk to Europe's coasts: Tsunamis and the vulnerability of Cadiz, Spain. *Natural Hazards and Earth System Sciences*, *10*, 2659–2675. https://doi.org/10.5194/nhess-10-2659-2010

Cantavella Nadal, J. V. (2015). La sorprendente fuerza del agua: los tsunamis. *Anuario del Observatorio Astronómico de Madrid*, (1), 409–436. https://astronomia.ign.es/rknowsys-theme/images/webAstro/paginas/documentos/Anuario/lasorprendete-fuerzadelaguaTsunamis.pdf

Castello, V. (2020). Desafíos y oportunidades para el turismo en el marco de la pandemia COVID-19. *Cuadernos de Política Exterior Argentina*, (131), 115–118. https://doi.org/10.35305/cc.vi131.85

Covarrubias Moreno, O. M. (2020). VUCA World y lecciones de interdependencia COVID-19. *GIGAPP Estudios Working Papers*, *7*(182–189), 513–532. https://www.gigapp.org/ewp/index.php/GIGAPP-EWP/article/view/225

Directorate General of Civil Protection and Emergencies. (2019). *Estrategia Nacional de Protección Civil*. https://www.proteccioncivil.es/documents/20121/57128/Estrate giaNacionaProtecci%C3%B3nCivil.pdf/ac29d248-6d09-6296-6b5b-8903ef84609 7?t=1608295060256

Directorate General of the National Geographic Institute and Directorate General of Civil Protection and Emergencies. (2021). *Plan Estatal de Protección Civil ante el riesgo de Maremotos. Edición comentada* [Archivo PDF]. Instituto Geográfico Nacional. https://www.ign.es/web/resources/acercaDe/libDigPub/Plan-Estatal-Maremotos. pdf

Duro, J. A., Pérez-Laborda, A., Turrión-Prats, J., & Fernández-Fernández, M. (2021). Covid-19 and tourism vulnerability. *Tourism Management Perspectives*, *38*, 1–12. https://doi.org/10.1016/j.tmp.2021.100819

EFE. (2020, 14 de marzo de). Municipios costeros de toda España cierran sus playas para evitar contagios. *La Vanguardia*. https://www.lavanguardia.com/vida/20200314/474132919017/municipios-costeros-de-toda-espana-cierran-sus-playas-para-evitar-contagios.html

El Confidencial. (2021, 20 de octubre de). Simulacro de tsunami sin precedentes en Huelva y Cádiz: así se enfrentan a un maremoto. *El Confidencial*. https://www.elconfidencial.com/espana/andalucia/2021-10-20/simulacro-tsunami-huelva-cadiz_3309902/

Fernández Alles, M. T. (2020). El impacto de la crisis sanitaria del Covid-19 en el sector turístico español. *Desarrollo, Economía y Sociedad, 9*(1), 36–40. https://doi.org/10.38017/23228040.655

Galeana, P. (2020). Las epidemias a lo largo de la historia. *Antropología Americana, 5*(10), 13–45.

Gómez Pina, G. (2016). ¿Qué es un tsunami?: importancia de la educación ciudadana. En IERD. Instituto Español para la Reducción de los Desastres. *El riesgo de maremotos en la Península Ibérica a la luz de la catástrofe del 1 de noviembre de 1755*. Jornadas técnicas IERD. https://ierd.es/wp-content/uploads/2017/03/El-riesgo-de-maremotos-en-la-Pen%C3%ADnsula-Ib%C3%A9rica.pdf

González Rodríguez, M. (2016). Desarrollo de metodologías para el cálculo del riesgo por tsunami y aplicación para el caso de Cádiz. En IERD. Instituto Español para la Reducción de los Desastres. *El riesgo de maremotos en la Península Ibérica a la luz de la catástrofe del 1 de noviembre de 1755*. Jornadas técnicas IERD. https://ierd.es/wp-content/uploads/2017/03/El-riesgo-de-maremotos-en-la-Pen%C3%ADnsula-Ib%C3%A9rica.pdf

Gracia Prieto, F. J. (2016). Registros de paleotsunamis en el litoral atlántico de la provincia de Cádiz: antecedentes del maremoto de 1755. En IERD. Instituto Español para la Reducción de los Desastres. *El riesgo de maremotos en la Península Ibérica a la luz de la catástrofe del 1 de noviembre de 1755*. Jornadas técnicas IERD. https://ierd.es/wp-content/uploads/2017/03/El-riesgo-de-maremotos-en-la-Pen%C3%ADnsula-Ib%C3%A9rica.pdf

Guirao-Goris, J. A., Olmedo Salas, A., & Ferrer Ferrandis, E. (2008). El artículo de revisión. *Revista Iberoamericana de Enfermería Comunitaria, 1*(1), 1–25. https://www.uv.es/joguigo/castellano/castellano/Investigacion_files/el_articulo_de_revision.pdf

Hernández Mateo, P. (2020, 01 de marzo de). Cádiz ya trabaja en su plan de emergencia ante un maremoto. *Diario de Cádiz*. https://www.diariodecadiz.es/cadiz/Cadiz-trabaja-plan-emergencia-maremoto_0_1441956218.html

Huertas, A., Oliveira, A., & Girotto, M. (2020). Gestión comunicativa de crisis de las oficinas nacionales de turismo de España e Italia ante la Covid-19. *Profesional de la Información, 29*(4), 1–18. https://doi.org/10.3145/epi.2020.jul.10

Mantecón, A. (2020). La crisis sistémica del turismo: una perspectiva global en tiempos de pandemia. In M. Simancas Cruz, R. Hernández Martín, & N. Padrón Fumero (Coord.), *Turismo pos-COVID-19. Reflexiones, retos y oportunidades* (pp. 19–29). Cátedra de Turismo CajaCanarias-Ashotel. Universidad de La Laguna. https://doi.org/10.25145/b.Turismopos-COVID-19.2020

Martínez Solares, J. M. (2016). El impacto del terremoto de 1755 en Portugal y España: efectos del maremoto de 1755 en las costas de Cádiz y Huelva (pp. 1–10). En IERD. Instituto Español para la Reducción de los Desastres. *El riesgo de maremotos en la Península Ibérica a la luz de la catástrofe del 1 de noviembre de 1755*. Jornadas técnicas IERD. https://ierd.es/wp-content/uploads/2017/03/El-riesgo-de-maremotos-en-la-Pen%C3%ADnsula-Ib%C3%A9rica.pdf

Ministry of Science and Innovation & Spanish National Research Council (CSIC). (2020). *Informe sobre transmisión del SARS-CoV-2 en playas y piscinas*. https://www.csic.es/sites/default/files/informe_playasypiscinas_csic.pdf

Ministry of Industry, Trade and Crafts. (2020). *Guías para la reducción del contagio por el coronavirus SARS-CoV-2 en el sector turístico.* https://www.mincotur.gob.es/es-es/covid-19/turismo/Paginas/Guias-sector-turistico.aspx

Ministry of Health). (2020a). *Materiales campaña coronavirus, Este virus lo paramos unidos.* Retrieved March 23, 2023, from https://www.sanidad.gob.es/campannas/campanas20/coronavirus/materiales.htm

Ministry of Health. (2020b). *Recomendaciones para la apertura de playas y zonas de baño tras la crisis del COVID-19.* https://www.sanidad.gob.es/profesionales/saludPublica/ccayes/alertasActual/nCov/documentos/Recomendaciones_apertura_playas.pdf

Ministry of Health. (2021). *Las 6M siempre en Mente [PDF file].* https://www.sanidad.gob.es/profesionales/saludPublica/ccayes/alertasActual/nCov/documentos/Infografia_6M.pdf

Moreno-Sánchez, F., Cross, R. M. F., Alonso, L. M. T., & Elizondo, O. A. (2018). Las grandes epidemias que cambiaron al mundo. *Anales Médicos de la Asociación Médica del Centro Médico ABC, 63*(2), 151–156. https://www.medigraphic.com/cgi-bin/new/resumen.cgi?IDARTICULO=80286

Pérez Guerra, R. (2020). Algunas notas sobre el derecho administrativo del turismo: Covid-19. *Revista General de Derecho Administrativo, 54*(4), 1–41.

Proes & Principia. (2017). Peligrosidad tsunamis en las costas españolas. *Principia.* https://principia.es/en/peligrosidad-tsunamis/

Rodríguez Vidal, J. (2016). Registros de paleotsunamis en las costas del litoral atlántico de la provincia de Huelva: antecedentes del maremoto de 1755. En IERD. Instituto Español para la Reducción de los Desastres. *El riesgo de maremotos en la Península Ibérica a la luz de la catástrofe del 1 de noviembre de 1755.* Jornadas técnicas IERD. https://ierd.es/wp-content/uploads/2017/03/El-riesgo-de-maremotos-en-la-Pen%C3%ADnsula-Ib%C3%A9rica.pdf

Rodríguez-Antón, J. M., & Alonso-Almeida, M. M. (2020). COVID-19 impacts and recovery strategies: The case of the hospitality industry in Spain. *Sustainability, 12*(20), 1–17. https://doi.org/10.3390/su12208599

Romero-Saritama, J. M., Simaluiza, J., & Fernández, H. (2021). Medidas de prevención para evitar el contagio por la COVID-19: de lo cotidiano a lo técnico-científico. *Revista Española de Salud Pública, 95*, 1–14. https://scielo.isciii.es/pdf/resp/v95/1135-5727-resp-95-e202104051.pdf

Royal Decree 1053/2015 of 2015. Approving the Basic Guideline for Civil Protection Planning in the Event of Tsunami Hazard. 20 November 2015. N° 279. https://www.boe.es/eli/es/rd/2015/11/20/1053/dof/spa/pdf

RTVE. (2022, 31 de enero de). Dos años del primer caso de COVID-19 en España: un turista alemán de vacaciones en La Gomera. *RTVE.* https://www.rtve.es/noticias/20220131/dos-anos-primer-caso-covid-19-espana/2275660.shtml

Sánchez-Arcediano, S., & Babinger, F. (2022). Covid-19 infection reduction measures as a safety certification in the Spanish tourism sector. *Revista de Estudios Andaluces,* (44), 72–89. https://doi.org/10.12795/rea.2022.i44.04

Statista. (2022b). Industries & markets. Coronavirus: Impact on the tourism industry worldwide. did-70298-1.

Statista. (2023). *Politics & society. The COVID-19 pandemic.* did-71007-1.

Trilla, A. (2020). One world, one health: The novel coronavirus COVID-19 epidemic. *Medicina clinica, 154*(5), 175–177. https://doi.org/10.1016/j.medcli.2020.02.002

Vega Falcón, V., Castro Sánchez, F., & Romero Fernández, A. J. (2020). *Impacto de la Covid-19 en el turismo mundial. Revista Universidad y Sociedad, 12*(S1), 207–216. https://rus.ucf.edu.cu/index.php/rus/article/view/1777

Velasco González, M. (2020). La pandemia como problema de política pública. In M. Simancas Cruz, R. Hernández Martín, & N. Padrón Fumero (Coords.), *Turismo pos-COVID-19. Reflexiones, retos y oportunidades* (pp. 131–145). Cátedra de Turismo CajaCanarias-Ashotel. Universidad de La Laguna. https://doi.org/10.25145/b. Turismopos-COVID-19.2020

Vizcaíno Ponferrada, M. L. (2015). Evolución del turismo en España: el turismo cultural. *International Journal of Scientific Management and Tourism, 4*, 75–95.

Chapter 13

Crime and Insecurity as Factors of Uncertainty and Erosion of the Tourist Image of Mexico

Carlos Mario Amaya Molinar and Irma Magaña Carrillo

The University of Colima, Colima, Mexico

Abstract

Mexico is a nation that attracts significant volumes of international tourists annually. The country possesses abundant natural and cultural assets, with significant opportunities for its tourism sector. Its geographical positioning, favourable weather, and the hospitality of its inhabitants enhance these prospects. Simultaneously, this country exhibits a heightened susceptibility to natural calamities and a dearth of public safety measures. The Mexican tourism industry encounters significant challenges within the framework of the VUCA (volatility, uncertainty, complexity, and ambiguity) model. These challenges include the inherent natural risks associated with the country, the escalating impact of global warming, and the proliferation of organised crime. Within this context, the management of tourist destinations in Mexico neglects significant factors highlighted in theoretical models associated with competitiveness and sustainability. These factors include public security, crisis and disaster management, political will, load capacity, and destination's image. The predicament encountered by Mexican tour operators is formidable, as the socio-political circumstances in Mexico facilitate the expansion of organised crime, leading to its infiltration into various sectors and regions of the country, with significant impacts on tourist operations. This chapter analyses the effects of organised crime on Mexico's tourism industry, utilising the VUCA framework as a conceptual lens.

Keywords: Tourist destinations; crisis; organised crime; insecurity; VUCA

Tourism in a VUCA World: Managing the Future of Tourism, 187–201
doi:10.1108/978-1-83753-674-020241013

Introduction

Mexican tour operators have effectively cultivated resilience to natural disasters through the acquisition of insurance and the assimilation of valuable experiential knowledge. Nevertheless, in recent times, Mexican tourist destinations have encountered a persistent and formidable challenge: organised crime. The observed detrimental social phenomenon experienced a significant surge in Mexico throughout the initial decade of the 21st century. It transitioned from being confined to specific sectors and regions within the country to actively challenging the authority of the state across a substantial portion of the national territory.

The proliferation of organised crime in Mexico is compatible with the conceptual framework of VUCA as delineated in scholarly discourse. This category of criminal activity is commonly linked to drug trafficking; however, it is regrettable that criminals have expanded their operations to encompass additional illicit practices, including extortion, kidnapping, human trafficking, and, inevitably, money laundering. The presence of organised crime activities is evidently contingent upon the complicity of governmental institutions, while simultaneously being influenced by socioeconomic factors such as poverty, marginalisation, and educational deficiencies among significant portions of the populace. According to Montero (2014), the impact of organised crime on tourism activities has been predominantly adverse.

This chapter is organised in the following manner: the initial section provides a comprehensive examination of the scholarly literature pertaining to the VUCA model (vulnerability, uncertainty, complexity, and ambiguity) as it relates to the field of tourism. The subsequent section provides a concise analysis of the genesis and progression of organised crime in Mexico, spanning from the post-revolutionary period to the contemporary era. The subsequent section of the chapter delineates the primary modalities through which organised crime exerts influence on the domestic tourism sector. The fourth section of this study examines the effects of organised crime activities on tourist destinations within the framework of the VUCA model. In conclusion, the information provided is thoroughly examined and conclusions are drawn regarding the content of the document. The methodology employed in the development of this chapter involves the utilisation of documentary research, including the examination of official statistics, academic journals, and online resources.

The Presence of Vulnerability, Uncertainty, Complexity, and Ambiguity (VUCA) within the Domain of Tourism is a Significant Concern

This section provides an overview of the key attributes of the VUCA theoretical framework, namely vulnerability, uncertainty, complexity, and ambiguity. Subsequently, it presents a range of applications of this model within the academic domain of tourism studies.

The concept of VUCA was originally introduced at the U.S. Army War College by Bennis and Nanus (1985) as a means to enhance the leadership capabilities of military officers in highly volatile, uncertain, complex, and ambiguous environments. Subsequently, the business literature adopted the VUCA framework, akin to the adoption of the term 'strategy', and it gained popularity in this domain.

In their study, Millar et al. (2018) emphasise the contemporary significance of the construction, noting the rapid and disruptive changes taking place on a global scale in areas such as climate, social dynamics, politics, demographics, technology, and commerce. Similarly, Wursten (2018) discusses a sense of restlessness or unease experienced by individuals, as they perceive untimely global transformations that distance them from their familiar traditional environment. Fig. 1 presents the acronym components and their utilisation according to Bennett and Lemoine (2014).

Šimková and Hoffmannová (2021) explicate the utilisation of the VUCA model in the context of rural tourism, characterising the business environment as intricate, volatile, dynamic, and exceedingly uncertain. This assessment remains valid even before factoring in variables such as criminal activities, natural calamities, and organised crime. In their study on the crises in tourist destinations, Petković et al. (2023) incorporate crime as one of the crises that can affect tourist locations. They identify various types of crises, including natural disasters, and economic, political, social, health, and infrastructure situations. Within this framework, the authors categorise the impact of organised crime as an economic and social event.

Ritchie and Crouch (2003) assert that crime plays a significant role in the realm of crisis and disaster management within tourist destinations. They argue that

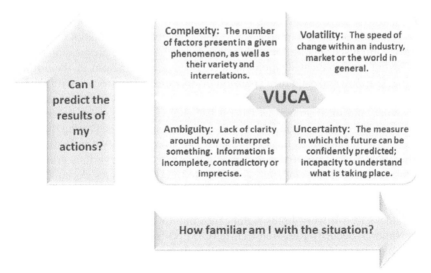

Fig. 1. VUCA and Its Application. *Source*: Adapted from Bennett and Lemoine (2014).

crime negatively impacts the destination's image, reduces its competitiveness, and dissuades potential tourists from visiting. The authors examine crime from three distinct perspectives: (a) crime resulting from heightened tourist activity, (b) dissemination of crime-related information and news about a destination, and (c) crimes specifically targeting tourists. Another crucial concept highlighted by the authors in relation to tourist competitiveness, consistent with the context of Mexico, is the political determination to enact measures aimed at enhancing the destination's competitiveness. Specifically, in the context of crime, it is pertinent to examine the extent to which governmental authorities possess the resolve to address this issue effectively. To what extent are the Mexican authorities politically inclined to address the issue of insecurity?

The Phenomenon of Organised Crime in Mexico

This section provides a concise analysis of the historical origins of organised crime in Mexico. It explores its emergence approximately a century ago, its gradual evolution throughout the twentieth century with the tacit approval of the authorities, and its rapid escalation in the first decade of the current century.

Background

The historical roots of drug trafficking in Mexico date back to a period spanning over a century. Valdés (2014) highlights the emphasis of indigenous drug traffickers on the cultivation and distribution of marijuana and opium destined for the United States. Since their inception, these groups have stood out by their considerable financial resources and propensity for employing violent tactics. With participants in an illicit market, traditional legal frameworks and judicial systems are ineffective in resolving commercial conflicts. The formidable capabilities of these criminal organisations coalesce with the inherent vulnerabilities of Mexico's security and justice institutions. The subsequent phase in the progression of drug trafficking was predicated upon the increased need for heroin in the adjacent nation, thereby catalysing the expansion of operations. Confronted with the burgeoning nature of this enterprise, individuals such as farmers, politicians, military personnel, and local as well as federal law enforcement agencies proceeded to partake in the cultivation and distribution of illicit substances. During the period outlined by the author as the second phase, spanning from 1940 to 1980, there is a discernible initiation of the consolidation process among various groups into sizable cartels. This development goes back to the United States' declaration of a war on drugs and its subsequent intense pressure on the Mexican government to combat these criminal organisations.

Valdés's (2014) work holds significance due to his tenure as the director of the National Security Research Centre (CISEN) from 2006 to 2011, despite its potential characterisation as an institutional approach. The author conducts an analysis of the initial institutional ambiguity surrounding the approach to drug trafficking pursued by the governments of Mexico and the United States. The Mexican government is purportedly complicit in the illicit operations of cartels (Ortiz, 2013), simultaneously benefiting from them, despite its ostensible efforts to combat them. Conversely, the US government attributes responsibility to the Mexican government for its leniency, all the while permitting the operation of extensive networks involved in drug distribution and money laundering within its own borders. The drug trade industry heavily relies on the substantial demand for illicit drugs within the United States. This demand generates significant financial resources for criminal organisations, while the accessibility of firearms in neighbouring countries enables them to establish private militias, often comprised of sicarios (hit men) who have previously served in law enforcement or the military.

Throughout the 20th century, a series of events transpired that transformed Mexican drug trafficking organisations into multinational corporations, establishing connections with partners from South America, Asia, and Europe. These organisations developed expertise in the importation of drug shipments into the United States from diverse global regions. In Mexico, there has been a consolidation of influential regional entities engaged in territorial disputes. The phenomenon of democratisation and decentralisation within national governments has resulted in the fragmentation of institutions, authorities, and security bodies. This fragmentation has created an environment conducive to the activities of criminal groups, who have strategically employed advanced intelligence technology and weaponry to counteract law enforcement agencies. According to Blanco and Cohen (2017), the absence of law and order provides organised crime with significant opportunities to exploit institutional and legal loopholes. Moreover, their access to substantial financial resources enables them to engage the services of various professionals specialising in areas such as arms management, law, finance, and technology. According to Valdés (2014), Mexican cartels experienced a bolstering of their capabilities in 2006 through the acquisition of high-powered weaponry sourced from the United States. This weaponry facilitated their engagement in inter-cartel conflicts, while also enabling them to expand their operations into areas such as extortion, kidnapping, and human trafficking.

A commonly employed metric for assessing the extent of organised crime activity in Mexico is the tally of intentional homicides perpetrated within the nation. Although it is indeed accurate that a majority of the victims are affiliated with criminal gangs, the available data presents a compelling case. Conversely, the high number of homicides poses challenges to their investigation and increases the potential for misidentifying unrelated conflicts. According to the report released by the National Institute of Statistics, Geography and Informatics in 2023, the homicide rate in the year 2022 stood at 12 per 100,000 inhabitants on a national scale. The report further reveals that 78% of these homicides were committed using firearms or bladed weapons, while 88% of the victims were male. Based on the data provided by the Council for Public Security and Criminal Justice (2023), it is evident that the majority of cities with the highest recorded murder rates are located in Mexico, with nine out of the top ten cities falling within this category. Fig. 2 illustrates the temporal progression of intentional homicides from 1990 to 2021.

Fig. 2.   Incidents of Deliberate Homicides in Mexico Spanning the Years from 1990 to 2021. *Source*: Instituto Nacional de Estadística, Geografía e Informática (INEGI) (2023).

The Influence of Insecurity on Tourist Destinations in Mexico

This section explores the impact of organised crime on the travel industry and hospitality sector in tourist destinations, with a particular focus on its disproportionate effects on the local population and small- to medium-sized tourist enterprises, as opposed to visitors.

In the realm of international tourism, a significant proportion of individuals who visit Mexico originate from the United States. The research conducted by Lozano Cortés (2016), Monterrubio (2013), de la Torre and Navarrete (2018), Mylonopoulos et al. (2016), and Corona (2018) provides evidence that the presence of organised crime has a detrimental impact on the perception of a tourist destination, leading to a significant decline in the number of potential tourists willing to visit locations deemed unsafe. According to a document published on the official website of the US State Department (2023), it is advised that American citizens refrain from travelling to 30 out of the 32 states in Mexico. The document highlights this recommendation in its summary section.

Violent offences, encompassing acts such as homicide, abduction, motor vehicle theft, and larceny, exhibit a pervasive and prevalent nature in Mexico. The US government possesses a restricted capability to provide emergency services to American citizens in various regions of Mexico, due to the travel restrictions imposed on US government personnel. Certain areas in the United States are subject to prohibitions or restrictions. In numerous states, the provision of local emergency services is constrained beyond the boundaries of the state capital or prominent urban areas.

Despite the advisory issued by the US government, a considerable number of over 9 million American tourists chose to travel to Mexico via air transportation in the year 2022. These individuals constituted a noteworthy portion of the overall 21 million visitors who typically enter Mexico through its land borders. Consequently, the influx of American tourists played a pivotal role in generating the majority of the $18.7 trillion in revenue generated by international tourism during that particular year. According to Centro de Investigación y Competitividad Turística Anáhuac (CICOTUR, 2023), the available data demonstrate that Mexico has the potential to become a prominent global tourist destination if it were not for the destabilising influence of organised crime. From a tourist perspective, Mexico and the United States share a close relationship, as Mexico serves as a significant source of international tourism for its northern neighbour, and vice versa. This interconnection derives from historical, economic, and demographic factors. Notably, approximately 38 million individuals in the United States trace their roots back to Mexico or have Mexican ancestry.

Insecurity impacts significantly border tourism. The northern border of Mexico, being a highly contested drug transit region among criminal organisations, is one of the most volatile areas globally. Nevertheless, it is worth noting that in the year 2022, the expenditure of visitors in border cities exceeded a staggering $1.5 trillion. The research conducted by Bringas and Verduzco (2008) reveals that a significant proportion of individuals residing in the southern border region of the United States exhibit apprehension towards travelling to the Mexican border due to concerns regarding security. Notably, approximately half of the American residents residing in this border area have never ventured into the Mexican side. Furthermore, it is worth noting that a substantial majority (82%) of individuals who do visit the border region either have migrated from Mexico to the United States or possess Mexican heritage.

Despite the presence of empirical evidence indicating that levels of criminal violence in Mexico remain unchanged, the influx of international visitors to the country continues to experience a steady increase (Oxford Analytica, 2018). This assertion derives from the observation that, in a broad sense, instances of violence perpetrated by organised criminal groups in tourist destinations affect mainly some sectors of the local population, leaving aside visitors. The perception of insecurity within the country often results in international visitors gravitating towards areas considered 'safe'. According to tourist statistics, there is a notable concentration of international visitors in a limited number of tourist destinations in Mexico. This phenomenon arises from a lack of confidence among tourists to traverse freely the entirety of Mexican territory. According to Enelow-Snyder (2018), Mexico possesses a significant array of tourist resources, including sun and beach destinations, viceroyal cities, 35 properties listed on the List of World Heritage of Humanity, 112 locations registered in the program *Magic Towns*, and pre-Hispanic archaeological sites. These attractions encompass a diverse range of offerings for visitors. Therefore, the majority of international visitors typically arrive at the airports depicted in Fig. 3.

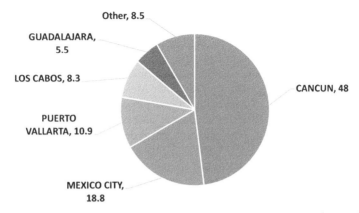

Fig. 3.   Distribution of International Tourist Arrivals at Airports in Mexico.
Source: Adapted from CICOTUR (2023).

Victims of Organised Crime in Mexican Tourist Destinations

One significant issue prevalent within the Mexican justice system pertains to the hesitancy of victims to report crimes. Official statistics from Instituto Nacional de Estadística, Geografía e Informática (INEGI, 2023a) indicate that victims do not report a staggering 91.5% of crimes committed within the country. This reluctance stems from various factors, including the perception that reporting is futile due to the absence of sufficient evidence or the perceived ineffectiveness of the authorities. Additionally, victims may be deterred from reporting crimes due to concerns such as fear of extortion, the perceived inefficiency of legal proceedings, lack of trust in the authorities, or negative past experiences with law enforcement. Of the criminal incidents, a little over 50% remain unresolved or lack an initiated investigation.

Regrettably, although it is indeed accurate that certain foreign tourists fall prey to organised criminal activities, their representation within the overall national criminal statistics is relatively insignificant, considering the substantial volume of data. Small- and medium-sized entrepreneurs are the primary targets of organised crime, frequently falling victim to activities such as extortion, theft, and abduction. In contrast, lower-income segments of the population are not a significant focus for organised crime, as their limited resources do not offer substantial profitability. In Mexico, a significant proportion of businesses operating within the country are categorised as micro, small, and medium-sized enterprises (MSMEs), constituting over 95% of the overall production units. Major multinational corporations in the domestic tourism sector possess the requisite capabilities to enforce more robust security protocols, alongside the financial and legal means to facilitate their recuperation from criminal activities.

Based on the findings of the National Survey of Victimisation of Businesses (Instituto Nacional de Estadística, Geografía e Informática INEGI, 2022), it is evident that a significant number of economic entities, totalling 1.2 million, fell victim to a considerable volume of crimes, amounting to 2.9 million incidents in the year 2021. Notably, in approximately 20.7% of these criminal acts, perpetrators employed firearms as a means of intimidation, while in 6.1% of instances, employees or proprietors of the businesses suffered physical assaults. The presence of organised crime compels businesses to allocate resources towards implementing security measures, thereby exerting financial strain on their operational expenses. Fig. 4 depicts the primary categories of offences experienced by companies in Mexico.

The majority of issues identified by the surveyed companies stem from actions or inactions of the government. These issues primarily include concerns related to insecurity and crime, followed by taxation, corruption, bureaucratic processes, and insufficient governmental assistance, among other factors. It is noteworthy that natural disasters, which occur with high frequency and inflict significant devastation in Mexico, are located towards the lower end of the list. Fig. 5 shows the data pertaining to the main problems identified.

In the year 2021, official statistical data documented a cumulative count of 829,000 incidents of extortion. This figure corresponds to a rate of 1,744 extortions per 10,000 economic units. The work of Le Cour Grandmaison et al (2022) on extorsion to small business in Tijuana, Mexico sheds light on the aggressive tactics employed by criminals in one of the globe's highly frequented border tourist destinations. This study highlights the imposition of illicit levies, commonly referred to as criminal taxes, which has resulted in a significant number of entrepreneurs, predominantly comprising small business proprietors and families, opting to cease operations and, in many cases, relocate to other regions.

Two previous governors of Quintana Roo, a prominent destination in Mexican tourism, currently serve time in prison due to their involvement in severe criminal activities. In the initial instance, Mario Villanueva Madrid, who served as governor from 1993 to 1999, faced legal charges related to drug trafficking, health offences, money laundering, organised crime, criminal association, and intimidation. Consequently, he went to jail in Mexico and was later extradited to

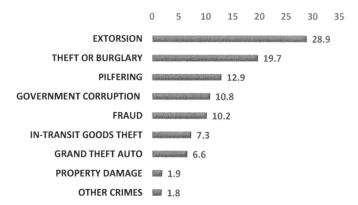

Fig. 4. The Main Categories of Offences Experienced by Companies in Mexico, as a Percentage. *Source*: Instituto Nacional de Estadística, Geografía e Informática (INEGI) (2022).

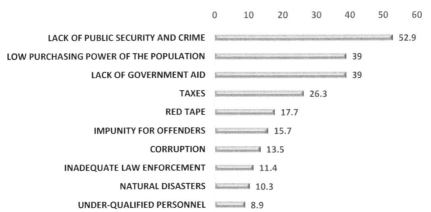

Fig. 5.   The Primary Challenges Identified by Companies in Mexico, as a Percentage. *Source*: Instituto Nacional de Estadística, Geografía e Informática (INEGI) (2022).

the United States. The second case pertains to Roberto Borge Angulo, who served as the governor of the state from 2011 to 2016. During his tenure, he devised legalistic strategies to seize individuals' assets and funds unlawfully from their bank accounts. In 2019, he went to jail on charges of organised crime, as well as alleged collusion with both public officials and private individuals in the illicit acquisition and sale of 22 real estate properties owned by the state government.

Money laundering is a clandestine form of organised criminal activity that occurs within the tourism sector, often operating covertly and evading detection. The potential for money laundering within tourism companies has been discussed in studies conducted by Schneider and Windischbauer (2008), Savona and Riccardi (2017), and Katsios and Dinu (2019). In the context of Mexico, the billing functionalities within the governmental tax system serve to streamline financial transactions; only a limited number of tourists request official receipts that comply with the necessary criteria for documenting expenses related to accommodation, tourist activities, meals, beverages, and entertainment. This situation allows for the possibility of reporting unusually high levels of service consumption. Organised crime poses a significant threat to tourism companies through various criminal activities, such as extortion, thereby negatively affecting their operations. Simultaneously, criminal entities exploit the tourism industry itself to legitimise their illicit earnings, creating an unfair competitive environment for legal tourist companies.

The Utilisation of the VUCA Model within Mexican Tourism Enterprises

This paragraph discusses the issue of insecurity caused by organised crime in tourist destinations with the VUCA model, while also discussing potential solutions with possibilities to address successfully this predicament.

The utilisation of the VUCA model in Mexican tourism enterprises solely permits the attainment of the variable description stage. The prevailing state of insecurity within Mexican society hinders the development of feasible response proposals to address their circumstances as outlined in Fig. 2. The organised crime groups present in Mexico exhibit a high degree of unpredictability, primarily due to territorial conflicts that can arise without warning. Additionally, it is common for individuals involved in criminal organisations to engage in illicit activities while under the influence of drugs. Following the approaches of Aimar & Smith (2021), it can be stated that, in the current situation of Mexico, the variable of the VUCA model more relevant is the vulnerability of the population and companies facing organized crime. Table 1 illustrates the utilisation of the VUCA model within the context of the Mexican tourism sector.

Table 1.   Utilisation of the VUCA Model in Mexican Tourism Enterprises.

Variable	Situation of Mexican Tourism Companys
Vulnerability	Obviously, Mexican tourism companies are vulnerable to the threat of organised crime and to the omitted or colluded position of government authorities
	In addition to the normal uncertainty faced by tourism companies due to the conditions of their activity, such as high volatility in demand, seasonality, and political and socioeconomic risks with the potential to affect tourism activity, Mexican tourist companies are at risk of becoming victims of organised crime at any time. In the different states and municipalities of Mexico, the change of political sign in elected authorities often brings changes in the correlation of forces of organised crime gangs. A change of government can generate sudden increases in the insecurity of a region by concluding agreements made with the outgoing authorities, generating periods of extreme violence as agreements with the incoming elected authorities are established
Complexity	In addition to the normal challenges that tourism companies generally face, such as the volatility and seasonality of tourism operations, intense competition, inflation, possible natural disasters, relations with staff, and government regulations, Mexican tourism firms must invest considerable resources and prepare to withstand possible outbursts of organised crime from gangs of different turns and inclinations
Ambiguity	Basically, the ambiguity in Mexican tourism companies, especially among SMEs, refers to the disjunctive that involves continuing to operate, facing the general challenges of insecurity, or, of course, closing the business, engaging in another activity, or emigrating

Based on the Mexican context, companies and individuals face limited capacity to address issues of insecurity. The documented instances of success in combating organised crime come from efforts of state governments that have implemented strategic measures and allocated significant resources towards the establishment of specialised law enforcement units. This is the approach implemented in the states of Coahuila, Yucatán, and, until the transition of governmental administration, Tamaulipas. The aforementioned entities exhibit the lowest levels of crime prevalence in economic units, as indicated by the Instituto Nacional de Estadística, Geografía e Informática (INEGI's) victimisation of enterprises report for the year 2022.

Various regions and countries across the globe have implemented successful strategies to combat organised crime. Paoli and Fijnaut (2006) provide a description of anti-crime policies in the European Union that centre around the internationalisation of law and police action. In contrast, the approach taken by law enforcement in New Zealand involves a certain level of tolerance towards criminal groups, with the aim of not completely eradicating them, but rather permitting their operation within specific boundaries. According to Newbold (2003), in a similar manner to European counterparts, the South African police force has adopted internationalisation strategies. These strategies involve the establishment of training programs and enhancements in police intelligence. Additionally, the implementation of risk assessment scales for various criminal organisations is the basis for prioritising effective objectives (Govender, 2015). In the Indian context, a comprehensive approach has been adopted, wherein various governmental entities collaborate with non-governmental and community organisations to implement a dual strategy (Verma & Tiwari, 2003). These strategies can serve as an illustrative model for the Mexican government in addressing organised crime; however, it is crucial to emphasise that political determination to combat crime is ultimately indispensable.

Discussion and Conclusions

According to Valdés (2014), the historical roots of drug trafficking date back to a century ago. While it is acknowledged that organised crime has long existed in Mexico, the recent surge in drug trafficking is noteworthy. Paradoxically, this surge comes from the advancements made in democratisation and decentralisation of decision-making within the country. In addition to the aforementioned point made by Montero (2014), it is important to acknowledge the failure of the regimes stemming from the Mexican Revolution of 1910 in addressing the significant disparities in income, opportunities, and education across different regions within the nation. Despite Mexico's vast territorial expanse, remarkable biodiversity, and abundant natural resources, it is disheartening to note that a considerable portion of its population, specifically 55 million individuals constituting 44% of the total population, were living in poverty as of 2020, as reported by the National Council for the Evaluation of Social Development Policy (CONEVAL, 2021).

The presence of organised crime exerts a multifaceted impact on Mexican tourism enterprises. One of the primary consequences stemming from the insecurity caused by organised crime is the degradation of a nation's tourism reputation, leading to apprehension and dissuasion of prospective tourists from visiting domestic tourist sites. The second impact that can be discussed pertains to the crimes that affect the majority of Mexican citizens from all walks of life, including extortion, kidnappings, robberies, assaults, and the corruption of government officials. Within this particular framework, the behaviours and inactions exhibited by government authorities position them on par with organised crime, functioning either as an accomplice or as a passive and compliant spectator. One additional manifestation of organised crime within the tourism sector involves the utilisation of tourist companies as a means for money laundering or the provision of financial support using funds derived from illicit sources.

The unique circumstances surrounding the presence of organised crime in Mexico hinder tourism companies from effectively applying the VUCA model to address the complexities associated with this issue. The national context highlights the necessity for state authorities to intervene with robust and timely strategies aimed at mitigating the impact of organised crime.

Bennett and Lemoine (2014) have presented a diagram that offers a means of applying the VUCA model to address effectively the rapid changes confronting contemporary society. However, it is regrettable that certain formidable forces, such as terrorism and international organised crime syndicates, surpass the capacity of this approach to respond adequately. This is primarily due to the substantial financial, technological, and political resources at their disposal. This assertion holds true for tourism companies in Mexico.

The statistics on the victimisation of Instituto Nacional de Estadística, Geografía e Informática (INEGI) companies (2022) discussed earlier encompass various sectors, including tourism. In the tourism industry, companies face challenges arising from criminal activities and the negative impact on the national tourist image. Additionally, they must contend with competition from tourism enterprises funded by illicit resources, as highlighted by Schneider and Windischbauer (2008), Savona and Riccardi (2017), and Katsios and Dinu (2019). In conjunction with the primary challenges encountered by tourism enterprises as identified by Šimková and Hoffmannová (2021), it is noteworthy that Mexican tourism entrepreneurs face security concerns that jeopardise the personal safety of their staff members and proprietors. In relation to the methodologies employed by Petković et al. (2023) and Ritchie and Crouch (2003), Mexico is currently confronting an enduring and escalating predicament of insecurity within its tourist destinations. While this issue does not directly compromise the safety of visitors, it consistently undermines the viability of tourist enterprises. According to Ritchie and Crouch (2003), the presence or absence of political will affects the progress of a tourist destination, positively or negatively. The association or tolerance of organised crime by Mexican authorities has had a detrimental impact on the country's national tourist image, despite its ample natural and cultural tourist assets.

The current study highlights several limitations. Firstly, it lacks specific information regarding various national tourist destinations. Additionally, the National Survey of Business Victimisation (ENVE) 2022 conducted by the National Institute of Statistics, Geography, and Informatics does not provide a stratification of data based on different lines of activity within companies. Consequently, it becomes challenging to determine the precise impact on tourist enterprises.

References

Aimar, C., & Smith, D. (2021). VUCA: A management tool for dealing with challenges in changing environments. *Global Journal of Entrepreneurship*, *5*(1), 140–152.
Bennett, N., & Lemoine, G. J. (2014). What a difference a word makes: Understanding threats to performance in a VUCA world. *Business Horizons*, *57*(3), 311–317.
Bennis, W., & Nanus, B. (1985). *Leaders: The strategies for taking charge*. Harper and Row.
Blanco, J., & Cohen, J. (2017). Macro-environmental factors driving organised crime. In *Using open data to detect organized crime threats: Factors driving future crime* (pp. 137–166). Cham: Springer International Publishing.
Bringas, N., & Verduzco, B. (2008). La construcción de la frontera norte como destino turístico en un contexto de alertas de seguridad. *Región y sociedad*, *20*(42), 3–36.
Centro de Investigación y Competitividad Turística Anáhuac (CICOTUR). (2023, February 15). *Panorama de la Actividad Turística en México. Año 11, N.0 37*. https://www.anahuac.mx/mexico/cicotur/sites/default/files/2022-11/PanoramaActTur37.pdf
Consejo Nacional para la Evaluación de la Política de Desarrollo Social (CONEVAL). (2021, March 31). *Pobreza en México*. https://www.coneval.org.mx/Medicion/MP/Paginas/Pobreza_2020.aspx
Council for Public Security and Criminal Justice, A. C. (2023, March 12). *2023 Boletín Ranking de las 50 ciudades más violentas del mundo*. https://geoenlace.net/seguridadjusticiaypaz/webpage/boletin.php
Corona, N. (2018). Does violent crime scare tourists away? Panel data evidence from 32 Mexican states. *EconoQuantum*, *15*(2), 21–48.
de la Torre, M., & Navarrete, D. (2018). Turismo y narcotráfico en México. *Estudios y perspectivas en turismo*, *27*(4), 867–882.
Enelow-Snyder, S. (2018). The resilience of the American vacation in Mexico. *Obtenido en*. https://skift.com/2018/10/15/the-resilience-of-the-american-vacation-in-mexico/
Govender, D. (2015). A conceptual analysis of strategies to combat organised crime in South Africa. *Insight on Africa*, *7*(2), 120–136.
Instituto Nacional de Estadística, Geografía e Informática (INEGI). (2023, February 22). Mortalidad: defunciones por homicidios. *Información de 1990 a 2021*. México. https://www.inegi.org.mx/sistemas/olap/proyectos/bd/continuas/mortalidad/defuncioneshom.asp?s=est
Instituto Nacional de Estadística, Geografía e Informática (INEGI). (2022, March 31). *Encuesta nacional de victimización de empresas (ENVE) 2022*. https://www.inegi.org.mx/programas/enve/2022/
Katsios, S., & Dinu, N. R. (2019). *Yellow Tourism: Crime and corruption in the holiday sector*. Springer.
Le Cour Grandmaison, R., Martínez Trujillo, M. T., Sorzano Rodríguez, D. M., & Ramírez, M. (2022, February 19). *Extorsión empresarial y seguridad pública en Tijuana: ¿quién protege a quién?* https://www.mexicoevalua.org/mexicoevalua/wp-content/uploads/2022/09/extorsiontijuanavf-15sept.pdf

Lozano Cortés, M. (2016). Inseguridad y turismo en Quintana Roo, México (1997–2013). *Revista Criminalidad, 58*(1), 159–169.

Millar, C. C., Groth, O., & Mahon, J. F. (2018). Management innovation in a VUCA world: Challenges and recommendations. *California Management Review, 61*(1), 5–14.

Montero, J. (2014). Historia del narcotráfico en México. *CONfines de relaciones internacionales y ciencia política, 10*(19), 151–157.

Monterrubio, J. C. (2013). Destination image and crime in Mexico: An analysis of foreign government travel advice. *PASOS Revista de Turismo y Patrimonio Cultural, 11*(3), 33–45.

Mylonopoulos, D., Moira, P., & Kikilia, A. (2016). The travel advice as an inhibiting factor of tourist movement. *Tims. Acta: naučni časopis za sport, turizam i velnes, 10*(1), 13–26.

Newbold, G. (2003). Organised crime: A perspective from New Zealand. In J. S. Albanese, D. K. Das, & A. Verma (Eds.), *Organised crime: World perspectives* (pp. 352–373). Prentice Hall.

Ortiz, M. (2013). Orígenes y desarrollo del crimen organizado en América Latina (1916–2013). *Política y estrategia, 121*, 119–150.

Oxford Analytica. (2018, March 24). Mexico tourism success disregards rising violence. *Emerald Expert Briefings, (oxan-ga)*. https://dailybrief.oxan.com/Analysis/GA231998/Mexico-tourism-success-disregards-rising-violence

Paoli, L., & Fijnaut, C. (2006). Organised crime and its control policies. *European Journal of Crime, Criminal Law and Criminal Justice, 14*, 307.

Petković, G., Bradić-Martinović, A., & Pindžo, R. (2023). Crisis management in the function of effective destination management. *Ekonomika preduzeća, 71*(1–2), 145–161.

Ritchie, J. B., & Crouch, G. I. (2003). *The competitive destination: A sustainable tourism perspective*. Cabi.

Savona, E. U., & Riccardi, M. (2017, March 29). Assessing the risk of money laundering in Europe. *Final Report of Project IARM*. http://www.transcrime.it/wp-content/uploads/2017/05/ProjectIARM-FinalReport.pdf

Schneider, F., & Windischbauer, U. (2008). Money laundering: Some facts. *European Journal of Law and Economics, 26*, 387–404

Šimková, E., & Hoffmannová, M. (2021, March 20). *Impact of VUCA environment in practice of rural tourism. Hradec Economic Days*. https://digilib.uhk.cz/bitstream/handle/20.500.12603/552/SIMKOVA_Eva_Martina_HOFFMANNOVA.pdf?sequence=1&isAllowed=y

US Department of State. Bureau of Consular Affairs. (2022, February 24). *Mexico Travel Advisory*. https://travel.state.gov/content/travel/en/traveladvisories/traveladvisories/mexico-travel-advisory.html

Valdés, G. (2013). Historia del narcotráfico en México. Ciudad de México: Editorial Libros Aguilar.

Verma, A., & Tiwari, R. K. (2003). Organised crime: A perspective from India. In J. S. Albanese, D. K. Das, & A. Verma (Eds.), *Organised rime: World perspectives* (pp. 240–266). Prentice Hall.

Wursten, H. (2018). Culture, VUCA and the all-encompassing unrest: What will happen? *Journal of Intercultural Management and Ethics, 1*(2), 25–30.

Chapter 14

Interfaces Between Biothreats, Biosecurity, and Tourism: Strategies for Indian Tourism

Manjula Chaudhary[a] and Naser Ul Islam[b]

[a]*Kurukshetra University Kurukshetra, Haryana, India*
[b]*Tata Institute of Social Sciences, Mumbai, India*

Abstract

COVID-19 has alerted all stakeholders to the serious challenges of bio-threats to humanity and its progress. Tourism as a business has been one of the worst sufferers from the COVID-19 impacts and has been held responsible to an extent for the spread of the virus. The 'containment, isolation, and restrictions' of biosafety and biosecurity measures exposed the vulnerability of the tourism industry. The densely populated urban areas in India can always be hot spots for the spread of biovectors from similar biothreats in the future, with a more significant threat to employment from mitigation measures. This theoretical paper combines research from medical science, biology, tourism, and other related areas to develop a thesis that social scientists can add value in designing socially acceptable measures for scientific solutions recommended by experts from medical and other related fields. The general environment of health and hygiene in India needs to be made safer for its population and tourists as a first-level strategy to reduce the risks of biothreats. The next level strategy shall be dominated by science to suggest mitigation measures with parallel action by tourism stakeholders for a socially acceptable face of safety measures.

Keywords: Biothreats; biosecurity; COVID-19; Indian tourism; microbial threats

Tourism in a VUCA World: Managing the Future of Tourism, 203–211
Copyright © 2024 by Manjula Chaudhary and Naser Ul Islam
Published under exclusive licence by Emerald Publishing Limited
doi:10.1108/978-1-83753-674-020241014

Introduction

The COVID-19 pandemic red-flagged the tourism industry about the signifi-cant dangers of microbial threats. The vulnerability of the industry to infectious diseases caused by microbes was known earlier as tourism has been adversely impacted with each spread of diseases. A global database study identified the association between eradicating Yellow Fever, Dengue, Malaria, and Ebola on international tourist arrivals and its nationwide economic impact at destinations through their tourism industries (Rosselló et al., 2017). The substantial financial, physical, psychological, and social burden of disease outbreaks from microbes has been documented worldwide in the cases of Spanish flu in 1918, swine flu in 2009, SARS CoV in 2002, AIDS in 1981, cholera, smallpox, leprosy, polio, mea-sles, and yellow fever (Shehri et al., 2022). The microbial threats are becoming a serious cause of concern for humanity across the globe, more so in the nations lacking resources to control these (Heymann, 2002). The prevalence of emerg-ing contagious diseases in humans has increased in the recent past or threatens to grow in the future, and developing countries such as India suffer significantly from the burden of contagious diseases given the confluence of existing environ-mental, socio-economic, and demographic factors (Dikid et al., 2013).

The microbial threat of COVID-19 has dominated global discussions and responses since 2020; however, the larger biothreat domain has always been a matter of concern.

Biothreats can come from plants or animals and can arise naturally or through sabotage. These pose severe problems to the human population and its activities, including travel-tourism. The movement of tourists, too, can spread vectors of biothreats (Hall, 2019), which has often led to the ban on tourism as a security measure. COVID-19 exemplified the responsibility of tourism in the dispersion of biotic agents with severe environmental, economic, social, and public health reper-cussions, thus needing an urgent rethink about the tourism growth trajectory and considering the biosecurity threats associated with mobility (Sacramento, 2023).

The containment strategy to control biothreats by restricting mobility can dev-astate tourism as tourists look out for alternate destinations, and tourism estab-lishments suffer losses, furthering the snowball effect on all connected businesses. The decisions on biosecurity, safety, and health risks lie with experts and are out-side the ambit of the tourism industry. However, during COVID-19, it has been observed that social behaviour and science are an essential part of preparations for the epidemic (May, 2021). The humanitarian and human rights dimension of COVID-19 highlights the inconsistent application of sanctions and their impacts on the general public and travel, which is gradually becoming familiar in work on mobility and tourism justice (Seyfi et al., 2023). Engagement of the tourism industry as an active partner in biosecurity preparedness at tourism destinations can support and encourage controlled tourism for a possible win-win proposition (Baker, 2015). WTTC's initiative during COVID-19 by creating the Safe Travels Stamp for travellers to recognise safe travel destinations and businesses around the world in line with WHO and CDC guidelines was one such step towards syn-ergy between safety and tourism (WTTC, 2020).

Biothreats and Biosecurity

The concept of biosecurity has changed over time with the changing spectrum of biothreats, from naturally occurring diseases to using diseases as weapons. The threat to human health from the continuous evolution of microorganisms has resulted in considering health issues as a security threat for the first time in 2000 by the UN Security Council for HIV/AIDS (McInnes & Rushton, 2010). Biosecurity is a comprehensive and integrated concept that covers the policies and regulations frameworks, including tools and actions to access and manage risk in food safety, public health, and animal and plant life-health, including associated environmental risk using primary devices such as exclusion, eradication, and control where travel is controlled that excludes long-distance commercial transport such as aircraft, ships, trains, and buses with continuous monitoring of travel in coordination with public health authorities (Ahmad et al., 2020). Biothreats and biosecurity are well-researched fields in health sciences. Tourism literature received attention whenever the disease spread impacted tourism, and the COVID-19 period witnessed a surge in such topical publications. It has been noted that research has mostly focused on previous outbreaks such as SARS whenever the impact of health crises on the tourism and hospitality industry was examined; however, from this time, the COVID-19 pandemic is expected to become a prominent reference point in the related studies (Kaushal & Srivastava, 2021).

Biothreats and Tourism

The biosecurity and safety measures change the ways of creating seamless and memorable tourism experiences. Most of the tourism literature on the subject deals with the effects of pathogens such as SARS, MERS, and COVID-19 on tourism, and these studies by tourism researchers are primarily concerned with recovery plans to avert losses to tourism. The advocacy of tourism promotion with requisite safety measures is often at a different wavelength from the thesis of health and medical researchers. A literature review on the impacts of COVID-19 and tourism also found that the bulk of publications can be described as opinion papers or research notes, out of which only a few have been written using an empirical approach, and none have discussed an evidence-based policy for tourism in light of the COVID-19 crisis (Kreiner & Ram, 2020). This paradox has been experienced by governments worldwide, particularly during the COVID-19 spread, wherein a multi-pronged strategy was adopted by engaging all stakeholders with a key focus on health and livelihoods. A brief of such important studies in tourism provides their perspective and covered space (Table 1).

Tourism literature addresses the prevailing issues of biothreats, but many areas of concern have not been adequately addressed. One such area of critical importance is human-primate interfaces and zoonotic diseases. The zoologists have well-researched this to bring out the threats (Lappan et al., 2020). The prevalence of such threats in tourism activities in parks, zoos, and entertainment involving other primates and animals needs proactive solutions for safe tourism. Tourism research has noted the transmission of diseases among tourists from

Table 1.   Focus Areas of COVID-19-Related Tourism Research.

Author/s	Focus/Main Point of Study
Bauer (2022)	Travel medicine and the tourism industry need to work together, yet there is little cooperation, collaboration, and acknowledgement of the other.
Kim et al. (2022)	Use an understanding of travel market attitudes to biosecurity measures to better target education and marketing communication campaigns for improving confidence among tourists, residents, and employees to adopt appropriate biosecurity measures and reduce the risks associated with international travel by COVID-19.
Selvanathan et al. (2022)	The threat of global tourism and the travel industry to global health security is evident from the association between the number of international tourism and COVID-19 cases and deaths across countries.
Gössling et al. (2021)	COVID-19 provides lessons about the impacts of global change. The challenge is to learn and accelerate the transformation of sustainable tourism.
Babii and Nadeem (2021)	Considering a serious threat to tourism, it suggested diversifying economies and investing in non-tourism sectors.
Fotiadis et al. (2021)	Predicts tourist arrivals with prevailing conditions of COVID-19 outbreak.
Thomas (2021)	While travellers spread infective pathogens, the latter also introduce other disease factors related to new farm technology, novel drugs, medical treatments, and chemicals and pesticides.
Jamal and Budke (2020)	With an increasing number of air travellers, greater responsibility and care will be called for important tourism stakeholders, such as tourism service providers, residents, and tourists, to manage the transmission and spread of infectious diseases.
Mohanty et al. (2020)	Relaunch tourism using augmented reality post-COVID-19.
Kreiner and Ram (2020)	Stresses the need for an evidence-based policy for handling COVID-19-related situations.
Qiu et al. (2020)	Proposes tourism recovery with resident's participation.
Duro et al. (2021)	Suggests for reduction of vulnerability of tourism destinations.
Karabulut et al. (2020)	COVID-19 impacted tourist arrivals everywhere but had more impact in low-income economies due to a lack of transparency and poor health infrastructure.

Source: The Authors.

animal contact. The high prevalence of free-roaming Non-Human Primates in urban settlements in India and at other places was found to be responsible for passing pathogens to humans when tourists were bitten for refusing to give food (Devaux et al., 2019). Similarly, the growth of eco-tourism in primitive settings with limited hygiene can be related to acquiring zoonotic agents (Chomel et al., 2007). The growing number of tourists now increasingly visiting regions away from traditional holiday destinations will result in the potential for tourists to not only inadvertently introduce alien species into new environments but also become exposed to zoonotic agents (Devaux et al., 2019; Hulme, 2020).

Infectious diseases pose health risks to tourists, particularly in developing countries. Infectious diseases in India contributed to 30% of its disease burden despite emerging as an economic hotspot (Kant, 2008), which was reported to be 27.5% in a current study (Ram & Thakur, 2022). The high presence of diseases in the environment can mar the attractiveness of any destination, and for this, tourism researchers need to broaden the scope of their inquiry by collaborating with scholars from life and physical sciences and offer evidence-based pragmatic solutions to address the requirements of both biosafety and tourism.

Management of Biothreats and Biosafety in India

The management of biothreats in tourism is derived from the general biosecurity guidelines at the destinations and varies across time and place. India, being a large and populous country, is vulnerable to biothreats. It is ranked 70 for biosafety and 58 for biosecurity in the Global Health Security Index 2021 despite its rank on international commitments on Global Health Security at 1 (Global Heath Security Index, 2021). The framework of biosafety regulations in India emanates from the Environment Protection Act 1986. It follows a dis-aggregated approach covering manufacturing, using, importing, exporting, and storing hazardous microorganisms/genetically engineered organisms and cells (Damodaran, 2005).

Biosafety guidelines in the country fall under the ambit of multiple organisations; Union Ministry of Science and Technology and the Ministry of Environment, Forest and Climate Change (MoEFCC), and researchers under the Indian Council of Medical Research and the Indian Council of Agricultural Research – research bodies set up under the Ministry of Health and Family Welfare (MoHFW) and the Ministry of Agriculture and Farmers' Welfare (Sharma, 2005). Biosecurity guidelines are issued by multiple bodies in their respective domains as per prevailing situations that also apply to the tourism industry.

Tourism and Biosecurity in India

Research on Indian tourism does not identify any significant biological factor directly impacting tourism except COVID-19. However, many studies found travel-borne illnesses among tourists returning from India. Angelo et al. (2017) noted that tourist to India accounts for nearly 60% of typhoid among international tourists returning to the US and the highest worldwide burden of rabies, resulting in increased numbers of individuals, including tourists, who may need post-exposure prophylaxis. A study among Thai tourists noted that over half (52%) of tourists experienced health problems during their visit to India, and the most common health problem was not tourists' diarrhoea but respiratory and musculoskeletal problems (Olanwijitwong et al., 2017). A review study on travel-related illnesses found travel-related illnesses among 43–79% of US and European tourists during or after travel to Asia or Africa (more specifically, India, Tanzania, or Kenya) (Angelo et al., 2017).

Concerns have been expressed about threats from medical tourism in India, particularly the spread of antibiotic-resistant superbugs (Hall, 2015). India has been identified as a top source of Antimicrobial Resistance (AMR), and travel advisories are issued for AMR pertaining to India. Research on biodiversity has identified tourism as one of the causal factors of biological invasions among many (Singh, 2005). The travel practices of medical tourism, mass travel to biodiverse areas, and travel, in general, can adversely affect the tourism industry in the long run if microbes and biothreats are not managed. Microbes and biothreats are much too complex to be addressed by medical or bioresearch only and require the participation of society as a whole (Gandra et al., 2017). Nair et al. (2021) emphasise the socioecological approach to control AMR.

India as a country is aware of its health-related challenges and has taken a number of initiatives to provide an overall hygienic environment. A comprehensive National Action has been adopted for control of AMR (Ranjalkar & Chandy, 2019). The decisions pertaining to biosecurity lie in the domain of experts in India, wherein the larger interests of the society are also considered. In tourism, the idea of bio-bubble was used in its state Kerala to revive tourism (Timestravel, 2021).

The tourism industry can expect innovative solutions for biosecurity from the collaborative research of tourism scholars and scientists. Biothreats cannot be eliminated but can always be contained with collaborative efforts. As suggested by Baker (2015), travellers should be considered an integral part of the global surveillance network for emerging infections. Research and the knowledge gained can be used to alert the global community to the presence or susceptibility patterns of pathogens in different regions and devise strategies to control infections in developing countries.

Conclusions

Biothreats pose big risks and challenges to the tourism industry by hurting the very foundation of the tourism industry, that is, human mobility and interface. Lately, the incidences of biothreats have increased, forcing all tourism stakeholders to plan for new models of tourism. Different strategies have been suggested worldwide, ranging from controlled tourism to reducing dependence on tourism. India has faced the burden of biothreats and has devised plans to contain these, but the high prevalence of microbial diseases in the country and disaggregated approach to biosecurity makes it more vulnerable. The Indian government has taken initiatives to address the health and hygiene issues of its population through the National Health Mission, Swach Bharat Mission (Clean India Mission), and

Mission Indradhanush. These plans aim to yield results consistently in the long run, and specific interventions are made during crisis periods such as during the spread of COVID-19. The government of India was able to deliver the indigenous vaccine 'Covaxin' to its large population. Such initiatives of many countries primarily targeted at saving lives could not save tourism. The Ministry of Tourism and the tourism industry in India used these downtimes for brand building by organising virtual tours that might have had a carry-over effect on the revival of tourism. A similar strategy was used in many countries. The response strategies used during COVID-19 can be taken as lessons for proactive strategies in the future to minimise the impacts of biothreats on the tourism industry.

The discussion in this chapter suggests unique weaknesses and threats to the Indian tourism landscape requiring solutions to sync with its opportunities and challenges. A few strategies are recommended to face biothreats with the underlying condition that tourism stakeholders shall play a pivotal role.

Improvement of general hygiene and health: The National Health Mission, Swatch Bharat Mission, and Mission Indradhanush initiatives can be taken forward as a Level 1 strategy to create barriers to germination and spread of vectors of biothreats wherein the tourism industry can be involved to sensitise and educate stakeholders at visit points. This will also change the image of the country for travel-borne illnesses.

Designing socially acceptable technical solutions: The tourism industry can engage with expert groups to suggest an easily diffusible and acceptable format of scientific solutions as a Level 2 strategy. The knowledge of tourism suppliers about an understanding of the behaviour of tourists and the host population will play a critical role in it.

Create a network of information sharing: Any spread of diseases at any point by tourists shall be immediately flagged by the tourism industry for corrective action. The tourism industry can support the mitigation of biothreats by being observant and responsible.

The above strategies can be effective if built into the system to tackle biothreats for continuous monitoring and management.

References

Ahmad, T., Haroon, H., Dhama, K., Sharun, K., Khan, F. M., Ahmed, I., & Hui, J. (2020). Biosafety and biosecurity approaches to restrain/contain and counter SARS-CoV-2/ COVID-19 pandemic: A rapid-review. *Turkish Journal of Biology, 44*(7), 132–145.

Angelo, K. M., Kozarsky, P. E., Ryan, E. T., Chen, L. H., & Sotir, M. J. (2017). What proportion of international travellers acquire a travel-related illness? A review of the literature. *Journal of Travel Medicine, 24*(5).

Babii, A., & Nadeem, S. (2021, April 10). *Tourism in post-pandemic world.* https://www.imf.org/en/News/Articles/2021/02/24/na022521-how-to-save-travel-and-tourism-in-a-post-pandemic-world

Baker, B. A. (2015). Tourism and the health effects of infectious diseases: Are there potential risks. *International Journal of Safety & Security in Hospitality & Tourism, 12*(1), 41–59.

Bauer, I. L. (2022). COVID-19: How can travel medicine benefit from tourism's focus on people during a pandemic? *Tropical Diseases, Travel Medicine and Vaccines, 8*(1), 26.

Chomel, B. B., Belotto, A., & Meslin, F. X. (2007). Wildlife, exotic pets, and emerging zoonoses. *Emerging Infectious Diseases, 13*(1), 6.

Damodaran, A. (2005). Re-engineering biosafety regulations in India: Towards a critique of policy, law and prescriptions. *Law Environment & Development Journal, 1*(1).

Devaux, C. A., Mediannikov, O., Medkour, H., & Raoult, D. (2019). Infectious disease risk across the growing human-non human primate interface: A review of the evidence. *Frontiers in Public Health, 7*, 305.

Dikid, T., Jain, S. K., Sharma, A., Kumar, A., & Narain, J. P. (2013). Emerging & re-emerging infections in India: An overview. *Indian Journal of Medical Research, 138*(1), 19–31.

Duro, J. A., Perez-Laborda, A., Turrion-Prats, J., & Fernández-Fernández, M. (2021). Covid-19 and tourism vulnerability. *Tourism Management Perspectives, 38*, 100819.

Fotiadis, A., Polyzos, S., & Huan, T. C. T. (2021). The good, the bad and the ugly on COVID-19 tourism recovery. *Annals of Tourism Research, 87*, 103117.

Gandra, S., Joshi, J., Trett, A., Lamkang, A. S., & Laxminarayan, R. (2017). Scoping report on antimicrobial resistance in India. *Center for Disease Dynamics, Economics & Policy*, 1–146.

Global Health Security Index. (2021). GHS Index Country Profile for India. https://www.ghsindex.org/country/india/

Gössling, S., Scott, D., & Hall, C. M. (2021). Pandemics, tourism and global change: A rapid assessment of COVID-19. *Journal of Sustainable Tourism, 29*(1), 1–20.

Hall, C. M. (2015). The coming perfect storm: Medical tourism as a biosecurity issue. In *Handbook on medical tourism and patient mobility* (pp. 193–204). Edward Elgar Publishing.

Hall, C. M. (2019). Biological invasion, biosecurity, tourism, and globalisation. In *Handbook of globalisation and tourism* (pp. 114–125). Edward Elgar Publishing.

Heymann, D. L. (2002). The microbial threat in fragile times: Balancing known and unknown risks. *Bulletin of the World Health Organization, 80*, 179.

Hulme, P. E. (2020). One Biosecurity: A unified concept to integrate human, animal, plant, and environmental health. *Emerging Topics in Life Sciences, 4*(5), 539–549.

Jamal, T., & Budke, C. (2020). Tourism in a world with pandemics: Local-global responsibility and action. *Journal of Tourism Futures, 6*(2), 181–188.

Kant, L. (2008). Combating emerging infectious diseases in India: Orchestrating a symphony. *Journal of Biosciences, 33*(4), 425.

Karabulut, G., Bilgin, M. H., Demir, E., & Doker, A. C. (2020). How pandemics affect tourism: International evidence. *Annals of Tourism Research, 84*, 102991.

Kaushal, V., & Srivastava, S. (2021). Hospitality and tourism industry amid COVID-19 pandemic: Perspectives on challenges and learnings from India. *International Journal of Hospitality Management, 92*, 102707.

Kim, M. J., Bonn, M., & Hall, C. M. (2022). What influences COVID-19 biosecurity behaviour for tourism? *Current Issues in Tourism, 25*(1), 21–27.

Kreiner, N. C., & Ram, Y. (2020). National tourism strategies during the Covid-19 pandemic. *Annals of Tourism Research, 89*, 103076.

Lappan, S., Malaivijitnond, S., Radhakrishna, S., Riley, E. P., & Ruppert, N. (2020). The human–primate interface in the New Normal: Challenges and opportunities for primatologists in the COVID-19 era and beyond. *American Journal of Primatology, 82*(8), e23176.

May, M. (2021). Tomorrow's biggest microbial threats. *Nature Medicine, 27*(3), 358–359.

McInnes, C., & Rushton, S. (2010). HIV, AIDS and security: Where are we now? *International Affairs, 86*(1), 225–245.

Mohanty, P., Hassan, A., & Ekis, E. (2020). Augmented reality for relaunching tourism post-COVID-19: Socially distant, virtually connected. *Worldwide Hospitality and Tourism Themes*, *12*(6), 753–760.

Nair, M., Zeegers, M. P., Varghese, G. M., & Burza, S. (2021). India's national action plan on antimicrobial resistance: A critical perspective. *Journal of Global Antimicrobial Resistance*, *27*, 236–238.

Olanwijitwong, J., Piyaphanee, W., Poovorawan, K., Lawpoolsri, S., Chanthavanich, P., Wichainprasast, P., & Tantawichien, T. (2017). Health problems among Thai tourists returning from India. *Journal of Travel Medicine*, *24*(4).

Qiu, R. T., Park, J., Li, S., & Song, H. (2020). Social costs of tourism during the COVID-19 pandemic. *Annals of Tourism Research*, *84*, 102994.

Ram, B., & Thakur, R. (2022). Epidemiology and economic burden of continuing challenge of infectious diseases in India: Analysis of socio-demographic differentials. *Frontiers in Public Health*, *10*, 1717.

Ranjalkar, J., & Chandy, S. J. (2019). India's National Action Plan for antimicrobial resistance: An overview of the context, status, and way ahead. *Journal of Family Medicine and Primary Care*, *8*(6), 1828.

Rosselló, J., Santana-Gallego, M., & Awan, W. (2017). Infectious disease risk and international tourism demand. *Health Policy and Planning*, *32*(4), 538–548.

Sacramento, O. (2023). Mass tourism, biosecurity and sustainability challenges: Prospects illustrated by the current COVID-19 pandemic. *Journal of Tourism Futures*, 1–14.

Selvanathan, E. A., Jayasinghe, M., & Selvanathan, S. (2022). International tourism and infectious disease transmission nexus: A cross-country and regional study. *Journal of Travel Research*, *61*(8), 1910–1927.

Seyfi, S., Hall, C. M., & Shabani, B. (2023). COVID-19 and international travel restrictions: The geopolitics of health and tourism. *Tourism Geographies*, *25*(1), 357–373.

Sharma, S. (2005, March 23). *Untold risks: India needs full-time body to tackle biological threats*. https://www.downtoearth.org.in/blog/governance/untold-risks-india-needs-full-time-body-to-tackle-biological-threats-76194

Shehri, S. A., Al-Sulaiman, A. M., Azmi, S., & Alshehri, S. S. (2022). Bio-safety and bio-security: A major global concern for ongoing COVID-19 pandemic. *Saudi Journal of Biological Sciences*, *29*(1), 132–139.

Singh, K. P. (2005). Invasive alien species and biodiversity in India. *Current Science*, *88*(4), 539.

Thomas, L. (2021, May 6). How Does Travel Influence Spread of Disease? *News-Medical*. https://www.news-medical.net/health/How-Does-Travel-Influence-Spread-of-Disease.aspx

Timestravel. (2021, April 25). *Bio-bubble model introduced by Kerala to revive tourism in the state*. https://timesofindia.indiatimes.com/travel/travel-news/bio-bubble-model-introduced-by-kerala-to-revive-tourism-in-the-state/articleshow/85295636.cms

WTTC. (2020, April 10). *'Safe Travels': Global protocols & stamp for the new normal*. https://wttc.org/initiatives/crisis-preparedness-management-recovery/safetravels-global-protocols-stamp

Chapter 15

Transformation of Tourist Regions Through the Recovery of Abandoned Rural Settlements – The Case of Croatia

Jasenka Kranjčević[a] *and Dina Stober*[b]

[a]*Institute for Tourism, Zagreb, Croatia*
[b]*Faculty of Civil Engineering and Architecture, Osijek, Croatia*

Abstract

For the last three decades, due to socio-economic and political processes such as Europeanisation and globalisation, Croatia has faced a population decline, leading to an increased number of abandoned settlements. During the COVID-19 crisis, rural areas in Croatia became areas of interest and rural tourism increased. However, the increased interest did not result in the revival of abandoned settlements but rather just in the construction of new facilities. According to statistical data, the majority of abandoned settlements are in regions with the highest tourist traffic or along the traffic corridor from continental Croatia to the Adriatic Sea. The superponing of statistical demographic data, tourism data, the spatial distribution of abandoned rural settlements, sectoral development plans, regional spatial characteristics, and types of construction related to tourism resulted in a proposal of a conceptual model for the reconstruction and inclusion of abandoned rural architecture and infrastructure settlements in the development of rural tourism.

Concerning the growth of certain tourist regions in Croatia, to achieve sustainability and resilience in managing territory, abandoned rural locations and infrastructure should be included in sectoral regional development plans in order to strengthen rural identity by preserving architectural heritage, landscape attractions, symbols, and all other identity contributors.

Keywords: Abandoned rural settlements; rural identity; resilience of rural area; recovery of rural area; transformation of tourist regions; Croatia

Tourism in a VUCA World: Managing the Future of Tourism, 213–229
Copyright © 2024 by Emerald Publishing Limited
All rights of reproduction in any form reserved
doi:10.1108/978-1-83753-674-020241015

Introduction

Despite the renewal of the Territorial Agenda – a future for all places on the European level (Ministers responsible for spatial planning, territorial development and/or territorial cohesion, 2020) and the adoption of the National Recovery and Resilience Plan 2021–2026 (Government of the Republic of Croatia, 2021a), Croatia, as a small European post-socialist country, has been facing pronounced depopulation (Croatian Bureau of Statistics, 2021a), brought about by deruralisation and deagrarianisation, which often leads to the extinction of some settlements. Furthermore, during the COVID-19 pandemic, one of the most affected sectors of the Croatian economy was tourism (taking into account its overall contribution to GDP) (Government of the Republic of Croatia, 2021a), despite the interest in staying in rural areas, primarily among domestic tourists. Therefore, Croatia's recovery and resilience plan proposed designing a new tourism development model with the purpose of making tourism sustainable, green and digital (Government of the Republic of Croatia, 2021a). Looking at tourist traffic, very large differences are visible at the level of regions (counties) between the two main spatial entities, the Adriatic and continental Croatia (Kranjčević & Stober, 2022) in favour of the Adriatic Croatia, while continental Croatia is neglected.

According to the last population census, carried out in 2021, as many as 195 Croatian settlements did not have a single inhabitant (Croatian Bureau of Statistics, 2022a). Besides these alarming statistical data, there is no data regarding the condition of traffic connections, technical infrastructure, residential buildings, social infrastructure facilities (shops, post offices, schools, etc.), landscape typology, property use, etc (Government of the Republic of Croatia, 2021b). Unfortunately, the trend of abandoning settlements will continue, especially settlements with one to five inhabitants because they lack vitality – young people.

On the one hand, it means the openness to new realities and meanings, and on the other, a constant need to problematise, a refusal to take anything for granted, to treat things as obvious and familiar (Kociatkiewicz & Kostera, 1999).

The question that arises is whether the function of some of the abandoned settlements can be changed (if they have good traffic accessibility, technical infrastructure, valuable regional architecture, etc.) through the recovery process.

This paper examines the relationship between tourist traffic and abandoned rural settlements by tourist regions (counties) to determine their potential, with the aim of designing the resilience concept and as a response to the Territorial Agenda – a future for all places and Croatia's National Recovery and Resilience Plan (Government of the Republic of Croatia, 2021a). The recovery concept of abandoned rural settlements can also be based on what happened in rural areas during the COVID-19 pandemic. During the pandemic, rural settlements showed greater resistance to changes and, in economic terms, had a lower loss of jobs (OECD, 2021). Also, during the pandemic, the interest in staying in rural areas (rural tourism) increased, primarily among domestic tourists. It was an attempt to protect workplaces and companies. Following the COVID-19 pandemic, many countries started to develop measures for building a more resilient tourism economy, including preparing plans for supporting sustainable tourism recovery, promoting digital transition, transitioning to a greener tourism system, and rethinking tourism for the future (OECD, 2020), and Croatia also developed these measures.

These several facts show the need for a conceptual review of rural tourism, *vis-à-vis* volatility, uncertainty, complexity, and ambiguity (VUCA) in the environment.

This research is based on available statistical and spatial planning data and domestic and foreign literature. In designing the recovery concept through the transformation of the function of abandoned settlements, the inductive-deductive and the time slice methods were used.

This work contributes to solving the concept of the recovery of abandoned settlements and their connection with tourism.

Literature Review

Rural studies cover various disciplines, such as spatial planning, architecture, sociology, economics and geography, and imply the use of qualitative, quantitative and mixed and hybrid methods. Researchers often use quantitative indicators to determine the differences between rural and urban areas, while qualitative research is used rarely (Hamilton, 2019; Kranjčević et al., 2018; Lukić, 2010; Strijker et al., 2020). The European Commission, at the EU level, determines the differences between urban and rural areas with such measurable indicators as the number of inhabitants living in rural areas, the number of apartments or houses, the use of digital skills, the share of overnight stays in tourist accommodation, etc. (Eurostat, 2019). The formal EUROSTAT definition of a rural area still relies on the urban-rural dichotomy and defines the rural area as the area outside urban clusters (Dijkstra et al., 2021). Quantitative data can be useful for determining social, economic and cultural trends in rural areas, as well as serve as the basis for rural development planning.

According to the EUROSTAT data (https://ec.europa.eu/eurostat/web/rural-development/methodology), only 458 of 1,514 NUTS3 regions are defined as 'predominantly rural', although agricultural topography and land use account for almost 80% of the EU's territory. Rural areas face various challenges.

Research mostly focuses on challenges specific to a distinctive region or geography relevance, while only several of them try to comprehensively aggregate general global rural issues and challenges. Health is one of the most relevant rural challenges (Bain & Adeagbo, 2022; Kumar et al., 2019; Morgan & Calleja, 2020; Strasser, 2003) directly linked to poverty and inequality (Rodriguez-Pose & Hardy, 2015) and unequal access to services (Cattaneo et al., 2021). Still, there are several thematic focuses that are identified to be common problems in rural areas throughout, such as lack of electricity (Javadi et al., 2013), international migrations (Woods, 2016), sustainable transition, renewable energies, the emergence of new technologies and growing awareness of environmental impacts (Ahlmeyer & Volgmann, 2023), social services provision (Manthorpe & Livsey, 2009), etc. In 2006, Dammers & Keiner (2006) elaborated in their article the comprehensive research results on trends and challenges of rural development in Europe, defining challenges for demography, economy, environment, energy and transport, and concluding that the diversification process is on the increase, as is the decline of rural areas. In 2014, Horlings and Marsden tried to identify new trajectories for European rural development and concluded that some shifts in rural areas are happening and can be expected, such as integrative development, place-based approach and rise of non-agricultural actors (Horlings & Marsden 2011). In the last 10 years, the European perspective revealed more detailed issues like the ageing population (Burholt & Dobbs, 2012), waste collection (Mihai, 2018), cultural heritage management (Gómez-Ullate et al., 2020), unequal development, decline of rural services, agro-economic developments, diversification of economy, migration patterns, sustainability transition and resilience and others (Ahlmeyer & Volgmann, 2023). The above research was further aggravated by the pandemic and its wider impact on society and the economy. Esteban-Navarro et al. (2020) presented results which show the digital vulnerability of rural areas during the COVID-19 pandemic, while Serrano and Fajardo (2023) pointed to possibilities for changing negative demographic trends in rural Spain. Lower mortality throughout the pandemic period appeared to be the most prominent fact for some rural areas in Europe (Amdaoud et al., 2021; Igari, 2023), but the picture of urban-rural disparities in COVID mortality was not very clear. It seems that less developed regions were more vulnerable to the consequences of the pandemic and that rural regions were not endangered in the first but in the second wave of the pandemic (https://cohesiondata.ec.europa.eu/stori es/s/The-regional-impact-of-COVID-19/24gj-n8r2/). The European Commission's strategy for supporting the development and recovery of rural areas until 2040 (European Commission, 2021a) is the long-term vision for rural areas to involve citizens and political actors at EU, national, regional and local levels to make rural areas and communities stronger, more connected, more resilient and more advanced. In contrast to securing the future of rural areas by reducing the differences in various urban-rural indicators, some people feel nostalgia, which is partly connected with the concept of place attachment (Belanche et al., 2021; Gillespie et al., 2022; da Silva et al., 2021; Štambuk, 1997; Tajfel, 1978). Also, rural area residents have a wide range of activities related to the natural environment (Hinds & Sparks, 2008).

Diversification of rural areas related to tourism activities has been discussed in the last 30 years (Hjalager, 1996). In order to promote rural tourism and rural development, the UNWTO (United Nations World Tourism Organization) declared 2020 as the Year of Tourism and Rural Development (UNWTO, 2020). The same organisation also launched the initiative 'Best Tourism Villages' (https://www.unwto.org/tourism-villages/en/).

Challenges for Rural Settlements in Croatia

Transformations of Rural Settlements Through the Aspect of Space, Demography, and Agriculture

Over the course of history, rural areas in Croatia have been transformed under the influence of natural and anthropogenic factors, changing their spatial structure and functional characteristics. Numerous villages emerged or disappeared because of specific political, economic, social, cultural, and natural conditions (wars, colonisation, landslides, earthquakes, fires, and diseases). Changes in socio-economic factors created conditions for new villages to emerge or for the existing ones to change and even disappear. In other words, external factors directly drove the change in the functions of the village, as well as in the spatial structure of the village, and consequently in the space in which the village is located (Kranjčević, 2018).

Already in 2002, Pokos (2002) called attention to the strong depopulation of rural areas in Croatia. Nejašmić and Toskić (2016) warned about the ageing population in rural settlements in Croatia. Štambuk identified modernisation processes in Croatian rural areas at the end of the 20th century (Štambuk 1997, 2002). Šundalić (2018) pointed to the lack of development potential in Slavonia and Baranja, the region with the strongest depopulation. Demographic data shows that Croatia lost 18.7% of its population in 30 years (1991–2021) (Croatian Bureau of Statistics, 2022a). The degree of depopulation within Croatia largely differs. Some counties, such as Osijek-Baranja County, a predominantly agricultural area that once had large villages, have lost 30% of their population since 1991, which is more than the average – primarily because of the emigration of young people (Croatian Bureau of Statistics, 2022a; Lukić 2012, 2022). Although the Croatian agricultural sector adapted to the market economy, it still faces several challenges, including the decline in arable land, fragmentation of land, deterioration of the ecological status of the environment due to the excessive use of fertilisers and pesticides, and the issue of food security (Global Monitor, 2020). Furthermore, Croatia's small agricultural population engages in low-level agricultural production for its own needs, finding it difficult to get a loan and pay it back. There is a lot of room for improvement in terms of an increased use of machinery and advanced technologies in agriculture; some activities related to the digital transformation of agricultural business have already begun.

Interest in the presentation of rural space and its architecture has a long tradition in Croatia. As early as the end of the 19th century, architects travelled around Croatia and recorded representative country houses (Doljak, 1885) in individual regions. At the beginning of the 20th century, these architects published five maps of Croatian building forms (Holjac & Pilar, 1904–1909), with the intention of providing the basis for the construction of new houses in certain regions. It was not unusual to see the most luxurious examples of rural regional architecture and their connection with the sale of industrialised agricultural food products presented at economic fairs in cities at the beginning of the 20th century.

Interestingly, during the 18th century (after the end of the war with the Ottoman Empire in 1699), strong spatial and economic transformation of rural areas was recorded in Croatia's geographical region of Slavonia because new, concentrated rural settlements were planned, built and populated with the aim of organised agricultural production and defence from a defeated enemy (Kranjčević, 2018).

Following the analysis of Croatian statistical data from 1875 to 2021, one can also speak of a kind of transformation of rural areas, as approximately 1,300 villages 'disappeared' (Dugački et al., 2021; Korenčić, 1979). Many of these villages were annexed to cities, and some were indeed left without a single inhabitant.

At the end of the 20th and the beginning of the 21st century, a new wave of demographic changes was recorded, bringing an end to many rural settlements.

According to the 2001 census, 105 settlements had no inhabitants; in 2011, the number of unpopulated settlements was 150, and in 2021 it went up to 195 (Croatian Bureau of Statistics, 2013, 2022a).

The Ageing Report of the European Commission (2021b) cites Croatia in the context that indicates an extremely unfavourable demographic situation, trend and forecast. Croatia had a negative migration balance from 2000 to 2018. It is in the same group with Latvia, Lithuania, Romania, and Bulgaria, countries expected to experience the strongest population decline in the range of 26–38% by 2070. For this group of countries, the number of working hours is expected to drop by 30–50% from 2019 to 2070. In addition, although the population of the entire European Union is expected to age, the share of population over 65 years of age in Croatia is expected to go up from 20% (2019) to 30% (2070). According to the census data of the Croatian Bureau of Statistics (2022b) from 1953 to the last census of 2021, the ageing index constantly increased, and so did the age coefficient. The population of Croatia crossed the age threshold of the definition of 'old population' (40% of the population over 60 years of age and the ratio of the population under 19 years old) in the 1960s (Fig. 1).

Encouraged by global trends and the rich architectural heritage of rural settlements, Croatian architects point to the necessity of looking at its regional architectural features. Freudenreich (1972), Čačić & Salopek (1971), and Salopek

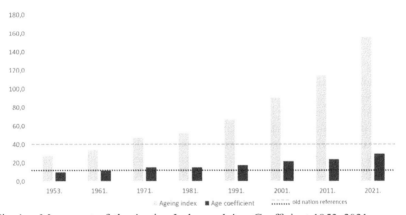

Fig. 1.   Movement of the Ageing Index and Age Coefficient 1953–2021.
Source: Croatian Bureau of Statistics (2013), https://web.dzs.hr/Hrv_Eng/publication/2012/SI-1468.pdf; Croatian Bureau of Statistics (2015), https://data.gov.hr/ckan/en/dataset/popisi-stanovni-tva-1953-2011-indeks-starenja-i-koeficijent-starosti/resourc.e/388f2b50-cf4e-4fe1-9911-895613ad6ff3 (for the years 1953–2011); Croatian Bureau of Statistics (2023a), https://podaci.dzs.hr/hr/podaci/stanovnistvo/popis-stanovnistva/ (for the year 2021), Adapted by Authors.

(1974) stand out among them. In several of his publications in 1992, mostly due to the suffering of rural settlements in the Homeland War (1991–1995), Živković (1992) highlighted the architectural values of rural architecture as part of spatial identity. Marinović-Uzelac (1992, 2002) pointed out the need to know regional specificities during spatial planning, as well as to know the typology of rural settlements. In Croatia, the situation is additionally burdened by fragmentised agricultural land, low price of agricultural land and rural houses, unsettled ownership relations, poor financial situation of municipalities, unfinished privatisation of agricultural assets (agricultural and industrial cooperatives), use of state-owned land, population's poor awareness of the importance of rural space and large areas of land under mines, etc.

A large building stock in need of renovation, especially abandoned and unused buildings, presents an additional burden on local governments and territories. The stock includes 110,143,965 m^2 of residential buildings in need of renovation and 58,722,937 m^2 of non-residential buildings in need of renovation, of which 16,099,527 m^2 are public buildings. In the Long-Term Strategy for the Restoration of the National Building Stock until 2050 (Ministry of Physical Planning, Construction and State Assets, 2020), the segment of the building stock out of use is described with the word *demolition* (demolition or abandonment), and the demolition rate is predicted at 25% by 2050. Urban and rural areas are equally burdened with residential buildings that require renovation, but there are more commercial and public buildings in urban areas.

Taking the above into consideration, the recovery of rural settlements should be viewed on the national and regional level through different sectors.

Transformations of Rural Settlements Through the Aspect of Tourism

Given that tourism was often an incentive for changing the way of life in villages, especially villages along the Croatian Adriatic coast, it does not surprise that some fishing settlements, notably in Kvarner, were transformed into exclusive tourist destinations (Opatija, Lovran, etc.) at the end of the 19th century. Through the construction of technical and transport infrastructure, they changed the function and purpose and influenced the change in employment.

The change continued after the Second World War, when tourism unstoppably penetrated the coastal area and to a higher or lesser extent paved the way for the transformation and modernisation of numerous settlements. Ensminger (1970) believed that the development of tourism served for the urbanisation of numerous rural settlements along the coast, and Mihletić (1962) indicated the possibility of a stronger connection between domestic agricultural production and tourism. Furthermore, Lukić (2000) pointed out that rural tourism could be a factor in the integral development of rural areas in Croatia.

During the COVID-19 pandemic, some geographical regions, such as Gorski Kotar, with very rural geographical characteristics and many abandoned settlements, but with a long tradition of rural tourism (Kranjčević et al., 2022b), became attractive and safe tourist rural areas.

Given that rural areas are increasingly becoming interesting to tourists, the Croatian Ministry of Tourism initiated the preparation of several manuals for the renovation of rural houses with the aim of preserving regional architectural design characteristics (Lončar & Stober, 2011; Salopek et al., 2006; Živković, 2015). Most abandoned settlements have residential and commercial buildings (in a better or worse condition) built with traditional design characteristics. The northeastern part of Primorje-Gorski Kotar County – Gorski Kotar – has the largest number of abandoned settlements. Although Gorski Kotar has a long tradition of rural tourism, dating back to the very beginnings of modern tourism, it was not tourism that was the driving force for the survival of the population. And there was no incentive for the development of tourism (Kranjčević et al., 2022b).

Throughout history, rural settlements have been shaped under the influence of natural and anthropogenic factors. Depending on the geographical region, rural settlements can largely be clearly identified through forms of spatial-architectural identity. It is known that, in certain periods, the states on the territory of today's Croatia (Kranjčević, 2018) influenced the development of agriculture and the formation of rural settlements in different ways.[1]

From the end of the 19th century until today (the beginning of the third decade of the 21st century) under numerous socio-economic and political processes, such as Europeanisation and globalisation, Croatia has faced strong depopulation, which has resulted in an increased number of abandoned settlements.[2] The cause can be found in the absence of recovery and resilience concepts.

Considering that these settlements most often have the basic technical infrastructure (electricity, some also water supply), the question arises as to whether these settlements can have a future, that is, whether they can get a new purpose and contribute to the recovery of the village area? Certainly, the recovery of settlements should be opposed to the development of 'uniformisation' and globalisation of space, landscape, living space and environment.

The conceptualisation of the recovery model of abandoned rural settlements should also be considered through the potential of tourist regions in Croatia, taking into account regional characteristics of architectural heritage. Those rural settlements that will change their function through tourism should be connected to the agriculture, culture, and construction sectors. In this way, the recovery of the settlement is linked to different sectors, the potential of sustainability and viewed through a tourist perspective.

---

[1]For example, the planning of rural settlements on the territory of Croatia is visible since the time of ancient Greece (Starigradsko polje on the island of Hvar, for example), the remains of which are still visible today. The planning of rural settlements in Croatia during the time of ancient Rome is also visible, the remains of which can be seen in the Tovarnik settlement, etc. (Kranjčević, 2018).
[2]Most of them were abandoned due to large population migrations caused by wars or the economic situation. At the end of the 19th century, there was a big wave of emigration from Dalmatia. In 2021, Croatia had 6,756 settlements, of which 127 cities. All other settlements can be characterised as rural.

Results and Discussion

By comparing the tourist traffic and the number of abandoned settlements by tourist regions (counties) in Croatia, it is evident that regions with strong tourist traffic have many abandoned rural settlements. As shown, even a good traffic situation in the region does not guarantee the survival of the settlement.

The increased number of abandoned settlements is not uniformly distributed. Out of 6,756 settlements in total, 195 were abandoned according to the 2021 census, which indicates a more intense spatial transformation of some tourist regions, especially in the northern part of the Adriatic Croatia (Croatian Bureau of Statistics, 2023b).

The biggest number of abandoned settlements – 54 – are in Primorje-Gorski Kotar County, followed by 30 settlements in Karlovac County, 18 in Istria and 18 in Požega-Slavonia County. These numbers represent the state of load and the potential for the consideration of solutions at the regional level. The result indicates the possibility of a synergy of locations in the network of settlements.

Data on tourist arrivals and overnight stays by county, collected and processed by the Croatian Bureau of Statistics (CBS, 2023b), indicate, on the one hand, the overload of certain areas with tourist activities and, on the other hand, abandonment of rural settlements (Figs. 2 and 3). Considering the data overview with the

Created with mapchart.net

Fig. 2. Tourist Arrivals to Commercial Accommodation Facilities in 2022. *Source*: Croatian Bureau of Statistics (2023b). https://podaci.dzs.hr/2022/hr/29506, adapted by Authors.

Created with mapchart.net

Fig. 3.   Overnight Stays of Tourists in Commercial Facilities in 2022. *Source*:
Croatian Bureau of Statistics, (2023b). https://podaci.dzs.hr/2022/hr/29506,
Adapted by Authors.

share of settlements with up to 5 inhabitants and the number of abandoned settlements, we can assume that abandoned and micro settlements in some regions
can be used for tourism and observed through the regional synergy and network-
ing of tourism activities. Primorje-Gorski Kotar and Istria are counties with a
high potential for settlement abandonment and large tourist burden, as well as
Split-Dalmatia County in the Adriatic Croatia; Osijek-Baranja County in continental Croatia has a greater number of settlement depopulation and a relatively
greater influx of tourists. For Požega-Slavonia County, which stands out with the
number of abandoned settlements, but has weaker indicators of tourist arrivals
and overnight stays, abandoned settlements should be viewed with other functional strategic ideas (Figs. 4 and 5).

The results showed that the county (tourist region) with the largest tourist
traffic has the largest number of abandoned rural settlements (Primorje-Gorski
Kotar County – 54 settlements in 2021). The second county in terms of the number of abandoned settlements is Karlovac County (30 settlements, 2021), and it
has good traffic connections. It is followed by counties with 18 abandoned rural
settlements each – Istria and Požega-Slavonia counties. Istria County is the region
with the largest tourist traffic, while Požega-Slavonia County has negligible
tourist traffic.

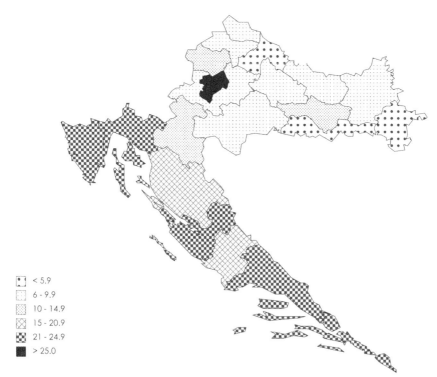

Fig. 4.   Tourism Development Index – County Data. *Source*: Institute for Tourism (2023), https://www.iztzg.hr/hr/itr/, adapted by Authors.

In addition to abandoned settlements, it is necessary to look at settlements with 1 to 5 inhabitants and where they are located. There are 72 settlements with 1 inhabitant in Croatia (19 in Primorje-Gorski Kotar County, 21 in Karlovac County, etc.). It can be assumed that by the next census in 2031, most of them will not have any inhabitants. Furthermore, Croatia has 61 settlements with 2 inhabitants (13 in Primorje-Gorski Kotar County, 12 in Karlovac County, etc.) and 46 settlements with 3 inhabitants (11 in Primorje-Gorski Kotar County, 12 in Karlovac County, etc.). In short, Primorje-Gorski Kotar County has 24.2% of settlements with 1–5 inhabitants, Karlovac County has 16.2% and Požega-Slavonia County has 15.9%.

It is not possible to understand the state of Croatia's rural area nor plan its recovery without understanding global and European processes and observing the opportunities and attitudes of different professions in Croatia. Different professions view the situation in the rural area from different aspects.

The Territorial agenda 2030 – a future for all places can serve as a framework for encouraging interdisciplinary reflection and research on the inclusion of abandoned rural settlements in the tourist offer.

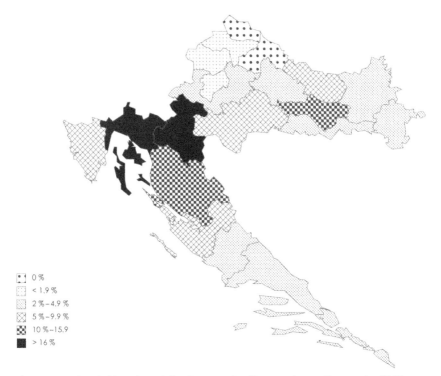

0 %
< 1.9 %
2 % – 4.9 %
5 % – 9.9 %
10 % –15.9
> 16 %

Fig. 5.   Ratio of Abandoned Settlements by County According to the 2021 Census. *Source*: Croatian Bureau of Statistics (2022a) Stanovništvo po naseljima. https://podaci.dzs.hr/media/rqybclnx/popis_2021-stanovnistvo_po_naseljima.xlsx, adapted by Authors.

Conclusion

Numerous technological changes, globalisation and depopulation have undoubtedly reshaped the space of regions and places, but if we want vital regions, we should think about the existing network of places, villages and towns and look at their future.

The development of tourism through different concepts should indeed get to grips with the new mechanisms of responsibility from tourism stakeholders because they are directly and indirectly related to different sectors (culture, construction, agriculture, economy, education, health, ecology, etc.). This chapter pleads to start an intersectoral debate on the impact of business reality at the national level. There is no doubt that space has constantly changed during the history, and the comprehensive transformation of regions can include the recovery of abandoned rural settlements by changing the traditional functions of settlements. Certainly, the functional changes of the village should be observed through the plans of different sectors such as tourism, agriculture, education, transport, etc. If some abandoned settlements are going to be recovered for the purpose of rural tourism development, it is necessary to look at the state of their infrastructure, traffic accessibility, spatial structure, regional architectural characteristics and so on and offer recognisability based on regional architectural characteristics shaped in a new way.

In addition to the presented quantitative data, it is necessary to take into account the first aspect of the qualitative approach, which is more often taken at the national level, but very little applied research has been conducted at the local level (Hauge, 2007; Rembold & Carrier, 2011).

This research should be deepened with field research to obtain data on the condition and quality of the building stock, spatial specifics, existence and condition of infrastructure, traffic accessibility, state of the landscape, etc., and the reason for abandoning the settlement. The database would serve as the foundation for creating guidelines for the recovery of abandoned settlements in the region.

It is important to sensitise and educate young experts involved in tourism and various creative industries (Kranjčević et al., 2022) in order to see and connect all challenges in the long term. Education and sensibility of experts and local residents can contribute to the recovery of abandoned settlements. The above means that if we want a vibrant future for all settlements, plans for abandoned settlements should be linked to a wider spectrum of challenges from different sectors, but also to the quality of life at the individual and community level.

Transformation and recovery of abandoned rural settlements should also be planned through digital and green transformation and creative industries that can provide momentum for designing a stimulus package.

References

Ahlmeyer, F., & Volgmann, K. (2023). What can we expect for the development of rural areas in Europe? Trends of the last decade and their opportunities for rural regeneration. *Sustainability*, *15*(6), 5485. https://doi.org/10.3390/su15065485

Amdaoud, M., Arcuri, G., & Levratto, N. (2021). Are regions equal in adversity? A spatial analysis of spread and dynamics of COVID-19 in Europe. *The European Journal of Health Economics*, *22*(4), 629–642.

Bain, L. E., & Adeagbo, O. A. (2022). There is an urgent need for a global rural health research agenda. *Pan African Medical Journal*, *43*(147). https://www.panafrican-med-journal.com//content/article/43/147/full

Belanche, A., Casaló, L. V., & Rubio, Á. (2021). Local place identity: A comparison between residents of rural and urban communities. *Journal of Rural Studies*, *82*, 242–252. https://www.sciencedirect.com/science/article/pii/S0743016721000036

Burholt, V., & Dobbs, C. (2012). Research on rural ageing: Where have we got to and where are we going in Europe? *Journal of Rural Studies*, *28*, 432–446. https://doi.org/10.1016/j.jrurstud.2012.01.009

Cattaneo, A., Nelson, A., & McMenomy, T. (2021). Global mapping of urban–rural catchment areas reveals unequal access to services. *PNAS*, *118*(2), 1–8. https://doi.org/10.1073/pnas.2011990118

Croatian Bureau of Statistics. (2013). *Popis 2011.* https://web.dzs.hr/Hrv_Eng/publication/2012/SI-1468.pdf

Croatian Bureau of Statistics. (2015). *Indeks starenja i koeficijent starosti.* https://data. gov.hr/ckan/en/dataset/popisi-stanovni-tva-1953-2011-indeks-starenja-i-koeficijent-starosti/resourc.e/388f2b50-cf4e-4fe1-9911-895613ad6ff3

Croatian Bureau of Statistics. (2021a). *Hrvatska u brojkama/Croatia in Figures.* https:// podaci.dzs.hr/media/fagflfgk/croinfig_2021.pdf

Croatian Bureau of Statistics. (2021b). *Population by age and sex, by settlements, 2021 CENSUS.* https://podaci.dzs.hr/media/rqybclnx/popis_2021-stanovnistvo_po_ naseljima.xlsx

Croatian Bureau of Statistics. (2022a). *Stanovništvo po naseljima.* https://podaci.dzs.hr/ media/rqybclnx/popis_2021-stanovnistvo_po_naseljima.xlsx

Croatian Bureau of Statistics. (2022b). *Procjena stanovništva Republike Hrvatske u 2021.* https://podaci.dzs.hr/2022/hr/29032

Croatian Bureau of Statistics. (2023a). *Stanovništvo prema starosti i spolu.* https://podaci. dzs.hr/hr/podaci/stanovnistvo/popis-stanovnistva/

Croatian Bureau of Statistics. (2023b). *Dolasci i noćenja turista u 2022.* https://podaci.dzs. hr/2022/hr/29506

Čaćić, B., & Salopek, D. (1971). *Hrvatska korablja – Saveza arhitekata Hrvatske, Zagreb-Rijeka.*

Dammers, Ed., & Keiner, M. (2006). Rural development in Europe. *The Planning Review, 42*(166), 5–15. https://doi.org/10.1080/02513625.2006.10556958

Dijkstra, L., Hamilton, E., Lakk, S., & Wahba, S. (2021). *How do we define cities, towns, and rural areas?* https://blogs.worldbank.org/sustainablecities/how-do-we-define-cities-towns-and-rural-areas

Doljak, I. (1885). Hrvatski građevni oblici. 1. iz Posavine. *Viesti družtva inžinira i arhitekata, 6*(1), 3–6.

Dugački, V., Peternel, L., & Škiljan, F. (2021). *Nestala naselja u Republici Hrvatskoj. Plejada; Institut za društvena istraživanja – Institut za migracije i narodnosti. Zagreb.*

Ensminger, S. (1970). Urbanizacija sela putem razvoja turizma. *Turizam, 18*(5), 10–12.

Esteban-Navarro, M.-Á., García-Madurga, M.-Á., Morte-Nadal, T., & Nogales-Bocio, A.-I. (2020). The rural digital divide in the face of the COVID-19 pandemic in Europe – Recommendations from a scoping review. *Informatics, 7*, 54. https:// doi.org/10.3390/informatics7040054

European Commission. (2021a). *Long-term vision for rural areas up to 2040.* https://rural-vision.europa.eu/index_en

European Commission. (2021b). *Directorate-general for economic and financial affairs the ageing report, underlying assumptions and projection methodologies.* European Economy Institutional Paper 142, pp. 238.

Eurostat. (2011). *Urban-rural typology update.* http://epp.eurostat.ec.europa.eu/statistics_ explained/index.php/Urban-rural_typology_update

Eurostat. (2019). *Urban and rural living in the EU.* https://ec.europa.eu/eurostat/web/ products-eurostat-news/-/edn-20200207-1

Eurostat. (2022). *Urban-rural Europe: Demographic developments in rural regions and areas.* https://ec.europa.eu/eurostat/statistics-explained/index.php?title=Urban-rural_ Europe_-_demographic_developments_in_rural_regions_and_areas

Freudenreich, A. (1972). *Kako narod gradi na području Hrvatske, Republički zavod za zaštitu spomenika kulture, Zagreb.*

Gillespie, R., DeWitt, E., Slone, S., Cardarelli, K., & Gustafson, A. (2022). The impact of a grocery store closure in one rural highly obese Appalachian community on shopping behavior and dietary intake. *International Journal of Environmental Research and Public Health, 19*(6), 3506.

Global Monitor. (2020). *Croatia agriculture market trends, statistics, growth, and forecasts.* https://www.globalmonitor.us/product/croatia-agriculture-market

Gómez-Ullate, M., Rieutort, L., Kamara, A., Santos, A. S., Pirra, A., & Solís, M. G. (2020). Demographic challenges in rural Europe and cases of resilience based on cultural heritage management: A comparative analysis in Mediterranean countries inner regions. *European Countryside, 12*(3), 408–431.

Government of the Republic of Croatia. (2021a). *Croatia's recovery and resilience plan.* https://planoporavka.gov.hr/

Government of the Republic of Croatia. (2021b). *Izvješće o stanju u prostoru Republike Hrvatske, 2013–2019, Zagreb.*

Hamilton, J. B. (2019). Rigor in qualitative methods: An evaluation of strategies among underrepresented rural communities. *Qualitative Health Research, 30*(2), 196–204. https://doi.org/10.1177/1049732319860267

Hauge, Å. L. (2007). Identity and place: A critical comparison of three identity theories. *Architectural Science Review, 50*(1), 44–51.

Hinds, J., & Sparks, P. (2008). Engaging with the natural environment: The role of affective connection and identity. *Journal of Environmental Psychology, 28*(2), 109–120. https://doi.org/10.1016/j.jenvp.2007.11.001

Hjalager, A. M. (1996). Agricultural diversification into tourism: Evidence of a European community development programme. *Tourism Management, 17*(2), 103–111.

Holjac, J., & Pilar, M. (1904–1909). *Hrvatski građevni oblici—Društvo inžinira i arhitekata, Zagreb.*

Horlings, L. G., & Marsden, T. K. (2011). *Towards the real green revolution? Exploring the conceptualdimensions of a new ecological modernisation of agriculture that could 'feed the world'.* [BRASSWorking Paper, Cardiff University, Cardiff].

Horlings, L. G., & Marsden, T. K. (2014). Exploring the 'New RuralParadigm' in Europe: Eco-economic strategies ASA counterforce to the global competitiveness agenda. *European Urban and Regional Studies, 21*(1), 4–20.

https://cohesiondata.ec.europa.eu/stories/s/The-regional-impact-of-COVID-19/24gj-n8r2/
https://ec.europa.eu/eurostat/web/rural-development/methodology

Igari, A. (2023). Spatiotemporal inequalities of excess mortality in Europe during the first two years of the Covid-19 pandemic. *Regional Statistics, 13*(3), 510–535. https://doi.org/10.15196/RS130306

Institute for Tourism. (2023). *Indeks turističke razvijenosti/Index of tourism development.* https://www.iztzg.hr/hr/itr/

Javadi, F. S., Rismanchi, B., Sarraf, M., Afshar, O., Saidur, R., Ping, H.W., & Rahim, N. A. (2013). Global policy of rural electrification. *Renewable & Sustainable Energy Reviews, 19*, 402–416. https://doi.org/10.1016/j.rser.2012.11.053

Kociatkiewicz, J., & Kostera, M. (1999). The anthropology of empty spaces. *Qualitative Sociology, 22*(1), 37–50.

Korenčić, M. (1979). *Naselja i stanovništvo SR Hrvatske 1857-1971. Djela JAZU, Knjiga 54, Zagreb.*

Kranjčević, J., & Stober, D. (2022). *Turizam: Regionalno promišljanje za revitalizaciju napuštenih ruralnih naselja Hrvatske.* In *Zbornik 3.* Konferencija o urbanom planiranju i regionalnom razvoju/3rd Conference on Urban Planning and Regional Development; Urbano - ruralna povezanost i regionalni razvoj/Urban - Rural Connectivity and REGIONAL DEVElopment. Udruženje Konsultanata Inženjera Bosne i Hercegovine (ed. Nataša Stanišić): održana 23. novembar 2021. Sarajevo, BiH, 185–198. https://uki.ba/download/zbornik-radova-3-konferencije-o-urbanom-planiranju-i-regionalnom-razvoju-urbano-ruralna-povezanost-i-regionalni-razvoj/

Kranjčević, J. (2018). *Zanemarena baština: Prostorne strukture sela.* Srednja Europa.

Kranjčević, J., Dolaček-Alduk, Z., & Stober, D. (2022). University education of architects for tourism planning in rural space. In *5th International Congress of Rural Tourism: Quality, Sustainability, Inclusiveness, Congress Proceedings 27–30* (pp. 180–192).

Kranjčević, J., Marković Vukadin, I., & Dumbović Bilušić, B. (2018). Qualitative approach to spatial identity evaluation of rural and suburban settlements. In *Congress proceedings:4th International congress of rural tourism, the era of rural tourism* (pp. 79–90).
Kranjčević, J., Tuhtan, G., & Marković Vukadin, I. (2022b). Rural tourism of Gorski Kotar – Between potentials and realities. In *Congress Proceedings, 5th international congress of rural tourism: Quality, sustainability, inclusiveness, congress proceedings 27–30* (pp. 276–290).
Kumar, V., Kumar, R., Singh, J., & Kumar, P. (2019). Contaminants in agriculture and environment: Health risks and remediation. *Agriculture and Environmental Science, India.* https://doi.org/10.26832/AESA-2019-CAE
Lončar, V. S., & Stober, D. (2011). *Tradicijska kuća Slavonije i Baranje – Pri ručnik za obnovu*, Ministarstvo turizma RH Sveučilište J.J. Strossmayera u Osijeku Građevinski fakultet Osijek.
Long-Term Strategy for the Restoration of the National Building Fund until 2050 [Dugoročna strategija obnove nacionalnog fonda zgrada do 2050. godine]. (2020). Narodne novine br. 140/2020. https://mpgi.gov.hr/print.aspx?id=9055&url=print&page=1
Lukić, A. (2000). Ruralni turizam-čimbenik integralnog razvitka ruralnog prostora Hrvatske. *Geografski horizonti, 6*, 7–31.
Lukić, A. (2010). O teorijskim pristupima ruralnom prostoru. *Hrvatski geografski glasnik, 72*(2), 49–73. https://doi.org/10.21861/hgg.2010.72.02.03
Lukić, A. (2012). *Mozaik izvan grada: tipologija ruralnih i urbaniziranih naselja Hrvatske.* Meridijani.
Lukić, A. (2022). Effects of economic restructuring and recent history: The case of Osječko-Baranjska County. *ESPON Conference: Challenges and Opportunities for Shrinking Areas, 16th February 2022.*
Manthorpe, J., & Livsey, L. (2009). European challenges in delivering social services in rural regions: A scoping review. *European Journal of Social Work, 12*(1), 5–24. https://doi.org/10.1080/13691450802567440
Marinović-Uzelac, A. (1992). *Regionalizacija iz vidokruga prostornog planiranja. In Država, regije, regionalni razvoj, Zbornik Društvena istraživanja*, (ed. M. Štambuk) (Vol. 1, pp. 69–85).
Marinović-Uzelac, A. (2002). *Morfološki tipovi hrvatskog sela, u: Prostor iza, Zbornik br.17 (ur. M. Štambuk, I. Rogić, A. Mišetić), Zagreb, Institut društvenih znanosti Ivo Pilar, 2002., str* (pp. 131–154).
Mihai, F. C. (2018). Waste collection in rural communities: Challenges under EU regulations. A case study of Neamt County, Romania. *Journal of Material Cycles and Waste Management, 20*, 1337–1347.
Mihletić, A. (1962). Turizam i planiranje poljoprivrede u jadranskom području. *Turizam, 11*(1962), 14–17.
Ministers Responsible for Spatial Planning, Territorial Development and/or Territorial Cohesion. (2020). *Territorial Agenda: A future for all places.* https://territoriala-genda.eu/library/
Ministry of Physical Planning, Construction and State Assets. (2020). Dugoročna strategija obnove nacionalnog fonda zgrada do 2050. *Godine, 2020*, 113.
Morgan, J. M., & Calleja, P. (2020). Emergency trauma care in rural and remote settings: Challenges and patient outcomes. *International Emergency Nursing, 51*, 100880. https://doi.org/10.1016/j.ienj.2020.100880
Nejašmić, I., & Toskić, A. (2016). Ostarjelost stanovništva seoskih naselja Republike Hrvatske. *Migracijske i etničke teme, 32* (2), 191–219.
OECD. (2020). *Rebuilding tourism for the future: COVID-19 policy responses and recovery.* https://www.oecd.org/coronavirus/policy-responses/rebuilding-tourism-for-the-future-covid-19-policy-responses-and-recovery-bced9859/#boxsection-d1e40

OECD. (2021). *The COVID-19 crisis in urban and rural areas.* https://www.oecd-ilibrary. org/sites/c734c0fe-en/index.html?itemId=/content/component/c734c0fe-en

Pokos, N. (2002). *Metodologija izdvajanja seoskog stanovništva, njegov raspored i popisne promjene 1953.-2001., u: Prostor iza, Zbornik, knjiga br. 17, (ur. M. Štambuk, I. Rogić, A. Mišetić), Zagreb, Institut društvenih znanosti Ivo Pilar, str.* (pp. 31–56).

Rembold, E., & Carrier, P. (2011). Space and identity: Constructions of national identities in an age of globalisation. *National Identities, 13*(4), 361–377. doi: 10.1080/14608944.2011.629425

Rodríguez-Pose, A., & Hardy, D. (2015). Addressing poverty and inequality in the rural economy from a global perspective. *Applied Geography, 61*, 11–23. doi: 10.1016/j. apgeog.2015.02.005

Salopek, D. (1974). *Arhitektura bez arhitekta:vitalne poruke narodnog graditeljstva, Mala arhitektonska bibliblioteka SAH-e, Zagreb, 1974.*

Salopek, D., Petrić, K., Mlinar, A., Horvat, M., Mavar, Z., Rajković, V., & Gugić, G. (2006). *Posavska tradicijska drvena kuća: priručnik za obnovu/izradili - Zagreb: Ministarstvo mora, turizma, prometa i razvitka: Ministarstvo kulture.* https://mint. gov.hr/UserDocsImages/arhiva/posavska-kuca-bez-c.pdf

Serrano, J. J., & Fajardo, F. (2023). Impact of COVID-19 on the territory and demographic processes: A view from Spanish rural and urban areas. *Sustainability, MDPI, 15*(10), 1–27.

Silva, S. M. D., Silva, A. M., Cortés-González, P., & Braziene, R. (2021). Learning to leave and to return: Mobility, place, and sense of belonging amongst young people growing up in border and rural regions of mainland Portugal. *Sustainability, 13*, 9432. https://doi.org/10.3390/su13169432

Strasser, R. (2003). Rural health around the World: Challenges and solution. *Family Practice, 20*, 457–463. https://doi.org/10.1093/fampra/cmg422

Strijker, D., Bosworth, G., & Bouter, G. (2020). Research methods in rural studies: Qualitative, quantitative and mixed methods. *Journal of Rural Studies, 78*, 262–270. https://doi.org/10.1016/j.jrurstud.2020.06.007

Štambuk, M. (1997). *Modernizacijski procesi i društvene promjene u hrvatskim ruralnim sredinama, Diss. doc. Filozofski fakultet, Sveučilište u Zagrebu, Zagreb.*

Štambuk, M. (2002). *Selo i modernizacija: kratka povijest nesporazuma, u: Prostor iza, Zbornik br. 17, (ur. M. Štambuk, I. Rogić, A. Mišetić), Zagreb, Institut društvenih znanosti Ivo Pilar, str.* (pp. 9–28).

Šundalić, A. (2018). O nedostatnim potencijalima razvoja Slavonije i Baranje. In: *Sudbina otvorenih granica. Zbornik radova sa znanstvenog skupa Globalizacija i regionalni identitet 2018.* (eds. Antun Šundalić; Krunoslav Zmaić; Tihana Sudarić; Željko Pavić). Filozofski fakultet Sveučilišta Josipa Jurja Strossmayera u Osijeku (pp. 36–151).

Tajfel, H. (1978). *Differentiation between Social Groups.* Academic Press.

The Ageing Report of the European Commission. (2021). *UNWTO – Best Tourism Villages.* https://www.unwto.org/tourism-villages/en/

UNWTO. (2020). 2020 Year Of 'Tourism and Rural Development' Background Notes, https://webunwto.s3.eu-west-1.amazonaws.com/s3fs-public/2020-09/wtdback-ground-note-en.pdf (Accessed 8/9/2023). https://www.unwto.org/tourism-villages/en/ (Accessed 6/9/2023)

Woods, M. (2016). International migration, agency and regional development in rural Europe. *Documents d'anàlisi geogràfica, 62*(3), 569–593.

Živković, Z. (1992). *Hrvatsko Narod no graditeljstvo – Istočna Hrvatska. Zavod za zaštitu spomenika kulture, Zagreb.*

Živković, Z. (2015). *Tradicijska kamena kuća dalmatinskog zaleđa – Priručnik za obnovu i turističku valorizaciju.* Ministarstvo turizma Republike Hrvatske, Ministarstvo van-jskih i europskih poslova.

Chapter 16

Challenges to Be Answered and Answers to Be Challenged

Izidora Marković Vukadin[a] *and Naser Ul Islam*[b]

[a]*Institute for Tourism, Zagreb, Croatia*
[b]*Tata Institute of Social Sciences, Mumbai, India*

Abstract

This chapter provides an overview of the key themes and takeaways discussed in this book, which explores the challenges and opportunities that the tourism industry faces in a volatile, uncertain, complex, and ambiguous (VUCA) world. Several reasons emphasise the importance of understanding the VUCA world, including risk management, innovation, resilience, evolving strategies, and anticipatory leadership. The book addresses the need to rethink tourism, community perspectives, and tourist behaviour in the VUCA context, which is vital for destination management. Stakeholders must adapt to changing conditions, implement effective crisis response strategies, and promote sustainability. Destinations and businesses must be proactive, adaptable, and forward-thinking, as well as foster cultures of innovation. Embracing digital technologies can enhance an organisation's ability to navigate the VUCA environment, and scenario planning can help identify and mitigate risks that can impact operations, financial stability, or reputation.

The future of the tourism industry in a VUCA world involves a holistic approach that prioritises healing, resilience, risk management, innovation, and sustainability. It requires a commitment to responsible tourism, nature and cultural preservation, and adaptability to changing conditions. By embracing these directions, the tourism industry can navigate the complexities of the VUCA environment and build a more sustainable and resilient future. Agility, adaptability, and innovative thinking are critical for long-term success and sustainability in an unpredictable and rapidly changing

Tourism in a VUCA World: Managing the Future of Tourism, 231–237
Published under exclusive licence by Emerald Publishing Limited
doi:10.1108/978-1-83753-674-020241016

world. Therefore, this book offers valuable insights into addressing the challenges of the VUCA world and provides a roadmap for the tourism industry's path forward.

Keywords: VUCA; tourism industry; rethinking tourism; community perspective and tourist behaviour; organisational and strategy transformation; future opportunities

Introduction

This book has discussed various ways for tourism to manage sustainability in an everchanging economic, social, and natural environment and challenging geopolitical landscape. Understanding the VUCA world is essential for several reasons, which were emphasised in this book: risk management, innovation, resilience as an ability to bounce back from setbacks and adapt to changing circumstances, strategies based on evolving conditions, and anticipatory leadership (Krawczyńska-Zaucha, 2019). Furthermore, the VUCA world is often characterised by global challenges such as climate change and pandemics that require international cooperation and collective action (Kaivo-oja & Lauraeus, 2018). Understanding VUCA is crucial for addressing these global issues effectively (Johansen & Euchner, 2013). Contributors to this book have used existing theories and practices to come to novel ideas and conclusions.

Rethinking Tourism

Rethinking tourism is essential for several compelling reasons, particularly in the context of the 21st century and the industry's challenges. Tourism significantly impacts the environment, from carbon emissions to overdevelopment and damage to natural habitats. Rethinking tourism is essential to minimising its ecological footprint and promoting sustainable practices that protect natural resources and ecosystems (Vărzaru et al., 2021). Furthermore, mass tourism can sometimes erode local cultures and traditions. New solutions and ideas for new ways to celebrate and preserve the unique cultural heritage of destinations can ensure that tourism benefits local communities (Al-Ababneh, 2019). Through such actions, economic resilience is built by diversifying revenue streams, preparing for unforeseen challenges, and evolving consumer preferences. Finally, through rethinking strategies, tourism aligns the industry with the United Nations Sustainable Development Goals (SDGs) and contributes to broader societal and environmental objectives (Sempiga & Van Liedekerke, 2023).

In the wake of the VUCA environment that the tourism industry faces, managing sustainable and responsible tourism trends post-2023 is paramount. As emphasised in the second chapter of this book, sustainability should not be a static goal but an evolving concept, adapting to the ever-changing landscape of tourism. In the face of new challenges, the industry must continue embracing responsible practices and innovative strategies. By monitoring trends, collaborating with stakeholders, and reevaluating sustainability measures, the tourism sector can move forward with resilience and a commitment to preserving the environment and local communities.

Furthermore, Chapters 3 and 4 focus on how the tourism industry must acknowledge and adapt to the new realities presented by global climate changes. Chapter 3 stresses the growing impact of climate change on destinations and traveller preferences; the sector faces a critical imperative to reduce its environmental footprint. In this VUCA context, the industry should focus on carbon reduction, disaster preparedness, and the promotion of sustainable practices. Chapter 4 highlights the need for adaptation and mitigation measures to protect destinations and promote responsible tourism. In the VUCA context, flexibility, and resilience are the key. Sustainable tourism practices, such as carbon offsetting and eco-friendly infrastructure, should be integrated into the industry's core strategies. By building capacities for climate change adaptation and mitigation, the tourism sector can navigate the uncertain future with a commitment to environmental stewardship.

As the hotel industry navigates the alternative reality created by technology, Chapter 5 underscores the need for adaptation and innovation. Virtual, augmented, and artificial technologies are transforming how travellers experience hotels and destinations. In a VUCA world, the industry must harness these technologies to enhance customer experiences, improve operational efficiency, and reduce environmental impact. Embracing digital advancements can enable the hotel sector to thrive in the evolving landscape and provide guests with immersive and sustainable options.

Community Perspectives and Tourist Behaviour in VUCA

This part of this book explored how communities in the tourism destinations and tourists themselves are influenced and respond to the challenges presented by the VUCA environment. Examining community perspectives and tourist behaviour in a VUCA context involves understanding how these communities and tourists react to these challenges. Overall, analysing community perspectives and tourist behaviour in a VUCA context is crucial for destination management, as it helps stakeholders adapt to changing conditions, implement effective crisis response strategies, and promote sustainability in the tourism industry. It also supports the development of resilient and adaptive tourism systems that can thrive despite the uncertainties and complexities of the VUCA environment. Therefore, a summary of chapters in this part of the book offers some challenges with the answers on how to deal with them.

Chapter 6 highlights the potential of nudging as a strategic tool for enhancing destination management. Nudging can contribute to a more prosperous and sustainable tourism industry by subtly influencing tourist behaviour and choices. As the world faces complex challenges, adopting behavioural interventions like nudging can lead to positive outcomes for tourists and destination management.

Chapter 7 focuses on the impact of cruise tourism on local communities and their way of life, which is a critical issue, especially in the context of the pandemic. This chapter underlines the need for balanced approaches that respect the local culture and environment. As we navigate through changing times, it is vital to reevaluate cruise tourism's role in local rhythms and work towards sustainable and mutually beneficial relationships.

The COVID-19 pandemic exacerbated tourism challenges, including tourist xenophobia, as presented in Chapter 8. This chapter examines the case of Japan and the importance of understanding residents' perspectives. As we operate in a VUCA world, fostering understanding and cooperation between tourists and locals is paramount for the sustainable recovery and growth of the tourism industry.

Understanding the psychological and socio-demographic drivers of pro-environmental behaviour in Generation Z is critical to promoting sustainable tourism. Chapter 9 sheds light on the motivations of the younger generation (in Croatia) to engage in environmentally responsible practices. In the VUCA context, harnessing the values and preferences of Generation Z is crucial for shaping a more eco-conscious and sustainable future in the tourism industry. The findings revealed that gender, education level, and residential area significantly influenced psychological drivers such as guilt feelings, and moral obligations. In contrast, women showed higher levels of guilt, moral obligations, and self-identity related to environmental responsibility.

Organisational and Strategy Transformations Under VUCA

Based on all stated challenges, there is a clear need for destinations, businesses, and institutions to adapt and evolve their organisational structures and strategies in response to the challenges posed by a VUCA environment. In this context, destinations and businesses need to make fundamental changes to how they operate and how they plan for the future (Bennett & Lemoine, 2014) through high-level agility and empowering managers and employees to make real-time decisions (Wakelin-Theron et al., 2019; Lubowiecki-Vikuk & Sousa, 2021).

A VUCA environment demands constant innovation and adaptability. Stakeholders should foster cultures of innovation, where employees are encouraged to generate new ideas and adapt existing practices to meet changing needs (Millar et al., 2018). Embracing digital technologies can enhance an organisation's ability to navigate a VUCA environment. For instance, businesses might invest in digital marketing, e-commerce, data analytics, or remote work solutions to remain competitive and responsive (Lubowiecki-Vikuk et al., 2023). Furthermore, given the uncertainty of a VUCA environment, organisations should engage in scenario planning (Johansen & Euchner, 2013; Mortlock & Osiyevskyy, 2023). They create scenarios for different possible futures and develop strategies for each, enabling them to adapt to the future. Through scenarios, destinations can identify and mitigate risks impacting their operations, financial stability, or reputation.

In essence, Organizational and Strategy Transformations under VUCA entail being proactive, adaptable, and forward-thinking to thrive in an environment characterised by unpredictability and complexity. These transformations enable organisations to navigate challenges effectively and seize opportunities in rapidly changing landscapes, as was highlighted in Chapters 10–15.

The COVID-19 pandemic was a global crisis that shook the tourism industry. Chapter 10 underscores the importance of healing as a central concept in recovery. As we emerge from this crisis, embracing healing – both physically and emotionally – will be vital for revitalising tourism. The COVID-19 pandemic has only heightened the need for healing tourism as people seek to fulfil their basic human needs for relaxation and rejuvenation. Studies have proven that travel can help reduce stress and improve mental health, making healing tourism an attractive option for many.

Chapter 11 highlights how adaptability, preparation, and the ability to bounce back from setbacks are central to the industry's survival. It assessed the resilience of tourism enterprises in Poland in the face of the pandemic crisis, the energy crisis, and the war in Ukraine. Companies undertook numerous innovative solutions in the organisational area, where resilience was a buzzword and a strategic imperative for navigating the complex and ever-changing tourism landscape.

Risk preparedness is essential for tourism destinations, whether the threat of a pandemic or natural disasters. Chapter 12 draws a parallel between COVID-19 and tsunamis, emphasising that rigorous risk preparation and effective response plans are crucial. It serves as a reminder that preparedness is the key to protecting coastal tourism areas through timely reactions and regulations.

Chapter 13 focuses on crime and insecurity in Mexico, which significantly impact a destination's image and tourism. This chapter explores how these factors contribute to uncertainty and erode the perception of Mexico as a tourist destination. It is revealed that the management of tourist destinations in Mexico neglects significant factors associated with competitiveness and sustainability such as security, crisis and disaster management, political will, load capacity and the destination's image. Addressing these issues is fundamental for rebuilding trust and ensuring the safety of travellers.

Biothreats and biosecurity have come to the forefront of tourism discussions, especially during the pandemic. Chapter 14 explores the intersections of these concepts in the context of Indian tourism. It emphasises the need for well-thought-out strategies to safeguard the health of tourists while promoting responsible travel.

Chapter 15 presents the case of Croatia as an example of how the recovery of abandoned settlements can breathe new life into tourism regions. Since abandoned rural settlements hold great potential for transforming tourist regions, this chapter demonstrates the power of creative revitalisation in the post-pandemic era. It was emphasised that abandoned rural locations and infrastructure should be included in sectoral, regional development plans to strengthen rural identity by preserving architectural heritage, landscape attractions, symbols, and all other identity contributors.

Way Ahead

The chapters in this book have provided valuable insights into the challenges and opportunities faced by the tourism industry in the VUCA world. As we look to the future, several vital directions emerge for the industry based on the chapters presented in this book. Here is a glimpse of the way ahead:

- The tourism industry should focus on providing experiences that address physical and emotional well-being, recognising the therapeutic benefits of travel.
- The concept of resilience is more than just a buzzword; it is a strategic imperative. Tourism enterprises need to be resilient and adapt quickly to changing circumstances. This involves innovative solutions, flexible organisational structures, and crisis preparedness.
- Risk management should remain a top priority, particularly in touristic coastal and mountainous regions. Destinations must be prepared to handle various risks, whether pandemics, natural disasters, or security concerns. Timely responses and effective regulations are essential.
- Wars, conflicts, and terrorism, along with biothreats and biosecurity, will continue to be significant concerns. Strategies should be developed to safeguard the health of tourists while promoting responsible travel through safety protocols, crisis response plans, and awareness campaigns.
- Creative revitalisation efforts can strengthen both rural and urban identities and preserve cultural heritage. Such initiatives should be integrated into regional development plans.
- Destinations, businesses, and all other stakeholders must remain innovative and adapt to evolving consumer preferences and technological advancements. Sustainability should be at the core of strategies, incorporating carbon reduction, eco-friendly infrastructure, and responsible tourism practices.
- Hospitality industry should focus on technology integration. Virtual, augmented, and artificial technologies should enhance the guest experience, improve operational efficiency, and reduce environmental impact. Embracing digital advancements is crucial for staying competitive and providing immersive and sustainable options.
- Collaborating with and understanding local communities is crucial to destination management. Fostering cooperation between tourists and residents, as well as promoting sustainability, is paramount.
- Continuous monitoring, collaboration with stakeholders, and re-evaluation of sustainability measures are essential for preserving the environment and supporting local communities.

Concluding Remarks

The way ahead for the tourism industry in a VUCA world involves a holistic approach that embraces healing, resilience, risk management, innovation, and sustainability. It requires a commitment to responsible tourism, cultural preservation, and adaptability to changing conditions. By taking these directions to heart, the tourism industry can navigate the complexities of the VUCA environment and build a more sustainable and resilient future. Furthermore, the VUCA world concept highlights the need for agility, adaptability, and innovative thinking in response to the unpredictable and rapidly changing environment in various aspects of life. Recognising and responding to VUCA conditions is critical for long-term success and sustainability. Tourism stakeholders must remain agile, responsible, and forward-thinking to navigate the ever-changing landscape and provide memorable and sustainable travel experiences.

References

Al-Ababneh, M. (2019). Creative cultural tourism as a new model for cultural tourism. *Journal of Tourism Management Research, 6*(2), 109–118.

Bennett, N., & Lemoine, G. J. (2014). What a difference a word makes: Understanding threats to performance in a VUCA world. *Business horizons, 57*(3), 311–317.

Johansen, B., & Euchner, J. (2013). Navigating the VUCA world. *Research-Technology Management, 56*(1), 10–15.

Kaivo-oja, J. R. L., & Lauraeus, I. T. (2018). The VUCA approach is a solution to corporate foresight challenges and global technological disruption. *Foresight, 20*(1), 27–49.

Krawczyńska-Zaucha, T. (2019). A new paradigm of management and leadership in the VUCA world. *Zeszyty Naukowe. Organizacja i Zarządzanie/Politechnika Śląska,* (141), 221–230.

Lubowiecki-Vikuk, A., & Sousa, B. (2021). Tourism business in a vuca world: Marketing and management implications. *Journal of Environmental Management & Tourism, 12*(4), 867–876.

Lubowiecki-Vikuk, A., Budzanowska-Drzewiecka, M., Borzyszkowski, J., & Taheri, B. (2023). Critical reflection on VUCA in tourism and hospitality marketing activities. *International Journal of Contemporary Hospitality Management, 35*(8), 2983–3005.

Millar, C. C., Groth, O., & Mahon, J. F. (2018). Management innovation in a VUCA world: Challenges and recommendations. *California Management Review, 61*(1), 5–14.

Mortlock, L., & Osiyevskyy, O. (2023). Strategic scenario planning in practice: Eight critical applications and associated benefits. *Strategy & Leadership, 51*(6), 22–29.

Sempiga, O., & Van Liedekerke, L. (2023). Investing in sustainable development goals: opportunities for private and public institutions to solve wicked problems that characterize a VUCA world. In G. Prelipcean (Ed.), *Investment strategies: New advances and challenges* (pp. 1–21). IntechOpen: London.

Vărzaru, A. A., Bocean, C. G., & Cazacu, M. (2021). Rethinking tourism industry in pandemic COVID-19 period. *Sustainability, 13*(12), 6956.

Wakelin-Theron, N., Ukpere, W. I., & Spowart, J. (2019). Determining tourism graduate employability, knowledge, skills, and competencies in a VUCA world: Constructing a tourism employability model. *African Journal of Hospitality, Tourism and Leisure, 8*(3), 1–18.

Printed and bound by CPI Group (UK) Ltd, Croydon, CR0 4YY